SOCIOLINGUISTIC VARIATION AND CHANGE

For Jean

SOCIOLINGUISTIC VARIATION AND CHANGE

Peter Trudgill

Edinburgh University Press

© Peter Trudgill, 2002

Edinburgh University Press Ltd
22 George Square, Edinburgh

Typeset in Sabon by
Hewer Text Ltd, Edinburgh, and
printed and bound in Great Britain by
MPG Books Ltd, Bodmin, Cornwall

A CIP Record for this book is
available from the British Library

ISBN 0 7486 1515 6 (paperback)

The right of Peter Trudgill
to be identified as author of this work
has been asserted in accordance with
the Copyright, Designs and Patents Act 1988.

CONTENTS

Acknowledgements   vii
Sources   ix

General introduction   1

I. Sociohistorical linguistics
Introduction: Sociohistorical linguistics   7
1. British vernacular dialects in the formation of
    American English: the case of East Anglian *do*   9
2. 'Short o' in East Anglia and New England   16
3. Sociohistorical linguistics and dialect survival:
    a note on another Nova Scotian enclave   21

II. Dialect change
Introduction: Dialect change   29
4. Two hundred years of dedialectalisation:
    the East Anglian short vowel system   33
5. New-dialect formation and dedialectalisation:
    embryonic and vestigial variants   40
6. Norwich revisited:
    recent linguistic changes in an English urban dialect   48

III. Language contact
Introduction: Language contact   65
7. Dual-source pidgins and reverse creoloids:
    northern perspectives on language contact   68
8. Language contact and the function of linguistic gender   76
9. Third-person singular zero: African American
    vernacular English, East Anglian dialects and
    Spanish persecution in the Low Countries   93
10. Language contact and inherent variability: the absence of
     hypercorrection in East Anglian present-tense verb forms   100

Contents

IV. Language creation and language death

Introduction: Language creation and language death   111
11. Ausbau sociolinguistics and the perception of
language status in contemporary Europe   114
12. Ausbau sociolinguistics and identity in modern Greece   125
13. Language maintenance and language shift:
preservation versus extinction   137

V. Englishes

Introduction: Englishes   147
14. English as an endangered language   150
15. Standard English: what it isn't   159
16. The sociolinguistics of modern RP   171

References   181
Index   193

ACKNOWLEDGEMENTS

The following people have helped with earlier versions of at least some of the chapters in this book. I am very grateful to all of them for their inspiration, information, suggestions, corrections, and erudition: Sasha Aikhenvald, Lyle Campbell, Andrew Carstairs-McCarthy, Jack Chambers, Sandra Clarke, Grev Corbett, Bill Croft, Alice Davison, R. M. W. Dixon, Malgorzata Fabiszak, Barbara Fennel, Paul Fletcher, George Grace, Michael Greengrass, Jean Hannah, Raymond Hickey, Ernst Håkon Jahr, Adam Jaworski, Marcin Kilarski, Jussi Klemola, Ian Kirby, Miklós Kontra, William Labov, Didier Maillat, Gunnel Melchers, Jim Milroy, Salikoko Mufwene, Frank Palmer, Harold Paddock, Shana Poplack, Dennis Preston, Klára Sándor, Daniel Schreier, John Singler, Janet Smith, Sali Tagliamonte, Milton Tynch, Theo Vennemann, Walt Wolfram and Laura Wright.

In addition I am also very grateful for discussions, many of them reflected in these pages, and assistance over the years, to: Enam Al-Wer, Lars Gunnar Andersson, David Britain, Jenny Cheshire, Donna Christian, Linda Compton, Jan Terje Faarlund, Ralph Fasold, Mike Garman, Elizabeth Gordon, Ian Hancock, Arthur Hughes, Brian Joseph, Mark Janse, Paul Kerswill, Ken Lodge, John Lyons, Lesley Milroy, Michael Montgomery, Terttu Nevalainen, Bengt Nordberg, Andy Pawley, Barbara Seidlhofer, Maria Sifianou, Mats Thelander, Dick Watts, J. C. Wells and Henry Widdowson. Special thanks also to John Laver, who inspired me when I was a student, and who now, thirty-five years later, has inspired me to produce this book.

SOURCES

The contents of this book are mainly derived from already published papers, some of them substantially revised here, as follows.

1. British vernacular dialects in the formation of American English: the case of East Anglian *do*. In: R. Hickey and S. Puppel (eds) *Linguistic History and Linguistic Modelling: a Festschrift for Jacek Fisiak on his 60th Birthday*. Berlin: Mouton de Gruyter, pp. 749–58, 1997.

2. 'Short o' in East Anglia and New England. In: J. Fisiak (ed.) *Studia anglica Posnaniensia* 33; 445–50. (Festschrift for K. Saajavara).

3. Sociohistorical linguistics and dialect survival: a note on another Nova Scotian enclave. In: M. Ljung (ed.) *Linguistic Structure and Variation*. Stockholm: Stockholm University Press, 2000.

4. Two hundred years of dedialectalisation: the East Anglian short vowel system. In: M. Thelander (ed.) *Samspel och variation: språkliga studier tillägnade Bengt Nordberg på 60–årsdagen*. Uppsala: Uppsala Universitet, 1996, pp. 471–8.

5. New-dialect formation and dedialectalisation: embryonic and vestigial variants. *Journal of English Linguistics* 1999; 27; 4, 319–27.

6. Norwich revisited: recent linguistic changes in an English urban dialect. *English World Wide* 1988; 9: 33–49.

7. Dual source pidgins and reverse creoles: northern perspectives on language contact. In: I. Broch and E. H. Jahr (eds) *Language Contact in the Arctic: Northern Pidgins and Contact Languages*. Berlin: Mouton de Gruyter, 1996, pp. 5–14.

8. Language contact and the function of linguistic gender. *Poznan Studies in Contemporary Linguistics* 1999; 35: 133–52.

9. Third-person singular zero: African American vernacular English, East Anglian dialects and Spanish persecution in the Low Countries. *Folia Linguistica Historica* 1998; 18.1–2: 139–48.

10. Language contact and inherent variability: the absence of hypercorrection in East Anglian present-tense verb forms. In: J. Klemola, M. Kytö and M. Rissanen (eds) *Speech Past and Present: Studies in English*

Dialectology in Memory of Ossi Ihalainen. Frankfurt: Peter Lang, 1996, pp. 412–25.

11. Ausbau sociolinguistics and the perception of language status in contemporary Europe. *International Journal of Applied Linguistics* 1992; 2.2: 167–77.

12. The Ausbau sociolinguistics of minority languages in Greece. *Plurilinguismes* 1992; 167–91.

13. Language maintenance and language shift: preservation versus extinction. *International Journal of Applied Linguistics* 1991; 1.1: 61–9.

15. Standard English: what it isn't. In: T. Bex and R. J. Watts (eds) *Standard English: the Widening Debate*. London: Routledge, 1999, pp. 117–28.

Other material has been taken from: Standard English and the national curriculum, *The European English Messenger* 1996; 5.1: 63–5; Dialect and dialects in the new Europe, *Etudes de lettres* 1997.4: 19–32 (Lausanne: Université de Lausanne, 1998); World English: convergence or divergence? In: H. Lindqvist, S. Klintborg, M. Levin and M. Estling (eds) *The Major Varieties of English*. Växjö University: Acta Wexionensis, 1998, pp. 29–36; Sociolinguistics and sociolinguistics once again. *Sociolinguistica* 2000; 14: 1–5; Language and nationalism in Greece and Turkey. In: S. Barbour (ed.) *Language and Nationalism in Europe*. Oxford: Oxford University Press, 2000.

GENERAL INTRODUCTION

People often think of me as being the first British sociolinguist. This is of course not at all true, although I was the first to apply Labovian methodology in the British context, even if, astonishingly as it now seems, I did not realise it at the time. There was already a long tradition in Britain, most notably in the work of Firth and Malinowski, of a socially informed linguistics. And the true father of British sociolinguistics in the modern sense is undoubtedly Robert Le Page, who has been enormously influential in the development of the thinking of British and British-based sociolinguists such as Jim Milroy, Lesley Milroy and Suzanne Romaine, as well as myself.

In my early work, it never occurred to me, as I worked my way into this milieu and tradition, that sociolinguistics was anything other than – in the words of William Labov – a way of doing linguistics. Firth was obviously a linguist. So were Le Page and Labov. Their linguistics was socially informed and socially sensitive, but it was linguistics. However, it gradually became clear to me in those early years that there were many other scholars doing what was, in my young opinion, very good work which they referred to as sociolinguistics which, however, seemed to have very little to do with what Le Page or Labov or I were doing.

This did not seem to me to be a particularly problematical matter, except insofar as it did seem to be giving rise to misunderstandings, not least on the part of the growing number of students who were being attracted to courses in sociolinguistics. The point was that the work of all the people who were carrying out research under the rubric of 'sociolinguistics' was valuable and insightful, but it seemed that not everybody involved was clear about the fact that scholars were working with different, sometimes very different, objectives. They were engaged in two – perhaps more – totally different enterprises which could interact in ways that were mutually beneficial but, I felt, it was as well to point out that they were different. The umbrella term 'sociolinguistics' had become at least potentially confusing.

1

I therefore gave a short presentation at the 1977 International Congress of Linguists in Vienna on this topic. I had been invited to contribute to a panel discussion following a paper by the leading ethnomethodologist Aaron Cicourel, and this seemed an appropriate moment. I simply suggested, rather nervously to the 3000 or so people present, that it was as well to be clear about the fact that some sociolinguistics, like Labov's, was aimed at answering questions which were, quite legitimately, of no professional concern to Aaron Cicourel, such as why are human languages like they are, how and why do languages change, and so on. Other people, such as Cicourel himself, were doing research which was aimed at answering questions which were, quite legitimately, of no professional concern to me (though as a human being I might be very interested), such as why are human societies like they are, and why is human social interaction like it is. I also pointed out that some work had mixed objectives – to find out more simultaneously about both language and society and their interrelationships and interactions, and to consider, for example, the effects of human interaction on the nature of human language.

This point was immediately misunderstood. I was accused of disparaging work in applied sociolinguistics, that is, work in the application of the results of sociolinguistic research to the solution of real-world (educational, political, social) problems. This was not what I meant at all. I had always believed, without articulating it to myself very clearly, that sociolinguists had a duty to help solve whatever social problems they could. I was therefore very grateful to another British linguist who was doing sociolinguistics well before me, Michael Halliday, for, in his turn, standing up in Vienna and pointing out that what I had said was quite valid and that both types of academic sociolinguistic work had applications in the non-academic world; and that to point out that social-scientifically oriented sociolinguistics was different from linguistically oriented sociolinguistics was in no way to argue against the social mobilisation of sociolinguistic research findings.

A longer version of my presentation subsequently appeared as the editorial introduction to my book *Sociolinguistic Patterns in British English* (1978). This introduction was somewhat facetiously but, I thought, relevantly entitled 'Sociolinguistics and sociolinguistics'. This was understood by the publishers and the other contributors as being modelled on the well-known English expression 'There's x and then there's x', implying in this case that sociolinguistics came in (at least) two different forms. Some people have professed to find this title 'strange' and, more seriously, have misunderstood my position and taken my argument to imply that I believe linguistically motivated sociolinguistics to be more important than social-scientifically motivated sociolinguistics. However, I wrote specifically in that introduction that it did not matter what an academic activity was called, that one activity was as valid and important as another, and that, following Hymes, I believed that there should be no demarcation disputes among scholars.

It is, however, perfectly true that I personally favour – which means 'prefer', not 'rate as superior' – linguistically motivated sociolinguistics. It is what I am interested in and it is what I do. I am a sociolinguist who is basically a linguist. The chapters that follow in this book are therefore studies in sociolinguistics as linguistics.

As to the applications of the findings of sociolinguistic research, I would additionally like to point out that people working in sociolinguistics are, sadly, familiar enough with the phenomenon of lay people ignoring what they have to say about linguistic variation and linguistic diversity. Much more regrettable, however, and much more disturbing, is the lack of awareness on the part of some of our non-sociolinguistic colleagues within general linguistics about these issues. I am here not referring to academic problems, although it is distressing enough to find colleagues supervising theoretical syntax theses on Standard Arabic in the belief that the student concerned is a native speaker, or to find scholars concerned with the latest syntactic theories enthusing about 'recent' discoveries of variability. Much worse, however, are pronouncements by linguists – and here I am concerned in particular about European linguists, including in some cases sociolinguists – which signal a woeful ignorance on their part about linguistic variability, the value of linguistic diversity, and the preservation of languages and dialects, as well as an unwillingness to fight for linguistically democratic and egalitarian issues which most sociolinguists have long taken for granted, following pleas for accountability on the part of linguists to the communities from which we have obtained data (for example, by prominent sociolinguists such as Labov and Wolfram – see Chapter 13).

Here are some examples of what I mean. In a recent issue of the *International Journal of the Sociology of Language*, under the general editorship of Joshua Fishman, in a discussion of linguistic minorities in Bulgaria, the prominent Bulgarian sociolinguist Michail Videnov writes (1999) in connection with suggestions by the large Turkish-speaking minority in Bulgaria that Turkish be granted some recognition in Turkish-speaking areas:

> Well aware of the significant role of language as means of national integration or disintegration, the Bulgarian government refrained from granting Standard Turkish the status of a regular school subject . . . Bulgarian sociolinguists have had a number of opportunities to express their views on the language situation in Bulgaria and to broach the hot issues of the regions with mixed populations. The conclusion we have arrived at is that general sociolinguistics should not be involved in the formulation of universal principles for the solution of problems of this kind.

Similarly, the Greek linguist Angelopoulos wrote (1979), apparently without any trace of irony, that 'Greece represents, in Europe, a country with practically ideal ethnic, linguistic and religious homogeneity and unity'. Similarly, the Hungarian linguistics professor László Deme argues (1998) against a particular Hungarian ongoing syntactic change (which is analogous to the English *Hopefully John will avoid further injury*) which research shows as being accepted by 50 per cent of Hungarians as 'correct', and which is produced by 25 per cent of informants in an oral sentence-completion task, by writing that it *must* be stopped because it is illogical and shows confused thinking. If, say, over half the population have caught cholera, he argues, should we bury the healthy? Similarly, Stein and Quirk recently wrote (1995), with considerable sociolinguistic naivety, that Standard English is not a social class dialect because the British tabloid *Sun* newspaper 'is written in Standard English'.

I would personally hope in future to see no more such abject failures of nerve, no more such failures to attempt to defend the rights of linguistic minorities, and no more such sociolinguistic sophistry. It is bad enough to have to fight battles about the legitimacy of linguistic variation with non-linguists; how much more distressing it is then to find academic linguists who have to be combatted in the same way. In the spirit of accepting the admonitions of Labov and Wolfram, and of counteracting sociolinguistic sophistry, this book also, then, contains studies in the applications of linguistic sociolinguistics to the solution of real-world problems.

I. SOCIOHISTORICAL LINGUISTICS

INTRODUCTION:
SOCIOHISTORICAL LINGUISTICS

Histories of the first thousand years or so of the English language obviously have to have a rather narrow geographical focus. Four hundred years ago, in 1600, English did not have a very important role as a foreign or second language anywhere, and was spoken as a native language in a very small area of the globe indeed: it was the native language of the indigenous population in most of England, and in the south and east of Scotland. It was, however, absent from much of Cornwall and from Welsh-speaking parts of Shropshire and Herefordshire; most of Ireland was Irish-speaking; nearly all of Wales was still Welsh-speaking; the Highlands and Hebridean islands of Scotland spoke Gaelic; Orkney and Shetland spoke Scandinavian Norn; the Isle of Man was Manx-speaking; and the Channel Islands were still French-speaking.

During the course of the 1600s this situation changed dramatically. English arrived, as a result of colonisation, as a native language in Ireland, in what is now the United States, and in Bermuda, Newfoundland, the Bahamas, and the Turks and Caicos Islands. It also spread during this time into many island and mainland areas of the Caribbean: Anguilla, Antigua and Barbuda, Barbados, the Cayman Islands, Jamaica, Montserrat, St Kitts and Nevis, the British Virgin Islands, the American Virgin Islands, and the mainland areas of Guyana and Belize. And it is not widely known that areas other than these – in modern times cricket-playing Commonwealth – countries were also settled by anglophones: eastern coastal and island areas of Honduras, Nicaragua and Colombia remain English-speaking to this day (see Chapter 14). The Dutch island colonies of Saba, St Maarten and St Eustatius have also been English-speaking since the early 1600s; and the mainly Papiamentu-speaking Dutch colony of Bonaire has a sizeable number of indigenous anglophones too.

During the eighteenth century, English began its expansion into Wales and north-western Scotland, and into mainland and maritime Canada. In the nineteenth century, again as a result of colonisation, English expanded to Hawaii, and into the southern hemisphere – not only to Australia, New

7

Zealand and South Africa, as is well known, but also to the South Atlantic Islands of St Helena, Tristan da Cunha and the Falklands, and in the Pacific to Pitcairn and Norfolk Island. There was also expansion from the Caribbean islands to eastern coastal areas of Costa Rica and Panama; and the repatriation of African Americans to Sierra Leone and Liberia, as well as an African-American settlement in the Dominican Republic. During this time also Caribbean Islands which had hitherto been francophone started on a slow process of becoming anglophone to different degrees: Dominica, St Lucia, Trinidad and Tobago, Grenada, and St Vincent and the Grenadines. Other little-known anglophone colonies which still survive today were also established during the nineteenth century in southern Brazil, by American Southerners fleeing the aftermath of the Civil War; and in the Bonin islands of Japan, by New England and Hawaiian whalers and seamen, and on one of the Cook Islands in the South Pacific (see Chapter 14). There are also today longstanding indigenous groups of British-origin native anglophones in Namibia, Botswana, Zimbabwe and Kenya.

In this section of the book we examine historical and sociolinguistic connections between some of the different varieties of English spoken around the world. Bailey *et al.* (1989: 299) state that 'present-day American English vernaculars evolved from earlier ones that differed remarkably from present textbook English. These earlier vernaculars, rather than the standard, clearly must be part of the focus of research into the history of American Black Vernacular English and American Southern White Vernacular English.' Scholars interested in the history of the development of varieties of North American English must then necessarily involve themselves in the history of nonstandard varieties of English from the British Isles. In this section we therefore focus in particular on connections between Britain, where English began, on the one hand, and varieties of English spoken in the Americas, where there are now many more native anglophones than in its original homeland.

1

BRITISH VERNACULAR DIALECTS IN THE FORMATION OF AMERICAN ENGLISH: THE CASE OF EAST ANGLIAN *DO*

Early explanations for why African American Vernacular English (AAVE) has the linguistic characteristics that it has have tended to focus on the inheritance of features of English derived originally from the British Isles (Krapp 1924; Kurath 1928). From the 1960s onwards, however, and with the work of Bailey (1965) and Dillard (1972) in the vanguard, it was also hypothesised that AAVE has instead, or as well, a creole history not unlike that of Gullah and the other Atlantic creoles (see also Chapters 3 and 9). In particular, a number of researchers pointed to similarities between the tense and aspect systems of AAVE and those of the English-based Atlantic creoles (see Dillard 1972; Winford 1992).

In the last few years, however, the creolist hypothesis has been supplemented by a renewed recognition that a number of AAVE features do seem to have non-creole or even British Isles origins, although at least some of these British Isles features may have an interlanguage (Selinker 1972) or interdialect (Trudgill 1986) history rather than having been inherited directly (see Schneider 1983). Notable in this area have been a number of papers concentrating on the history of AAVE verb forms including, for example, Poplack and Tagliamonte (1989; 1993), and Montgomery *et al.* (1993). Montgomery *et al.* in particular have pointed out close parallels between certain linguistic forms found in early AAVE and those found in British Isles dialects. They also stress the heterogeneity of earlier AAVE, as well as the degree and complexity of interaction between Black and White varieties of American English.

Very many of the ancestors of the speakers of modern AAVE came, obviously, from Africa. Equally obviously, the English language itself came originally from Britain. While I am therefore not in principle at all opposed to the suggestion that AAVE owes much to a creole and/or African background, in this chapter I support the view of Bailey *et al.* and the arguments of Montgomery *et al.* that AAVE also owes at least something to a British Isles background. I do this by examining a feature of American English which demonstrates reasonably unambiguously that at least some varieties of AAVE inherited at least one nonstandard British grammatical dialect structure directly. The presence of this feature in both black and white American dialects, moreover, testifies to a close interaction between the two. It is most unlikely that this feature has any kind of creole background, and its presence in a geographically rather restricted area of the USA in both AAVE and local nonstandard White dialects indicates the continuing importance of settlement patterns for an understanding of the heterogeneity of Black and White speech to which Montgomery *et al.* refer.

BRITAIN: THE EAST ANGLIAN CONJUNCTION *DO*

In the older traditional dialects of East Anglia, the obviously originally verbal form *do* functions as a conjunction which is approximately semantically equivalent to the conjunction *otherwise*. East Anglia has always been a distinctive dialect area within England (see Fisiak 1990) and this usage does not ever appear to have extended outside this area at all. The *English Dialect Dictionary* shows that the usage was once found in the rural dialects of Norfolk, Suffolk, Cambridgeshire and northern Essex, but in more recent decades it is probable that the phenomenon has been confined to the core East Anglian area of Norfolk and Suffolk. It has also become rare in the urban speech of younger East Anglians, and it seems destined to disappear from the English of this area within the next few decades. In Trudgill (1995) I have argued that the origins of this usage lie in a process of grammaticalisation that is ultimately phonological in origin. The examples supplied below are taken from dialect literature written in East Anglia in the last hundred years (see Sources). Dialect literature is, of course, not always the best source of reliable data. My own lifelong residence in the area, however, together with more than thirty years of academic work on the dialects of the region, leads me to accept all the examples below as entirely genuine.

From a diachronic point of view, the most advanced East Anglian traditional dialect function of *do* as a conjunction is illustrated in the following example:

1. You lot must have moved it, do I wouldn't have fell in.
   'You lot must have moved it, or I wouldn't have fallen in.'

It is clear here that *do* is functioning as a non-verbal form with no semantic content connected to 'doing' anything, and with a function entirely equivalent to Standard English *otherwise*. I hypothesise (Trudgill 1995) that the development of this function in East Anglian English is probably initially due to phonological developments involving the loss of phonetic material. This is confirmed by the continued usage of somewhat less advanced, less completely grammaticalised forms in the dialect area. That is, many of the hypothesised different stages of the diachronic development of *do* as a conjunction can actually be found in a synchronic examination of different dialect texts.

Consider, for example, the following:

2. Don't you take yours off, do you'll get rheumatism.
3. Don't you tell your Aunt Agatha about the coupons, do she'll mob me.
4. Don't you walk upstairs yet, do you'll whitewash the whole stair carpet.
5. Don't sleep there, do you'll be a-laughing on the wrong side of your face.
6. Don't you put her proper name in, do she'll pull both of us for libel.

The forms in examples 2–6 would appear to represent the earliest stage in the grammaticalisation process, that is of simple omission of lexical material. In these examples, the insertion of *and/because if you* will provide forms readily comprehensible to speakers of all English dialects, for example:

2* Don't take yours off, [because if you] do you'll get rheumatism.

Similar reconstruction is possible in the case of the following examples where *don't* appears rather than *do*:

7. Put that there antimacassar over her face, don't she'll give me nightmares.
8. You'd better turn that broom the other way up, don't you'll be breaking someone's neck.
9. Put your hand in front of your mouth when you cough, don't you'll have them germs all over the house.

Once again, insertion of *and/because if you* supplies sentences which are grammatical in all varieties of English:

7*. Put that antimacassar over her face, [because if you] don't she'll give me nightmares.

The grammaticalisation of *do*, then, resulted from an initial stage which consisted of the omission of phrases such as *because if* + pronoun. In examples 2–9, however, grammaticalisation is only partial in that a verbal-type negative/positive distinction between *do* and *don't* is still maintained, together with the grammatical (tense) link between the verb in the first clause and the quasi-auxiliary verb form in the second.

The second stage in the grammaticalisation process shows a weakening of this link and is illustrated by the following:

10. Have the fox left?
    No that ain't, do Bailey would've let them went.
    'No it hasn't, or Bailey would've let them [the hounds] go.'

Similar forms occur with *don't*:

11. He pinned ahold of her other leg, don't she'd have been in.

Here a distinction between positive and negative quasi-verbal forms is still maintained, since we have a positive form *do* in the second clause corresponding to a negative form in the first clause in 10, and vice versa in 11. But some regrammaticalisation has clearly taken place since the grammatical link with the verb in the first clause has been broken in that (a) the originally present-tense forms *do* and *don't* are now being applied in past-tense contexts; and (b) expansion to sentences with fully verbal *do* and *don't* is no longer possible – we would rather expect *had* and *hadn't*. The correct paraphrase for 10 would include not *because if it does* but *because if it had*. The verbal history of the form is thus still apparent in the *do/don't* distinction, but the grammatical link to the verb in terms of the tense of the preceding clause has been lost; and the semantic content is now almost entirely equivalent to Standard English *or/otherwise*:

The final stage in the grammaticalisation process is demonstrated in examples 12–14:

12. Sing out, do we shall be drownded!
    'Call out, or we shall be drowned!'
13. Where's the ladder?
    That stand in the stackyard, do that did do.
    'It's standing in the stackyard, or at least it was.'
14. Keep you them elephants still, do we shan't half be in a mess.
    'Keep those elephants still, or we won't half be in a mess.'

In these three examples, as it happens, there still appears to be grammatical agreement between present-tense forms in both clauses, but we see that the originally verbal negative/positive distinction has now been entirely lost, with *do* appearing where in earlier stages *don't* would have been expected i.e. the *do/don't* distinction has been neutralised in favour of *do*.

Examples 1 and 15–19 show more clearly that the process has now gone to completion, in that there is no quasi-verbal grammatical link at all either to the tense or to the negative/positive polarity of the preceding clause.

15. That's a good job we come out of that there field, do he'd've had us!
16. She say that wouldn't have done to have done nothing to the boy, do I might have gone round for nothing, not knowing.
    'She said that it wouldn't have done to do anything to the boy, or I might have gone round for nothing, not knowing.'
17. That was up to him to do his job proper, do there wouldn't be nothing yet nobody to start things off again.
18. We stabled them elephants right in the middle, do we should've capsized.
19. Things must be wonderful bad, do master would never have broke.

'Things must have been extremely bad, or master would never have gone bust.'

The development of the East Anglian conjunction would thus appear to have gone through the following stages:

a. Phonological reduction and loss of lexical material of the type *because if* + pronoun.

b. Loss of tense-marking of *do* and *don't*, and extension to grammatical environments where a fully verbal *do* would not have been possible and some other operator would have been expected.

c. Loss of negative/positive polarity and neutralisation in favour of *do*.

THE USA: THE SOUTH ATLANTIC STATES
CONJUNCTION *DO*

The conjunction *do* is not found anywhere in the British Isles outside East Anglia. Nor, as far as I know, is it found anywhere else in the English-speaking world, with one exception – in the south-eastern United States.

The *Dictionary of American Regional English* (DARE) cites a number of examples of conjunctional *do* in AAVE from works set in Florida by the novelist Zora Neal Hurston. Hurston was born in Eatonville, Florida, the first incorporated Black town in the United States, in 1903. She was a folklorist as well as a novelist, and she studied under the famous linguist and anthropologist Boas. There is every reason to believe that her renderings of Black Florida dialect are authentic. The examples are as follows:

20. Dat's a thing dat's got to be handled just so, do it'll kill you. (*Mules and Men*, 1935)
21. Don't you change too many words wid me dis mawnin', Janie, do Ah'll take and change ends wid yuh!
22. You got to have a subjick tuh talk from, do you can't talk.
23. Yuh can't live on de muck 'thout yuh take uh bath every da – Do dat muck'll itch yuh lak ants. (*Their eyes*, 1937)
24. Git this spoon betwixt her teeth do she's liable to bite her tongue off. (*Seraph*, 1948)

The editors of DARE conjecture that the origins of conjunctional *do* probably lay in an 'abbreviation of *do you* (= *if you do*) etc. following negative statements or commands' (p. 94). As can be seen, this explanation works for example 21, but the other examples show progress towards the fully completed grammaticalisation also typical of East Anglia in that *do* is employed where *don't* might have been expected. It is also of considerable interest that Hurston supplies an incompletely grammaticalised example of a type unknown in England, in which stage 3 seems to have preceded stage 2:

> 25. Ah never dreamt so many different kins uh black folks could colleck in one place. Did Ah never woulda come.

Interestingly, we also have conclusive evidence that conjunctional *do* is used elsewhere in the American south-east, and that it continues to be used to this day. In the 1994 field recordings carried out by Milton Tynch (see Tynch 1994), we find the following example from a Black speaker from the area of Edenton, Chowan County, in north-eastern coastal North Carolina:

> 26. And she come pull the covers back off that baby's face, don't that baby would have been dead.

Here we have the not fully grammaticalised negative form *don't*, but considerable grammaticalisation has occurred, since *don't* is being used here in a past-tense context and is equivalent in meaning to *and if she hadn't*, as in some of the East Anglian examples.

Tynch (pers. comm.), who is a native of the area, further points out that not only does conjunctional *do* occur as well as *don't* in contexts similar to those in East Anglia, but that it also occurs in the speech of Whites in Chowan County. This is further confirmed by one of the DARE informants, who writes that in eastern North Carolina, during the period approximately from 1915–30:

> I remember hearing White people, speakers with moderate education, saying things like 'Shut the door tight, do it'll blow open before morning' and 'Leave the note in the middle of the table, do she won't see it'. (p. 94)

CONCLUSION

It is possible that East Anglia and south-eastern USA conjunctional *do* represent independent developments. This seems unlikely, however. A much more likely scenario is that this feature, which has never been available in any form of Standard English, was brought to eastern North Carolina by settlers who were speakers of East Anglian dialects. In (at least some parts of) the south-eastern United States, it was then not only retained in White nonstandard dialects of English but also acquired by speakers of AAVE. The analysis by Montgomery *et al.* (1993) of third-person plural present tense verb-marking shows 'a strong similarity between white and black English in the nineteenth-century south Atlantic states' in the use of a nonstandard grammatical feature derived from the north of Britain which 'does not necessarily argue against the hypothesis of a creole origin of some varieties of AAVE' but 'does suggest . . . more diversity in mid-nineteenth-century AAVE than has usually been acknowledged'. Much more research is required on the history of conjunctional *do* in the United States before we can with confidence add it to the same overall picture which Montgomery *et al.* have painted. It is undoubtedly true, however, that there is at least one nonstandard dialect feature with its origins in the British Isles, in addition to the ones they describe, which has been retained by some AAVE speakers, as well as by some White speakers, in at least some areas of the southern Atlantic states.

EAST ANGLIAN SOURCES

Benham, C. E. (1895) *Essex ballads*. Benham Newspapers (reissued 1960).

Claxton, A. O. D. (1954) *The Suffolk Dialect of the Twentieth Century*. Woodbridge: Boydell Press (3rd edn 1968).

Cooper, E. R. (1932) *Mardles from Suffolk*. Newbury: Countryside Books (reissued 1984).

Grapes, S. (1958) *The Boy John Letters*. Norwich: Wensum Books (reissued 1974).

Mardle, J. [alias of E. Fowler] (1973) *Broad Norfolk*. Norwich: Wensum Books.

Riches, C. (1978) *Orl Bewtiful and New*. Norwich: F. Crowe & Sons.

West, H. M. (1966) *The East Anglian and his Humour*. Ipswich: Anglian Publications.

West, H. M. (1983) *East Anglian Tales*. Newbury: Countryside Books.

2

'SHORT O' IN EAST ANGLIA
AND NEW ENGLAND

The New England 'short o' has been discussed in the literature on American dialects a number of times (see Avis 1961; Kurath and McDavid 1961: 12). Kurath (1964: 150) introduces this phenomenon as follows. He discusses the loss in American English of the original Middle English (ME) distinction between monophthongal ǫ: and diphthongal *ou*, and writes:

> Only New England [in the USA] preserves the original [ME] distinction, though to a limited extent. Here the old monophthong survives in checked position as a short and fronted mid-back vowel /ə/ as in stone, *road, coat* /stən, rəd, kət/, contrasting with up-gliding /o/, as in *know, grown* (but also, e.g., in *no, rode*). This so-called 'New England short' is somehow related to regional English folk speech.

Avis (1961) further tells us that the heartland of this phenomenon in North America lies, for the USA, in eastern Vermont, New Hampshire, north-eastern Massachusetts, and Maine, and in Canada in south-western New Brunswick.

Kurath (1965 [1971]) asks the interesting question: 'Is the survival of contrasting vowels in New England to be attributed to English folk speech?' and answers it as follows: 'New England usage in this matter probably derives from English folk speech or from a regional type of Standard British English reflecting folk usage.' In a much earlier publication (1928 [1971]) he actually appears to give a more geographically detailed answer to the question when he says: 'The population of the seaboard of New England had come for the most part from south-eastern counties of England'; and 'the shortened vowel of *coat, whole,* and *home* is recorded for East Anglia'. It is definitely tempting to see a connection. This was certainly also the link I was suggesting myself when I wrote (1974) that there was a 'clear resemblance' between the two phenomena in East Anglia and New England.

Further linguistic evidence in favour of Kurath's linkage to East Anglia is as follows. In the case of both East Anglia and New England, the phenom-

enon of shortening is confined to items descended from Middle English ǫ: –
it never occurs in either area in words such as *grown, soul.* Both features,
moreover, are recessive, and both vary widely in their incidence from word
to word, style to style, and speaker to speaker.

The East Anglian facts are as follows. The vowel of English labelled by
Wells (1982) as the GOAT vowel has, as in New England, maintained two
counterparts in the vowel system of the dialects of northern East Anglia,
that is Norfolk and northern Suffolk. Paralleling a now vestigial distinction
in the front vowel system between the sets of *made* and *maid,* corresponding
to the distinction between the Middle English monophthong and
diphthong, there is in northern East Anglia a similar contrast in the back
vowel system which, however, is by no means vestigial (see Trudgill 1998
on why the one distinction has survived longer than the other). The
distinction is between /uː/ = [ʊu], descended from ME ǫ:, and /ou/ =
[ɐu], descended from ME *ou.* Thus pairs such as *moan–mown, road–
rowed, nose–knows, sole–soul* are not homophonous.

The important thing to notice for our purposes is that the FOOT vowel /ʊ/
was much more frequent in the older East Anglian dialect than in General
English (in the sense of Wells 1982). There has been a strong tendency in
East Anglia for the /uː/ descended from ME ǫ: to be shortened to /ʊ/ in
closed syllables. Thus *road* can rhyme with *good,* and we find pronunciations such as *toad, home, stone, whole, coat* /tʊd, hʊm, stʊn, kʊt/. Distribution is unpredictable: /ʊ/ does not occur, at least in current dialects, in
foam, load, moan, coal, vote, for example.

The extent of this East Anglian 'short o' phenomenon is indicated in the
work of a number of writers. Kökeritz (1932), for example, writing about
the dialects of northern Suffolk, lists the following items as having the same
vowel as *pull: boast, boat, bone, choke, cloak, clover, coach, coast, coat,
don't, folk, goat, hole, home, hope, load, loaf, moat, most, oak, oath, oats,
over, poach, pole, post, road, rope, smoke, stone, toad, whole, wholly.*

Lowman's records (see Trudgill 1974) also show a large number of
examples of the 'short o', although (possibly incorrect) transcriptions such
as [ston] *stone* make it unclear as to whether he regards such words as
having a vowel identical to that of *foot.* Words in his records that have the
'short o' are: *froze, posts, comb, bone, oats, whole, home, boat, stone, yolk,
poached, hotel, ghosts, don't, won't, woke, wrote, over, toad*

It is difficult to judge, but the usage of 'short o' in East Anglia seems to
have declined by the 1950s, as revealed by the *Survey of English Dialect*
records. The fieldworker, W. Nelson Francis, shows the following items
with some form of short vowel in the Norfolk localities: *both, broke, comb,
road, spoke, stone, throat, whole.*

In his field notes, Francis mentions the occurrence of short forms, and
writes of Pulham, Norfolk: 'Evidence of shortened lax forms, apparently
much more prevalent in the dialect 50–75 years ago, was rather plentiful in

the speech . . . of the oldest informant; thus [rʊd, stʊn, kʊm, spʊk, trʊt] [= *road, stone, comb, spoke, throat*].'

Trudgill (1974) showed that by 1968 it was only the working class for whom the 'short o' was a characteristic feature of the urban dialect of Norwich. Items on my tapes with 'short o' are: *aerodrome, alone, bloke, both, broke, Close, coats, comb, combed, don't, drove, Holmes, home, most, notice, only, over, photo, post, road, spoke, stone, suppose, whole, woke, won't.*

Note that even the lower working class used only 42 per cent of possible forms with 'short o', which suggests that this had now become something of a relic form. This is stressed by the fact that this figure is largely made up of a relatively small number of common lexical items, notably *don't, home, suppose, only*. On the other hand, the shortening process has clearly been a productive one, suggesting that knowledge of the stylistic relationship between /u:/ and /ʊ/ has continued to be part of competence of local speakers: Norwich, for example, until the 1960s had a theatre known as The Hippodrome /hipədrʊm/, and trade names such as Kodachrome can be heard with pronunciations such as /kʊdəkrʊm/. The feature thus survives in modern speech, but a number of words appear to have been changed permanently to the /u:/ set as a result of lexical transfer.

It would therefore be very easy to look favourably on an answer to Kurath's question which focuses on the role of East Anglian English in the formation of the English of New England. We can suppose, that is, that the New England 'short o' phenomenon was transplanted to the United States from East Anglia.

There are, however, a number of problems with this interpretation. One is that, while it is certainly clear that the northern East Anglian 'short o' is of some antiquity, it is not at all clear that it is of sufficient antiquity for it to have been taken to North America. Forby (1830 [1970]: 90) writes:

> The long o . . . has also in some words the common short sound of the diphthong oo (in foot), or that of the vowel u in pull: Ex. Bone–stone–whole.

He was, however, writing about the dialect of northern East Anglia as it was spoken in the late 1700s, and we will need to push the date of East Anglian 'short o' further back than that if we are to accept it as the progenitor of the New England form. This is, moreover, not the only problem. There is an additional East Anglian complication. The first concerns the GOOSE vowel. This vowel, /ʉ:/, is a central diphthong [ʉ̞u] with more lip-rounding on the second element than on the first. Since northern East Anglian English demonstrates total yod-dropping (see Trudgill 1974), there is complete homophony between pairs of words which have this vowel, such as *dew–do, Hugh–who, cute–coot*. However, many words from the set of GOOSE which are descended from ME ǫ: may have /u:/ rather than /ʉ:/. That is, words such as *boot* may be pronounced either /bʉ:t/ or /bu:t/. In the latter case, they are of course then homophonous with words such as *boat*. Thus *rood* may be homophonous either with *rude* or with *road* which, however, will not be homophonous with *rowed*. Note that this alternation never occurs in the case of those items such as *rule, tune, new* etc. which have historical sources other than ME ǫ: – for very many speakers, then, *rule* and *school* do not rhyme.

Our problem is that in northern East Anglia a shortening process similar to that which produced 'short o' has also been rather extensively operative in the case of GOOSE words. That is, the FOOT vowel is usual as a result of shortening not only in *foot, look, soot, good* etc. but also in the lexical sets of *hoof, roof, proof* and *room, groom, broom*. Crucially, it also occurred in the older dialect in large numbers of other words such as *boot, goose, moon, move, noon, root, soon, spoon, tooth* as well as in compounds such as *afternoon* /a:tənʊn/. The question then is, given the convergence in pronunciation on /u:/ of items from both the GOOSE and GOAT sets, whether the northern East Anglian 'short o' has any connection with the compli-cated shortening process which led to short /ʊ/ in *good, foot*, and, variously in different accents, in *look, tooth, room* etc. That is, does the change from /u:/ to /ʊ/ in *boot* represent the same phenomenon as (a putative) change from /u:/ to /ʊ/ in *boat*? This situation appears to have no parallel in the USA. In order to rescue our hypothesis, however, we could perhaps quite legitimately argue that it represents a complication which postdates the emigration of East Anglians to New England.

Turning now to the American evidence, we have to observe that another difficulty is that items listed by Avis (1961) as occurring with the New England 'short o' include the following, which also demon-strate 'short o' in East Anglia: *boat, bone, broke, coat, goat, home, most, oats, post, road, stone, toad, toast, suppose, whole*. Avis, however, also cites a number of words which do not have 'short o' in New England but which I know to have it in East Anglia: *coast, drove, froze, over, rode, yolk*.

This can perhaps be explained away in terms of dedialectalisation and the loss of this recessive feature in New England in these words. We can suppose that these items formerly had 'short o' in New England, but had lost them by the time the research on which Avis' paper was based was carried out in the 1930s – or, more prosaically, that the fieldworker simply failed to elicit this (stigmatised) pronunciation.

However, there are also two further issues which are problematic if we wish to establish any connexion. First is the fact that, while in neither dialect can shortening occur, for obvious phonotactic reasons, in open syllables, East Anglia retains a distinction in such syllables between the two original Middle English lexical sets, while New England does not:

	hood	*road*	*go*	*low*
East Anglia	/ʊ/	/ʊ/	/uː/	/oʊ/
New England	/ʊ/	/ə/	/oʊ/	/oʊ/

The number of problematical words involved here is rather small. GOAT items, which in northern East Anglian English have stressed syllable final /uː/, are few: *Coe, foe, go, Joe, no, roe, so, toe, woe.*

Again, perhaps, we can therefore argue that this difference between East Anglia and New England can be accounted for by dedialectalisation. We could hypothesise that New England English formerly had a distinct vowel also in open syllables, but that it has lost it under the influence of more mainstream forms of English.

Second, and more damagingly for this thesis, there is the perplexing fact that the New England 'short o' contrasts with the FOOT vowel as /ə/ versus /ʊ/, while in northern East Anglia it is identical and *road* and *hood* rhyme. Here one could argue that it is in this case in East Anglia that dedialecta-lisation has taken place. This would have to have happened some con-siderable time ago, however, since we have seen above in the quotation from Forby (1830 [1970]) that *road* and *hood* already rhymed at the period when he was writing. Moreover, the putative East Anglian replacement of /ə/ by /ʊ/ is not the kind of development that is to be expected during dedialectalisation: a dialect vowel which does not exist in the prestige variety is usually replaced by another dialect vowel which bears a closer phonetic resemblance to that which occurs in the prestige variety, as when for example /ie/ in *home* changes to /uo/ in dialectal English in north-eastern England under the influence of Received Pronuniciation (RP) /oʊ/. The vowel /ʊ/, however, can hardly be said to bear a greater phonetic resem-blance to RP /oʊ/ than does /ə/. Perhaps we could argue that /ə/ was replaced by /ʊ/ because, while the former did not exist in RP, the latter did, even if not in that lexical set. We could, alternatively, simply argue for a merger in East Anglia of two phonetically rather similar vowels as a sound change which occurred after the emigration to North America had taken place and which did not take place in New England, but there is as yet no evidence at all of this.

The conclusion has to be that the resemblance between the two different forms of 'short' is indeed striking, but that we still have quite a bit of explaining to do if we are to argue convincingly for a common origin.

3

SOCIOHISTORICAL LINGUISTICS AND DIALECT SURVIVAL: A NOTE ON ANOTHER NOVA SCOTIAN ENCLAVE

In this chapter I look at a rather unusual community and take up the issue of the light it can shed on a currently ongoing controversy in North American sociohistorical linguistics.

Shana Poplack and her associates (see especially Poplack and Tagliamonte 1993; Poplack 1999), in their work on the sociolinguistic history of African American Vernacular English, have argued that it is possible to shed light on the history of AAVE – a variety for which we have few reliable records until the modern period – by examining the English spoken in a number of AAVE exclaves, notably the AAVE spoken by the descendants of escaped or liberated slaves from the USA in Samaná, Dominican Republic, and in two different locations in Nova Scotia, Canada. As was dicussed in Chapter 1, the work has focused especially on whether AAVE has come to have the distinctive characteristics it has as a result of a creole history plus independent developments (see, for example, the exciting, insightful and careful work reported on in Mufwene *et al.* 1998; and Rickford 1999) or as a result of the inheritance of original British Isles dialect features plus independent developments – or of course, as often seems most reasonable (see Trudgill 2000) both.

Of crucial importance is Poplack's argument that some modern AAVE features that would be diagnostic for a creole origin are actually not present in, for example, the AAVE of the Black communities of Guysborough and East Preston, Nova Scotia. A crucial assumption is, of course, that the exclaves, as isolated linguistic communities cut off from mainstream USA AAVE, can shed light on the history of AAVE in the sense that they have not participated in recent developments and can therefore legitimately be regarded as being more conservative. (I am of course not doing justice here to the large amounts of data investigated by Poplack and her team, nor to the subtleties of their analyses, insights and argumentation.)

I am on record as an admirer of the work of Rickford on the creole origins of AAVE and of Poplack's interesting work (see my editor's prefaces to Rickford 1999, and Poplack 1999). As Poplack and her associates acknowledge, however, there is an obvious problem with the methodology that they have employed. It is true that there is a *prima facie* case for supposing that the English of small groups of speakers in the exclaves is likely to be more conservative in many respects than that of the millions of AAVE-speakers in the USA (see Trudgill 1996). On the other hand, it obviously has to be recognised, as has very reasonably been pointed out by Singler (1997), that these exclave speakers have not been living in a vacuum since their departure from the USA. In spite of a certain amount of geographical isolation and racial segregation in residence patterns, and in spite of the maintenance of some sense of a separate history and identity among the members of the communities themselves, the exclave speakers have been living in environments where they have been surrounded by and in contact with speakers of other language varieties and, importantly, in the case of the Nova Scotia speakers, of other varieties of English. There can therefore be in principle no guarantee, in the absence of evidence to the contrary, that even the oldest speakers in the community have not lost linguistic features that were formerly part of AAVE as a result of contact with local non-AAVE varieties, nor that they have not acquired features that were originally not present in AAVE from these same local varieties. I say 'in principle' because in many cases Poplack *et al.* are able to call on additional evidence, particularly comparisons between the Dominican Republic and Nova Scotia. The methodological problem remains, however, a very interesting one, not least because of the time-depth involved. American Blacks first arrived in Nova Scotia in the households of New England planters in the 1760s, but they came in greater numbers in the aftermath of the American Revolution in the 1780s, and more especially between 1813 and 1816, in the aftermath of the 1812 British–American war.

In the rest of this chapter I attempt to shed some light on this interesting methodological problem by looking at another Nova Scotian enclave which is very similar to the AAVE-speaking exclaves in many ways, and by making comparisons between them. Much work remains to be done, and what I have to say is very speculative. I also have to acknowledge that I am addressing myself to phonetics and phonology, while Poplack and her collaborators have been concerned with grammatical features. Nevertheless, it seems to me that there are some interesting parallels, and I hope that this exploratory note will be suggestive.

In Nova Scotia, about 190 miles south-west of Guysborough, and about 70 miles south-west of East Preston, lies the coastal town of Lunenburg, in Lunenburg County. This area is well-known, at least among Canadian linguists (see Chambers 1991), as a dialect enclave. In particular, it is known to be the only mainland White Canadian community to be non-rhotic. This non-rhoticity has been ascribed (see Emeneau 1935) to the sociolinguistic origins of the community. Lunenburg was settled between

1750 and 1752 by approximately 2700 'foreign Protestants'. Some of these were francophone, but the vast majority were German-speakers from Germany and Switzerland. A form of German, indeed, survived as a spoken language in some parts of the county until the 1940s.

It is clear, however, that this German background does not in fact work as an explanation for the non-rhoticity. There is no reason at all why interference from German should lead to non-rhoticity: nearly all forms of eighteenth-century German were highly rhotic. And in any case, it is clear that Lunenburg County English differs from the surrounding areas of Nova Scotia in many particulars other than in lacking rhoticity – particulars which need to be explained.

My research in Lunenburg employed time-honoured dialectological methodology: I went there and talked to people. The area involved is very small: local people report that the area in question, which they are well aware of as being distinctive, extends to a radius of no more than 7 or 8 miles from the town of Lunenburg. The town itself, moreover, is for the most part no longer distinctive in the same way.

The phonological facts are these. Rural Lunenburg County speakers who have preserved the local dialect are indeed non-rhotic, except that they are consistently rhotic in the case of words such as *first, work, turn* where /r/ occurs after /ɜ:/. They also demonstrate, moreover, intrusive /r/, in for example *saw it*, in the manner of most non-rhotic anglophone communities around the world. This complexity is of course particularly unlikely to be the result of a German substratum.

Other features which clearly demarcate local dialect speakers from their Nova Scotian neighbours include the following. First, word-final /t/ in very many forms of, particularly, rural Atlantic Canadian English is, unusually in a world-wide anglophone context, a released, aspirated stop, including in some areas the slit-fricative variant associated with some Irish English varieties (see Wells 1982). The only other varieties where this is usual – and this is presumably not a coincidence – are the Englishes of Ireland as just mentioned, the Scottish Highlands and parts of Wales, as well as of certain other places such as Liverpool, England, which have experienced heavy Irish immigration. In Lunenburg County, however, word-final /t/ is un-released and may in some contexts be a glottal stop.

Second, in very many forms of rural Atlantic Canadian English, syllable-final /l/ is 'clear', i.e., palatalised. In rural Lunenburg, however, it is 'dark', i.e. velarised, with some tendency to vocalisation.

Third, the vowel of STRUT, which is typically a back and even in some cases rounded vowel in rural Atlantic Canadian English (see for example Clarke 1991), is in rural Lunenburg a central unrounded vowel.

Fourth, and especially strikingly, the vowels of FACE and GOAT are very distinctive. In most of rural Nova Scotia and indeed beyond, these vowels are monophthongal [e:] and [o:] or very narrow diphthongs starting on [e] and [o] respectively. In rural Lunenburg, on the other hand, we have wider diphthongs. FACE typically begins at a point around [æ] and GOAT has a very characteristic front rounded onset around [œ].

Perhaps even more striking in the general Canadian context is the fact that speakers of this variety do not have the merger of the vowels of LOT and THOUGHT. In most of Atlantic Canada, speakers have a very distinctive front vowel, around [a], in both these sets, so that unsuspecting Britons find it easy to process, say, *caught* as *cat*. In rural Lunenburg, however, these two vowels are neither front nor merged. LOT has a low central vowel around [ʌ] = /ɑ/ in LOT, and a very different long, back, mid-open rounded vowel in THOUGHT.

None of this suggests German influence. What it does suggest, however, is an origin for this variety in the English of New England – indeed, North American speakers hearing this variety for the first time often identify it in this way – although the phonological system is not that of modern Boston (see Wells 1981). As we have already seen, the LOT/THOUGHT merger has not occurred. And there has been no development of the new long vowel /aː/: words such as *car, hard* have the /a/ vowel such that *cod = card, market = mock it. Dance* and *bath*, moreover, have /æ/ and not /aː/. Similarly, words such as *north, four* have the same vowel as THOUGHT so that *sore = saw, court = caught.*

One explanatory sociohistorical linguistic scenario for this extreme distinctiveness would be as follows. The eighteenth-century German-speaking migrants for the most part, obviously, acquired English after their arrival, although some of their descendants remained bilingual for nearly 200 years. The point is that they had, of course, to learn English from someone. What better candidates for this role (as suggested to me by J. K. Chambers) than the 8000 New Englanders often known as 'pre-Loyalists' or 'Planters' who arrived in Nova Scotia between 1759 and 1768? These were people who came from coastal Connecticut, Rhode Island and Massachusetts, who arrived in Nova Scotia before the American Revolution just seven or eight years after the 'foreign Protestants', and some of whom settled in neighbouring areas such as Liverpool, Nova Scotia (see Cuthbertson 1998). The model they provided might then have been reinforced later by the English of at least some of the thousands of Loyalists who came to Nova Scotia in the 1770s and 1780s.

My suggestion, then, is that the English of Lunenburg County represents a 250-year survival in an ethnically distinct community of a distinctive dialect which has remained phonologically intact while, all around it, a new form of English was being formed, especially during the nineteenth century, out of the English of later arrivals, notably non-New England Americans and perhaps more especially Highland Scots, Lowland Scots, Scots-Irish, and southern Irish (see Clarke 1997; Trudgill 1986). The moral is, of course, that distinctive linguistic features imported from elsewhere can survive in enclaves to tell a particular historical story even in small communities surrounded and outnumbered by very different dialects.

It turns out, however, that this is not the whole story. There are a number of caveats to make here which stress that this methodology does in fact have to be used with great care. The fact is that rural Lunenburg English does have some features that were almost certainly acquired from neighbouring non-New England-origin varieties, and others which may or may not have been so acquired but which in any case do not appear to be of New England origin.

First, the dialect does have th-stopping: that is *three* can be identical to *tree*, and *then* can be homophonous with *den*. We shall never know, of course, whether this is the result of German substratum influence, or of influence from rural Atlantic Canadian English, or both, but we certainly cannot rule out general Nova Scotian influence. Presumably, therefore, the same kind of scenario could be true in principle of features found in the AAVE-speaking exclaves.

Second, the dialect also has the PIN/PEN merger. This is usually thought of as having its origins in the southern USA but in fact it was almost certainly brought there from Ireland (O Baoill 1997), and is common in Newfoundland (Paddock 1981). This feature is unlikely to be a New England survival, and, like th-stopping, can also be interpreted as an indication that the Nova Scotian AAVE exclaves could have been the recipients of certain features from neighbouring Nova Scotian dialects.

Finally, the dialect has a merger of the vowels of NEAR and SQUARE, as [e:]. This does occur in certain other Atlantic Canadian varieties – it is certainly attested in Newfoundland, for instance (Story *et al.* 1982) – and could therefore have been imported into Lunenburg English from these. It could also of course, and crucially, be an independent innovation. It is after all a merger which has also occurred independently in East Anglia and New Zealand.

It goes without saying that rural Lunenburg English, like all other language varieties, is not static, and that it does produce internally generated changes of its own. Obviously this is undoubtedly true also of the AAVE-speaking exclaves in Nova Scotia – another challenge, of course, for this useful and interesting sociohistorical linguistic methodology.

II. DIALECT CHANGE

INTRODUCTION: DIALECT CHANGE

In this section we deal with dialect change, dedialectalisation and dialect death. There are specific reasons in the European context to feel particularly anxious about the effects of dialect death. It may not be immediately obvious that dialects are just as intimately linked to cultures as are languages (we shall return to this issue in Chapter 14). But just as there are national cultures, so there are local cultures, and dialects symbolise these local cultures, and help to maintain and defend them. Indeed, in the new Europe, it is possible to argue that, at least in some cases, local identities as symbolised by dialects are actually more desirable than national identities as symbolised by standard languages. In some situations, regional dialects, by reinforcing local cultures and local identities, may act as a counter to nationalism.

In most parts of Europe, though, we are witnessing this phenomenon of dialect death. We are seeing less and less regional variation in language, less and less dialect variation, the loss of patois/traditional dialects, increasing standardisation, increasing homogenisation. Do these processes matter? Why should we worry if most of the dialects of the world disappear? Specifically, does it matter if Europe becomes linguistically more homogeneous?

This is a question that linguists should be prepared to answer as often as possible, and as publicly as possible. No one else will do it for us, and many non-linguists are quite understandably unaware, unconcerned, misinformed or even hostile about the issues involved. A frequent, non-linguistic view of language and dialect diversity is that dialects are a nuisance. Dialects are regarded as impeding communication, delaying modernisation, damaging education and slowing down nation-building. To argue for the desirability of the preservation of linguistic diversity is therefore no easy matter.

I believe that an intellectual position we can call the denigration of vernacular varieties plays a role in dialect loss. It is therefore necessary to point out to those intellectuals who despise regional dialects that dialect

29

death and standardisation can actually cause rather than solve communication problems. This is particularly likely to be the case where, as in many parts of Europe, we find a geographical dialect continuum. Take, for example, the border between The Netherlands and Germany. As is well known, this is a border without an isogloss. Speakers on either side of the border speak dialects which are the same or very similar; this has meant that for generations there has been ready and easy cross-border communication, as there continues to be today. Working-class Dutch people from Nijmegen, for example, travel across the border to the German town of Cleves to visit, to shop and to work – something which the European Union has made much easier. Working-class Germans travel in the opposite direction. Notice, however, that just as the new Europe is breaking down barriers to cross-border travel and employment, middle-class Dutch and German people from Nijmegen and Cleves are no longer able to participate so readily in this cross-border traffic. This is because they can no longer speak the local dialect. If middle-class Dutch people who can only speak Standard Dutch want to travel to work in Germany, they have to study and learn Standard German because the people of Cleves cannot understand Standard Dutch. Many of them, of course, have done so. Many fewer Germans, however, have learnt Standard Dutch. The dialect continuum which permitted easy communication has, at least for middle-class speakers, been cut and broken by standardisation.

The connection between dialect death, on the one hand, and the denigration of vernacular varieties, on the other, is clear. If we wish to maintain linguistic diversity and oppose linguistic homogenisation (see also Chapter 13), we have to consider speakers' attitudes to their own dialects. We have to acknowledge that much dialect loss in modern Europe is due to processes which are probably sociolinguistically inevitable. Increased geographical mobility and urbanisation lead to contact between dialects and thus dialect-levelling and koinéisation. There is nothing we can or would wish to do about that. What we can work against is that kind of dialect loss which is the result of attitudinal factors. In most European countries, the majority of the population that does not speak the standard variety is discriminated against in various ways, and made to feel that their native vernacular dialects are inferior, not only socially, which is unfortunately true, but also linguistically, which is most emphatically not true. It is hardly surprising, therefore, if many of them try to shift to the standard variety even if, at some level of consciousness, they do not really want to. In this kind of atmosphere, traditional dialects or patois can disappear surprisingly quickly. There is often a direct relationship between the degree of hostility to dialects, the amount of denigration of vernacular varieties, and the rate at which they disappear.

One way of combatting this hostility is to point to those fortunate, more tolerant societies which do have greater respect for language varieties as good examples to be followed. In many dialect-hostile parts of Europe, including England, there is a widespread view that dialects are out-of-date, old-fashioned, unsophisticated, divisive, even economically disadvantageous. However, we can point to the following very interesting fact. In 1990, according to many measurements of per capita income, the three richest countries in Europe were Luxemburg, Norway and Switzerland. The entire indigenous population of Luxemburg is dialect-speaking. They learn and use German, they learn and use French, but their mother-tongue is Luxemburgish/Letzeburgisch, which is widely regarded as a dialect of German. Norway is also one of the most dialect-speaking countries in Europe: some people do speak Standard Norwegian, but the majority do not, whatever the social situation. People speak dialect on radio and TV, professors give lectures in dialect, and authors write poems and novels in dialect. The most important aspect of the Norwegian language situation, however, is that there is an enormous societal tolerance for linguistic diversity and that, what is more, linguistic diversity in Norway is officially recognised and officially protected. This is most clearly illustrated by the fact that in Norway there is a law stating that teachers are not allowed to try and change the way children speak in the classroom. If, as most of them do, children come into school speaking dialect, they must be allowed to continue to do so. In Switzerland, in German-speaking areas of the country, all the indigenous inhabitants are dialect speakers. These richest of Europeans are paradigm examples of extremely desirable sociolinguistic situations that the rest of us would do very well to imitate.

It would be too much to claim, of course, that Luxemburg, Norway and Switzerland are rich because they are dialect-speaking. But I also think that we should not underestimate the degree of alienation that occurs in situations where people are denied the dignity of having respect accorded to their vernacular speech. Nor should we underestimate the advantages of having a population able to express itself fluently and clearly in its own vernacular, without having to monitor the extent to which they are speaking 'correctly' or not. It is the job of linguists, I would argue, to persuade such people that all dialects are structured, grammatical systems of equal correctness, clarity and adequacy.

There is an obvious moral issue here, concerning the human rights of dialect speakers. If individuals suffer discrimination as a result of racism, we do not suggest that they change their race, although of course in places such as the United States there was a long and sad history of black people doing their best to look as much like white people as possible. If individuals suffer discrimination as a result of sexism, we do not suggest they change sex, although of course there are celebrated cases in history of women pretending to be men to be taken seriously. If individuals suffer discrimination because of the dialects they speak, then it is the discrimination that should be stamped out, not the dialects, although of course we cannot blame people if, in the meantime, they try to protect themselves against discrimination by acquiring another dialect. Linguists are in a particularly strong position to oppose this discrimination and consequent homogenisation because they, as experts on language, have the knowledge and ability to engender positive attitudes and to counter the denigration.

One of the better-known maxims of William Labov is that 'the more we know, the more we can find out'. This observation is amply borne out by the very fruitful work that has been carried out by many sociolinguists, although ironically not by Labov himself, into their own dialects. Sadly, however, it is not entirely clear to what extent such work on distinctive linguistic varieties will continue to be so fruitful in modern Europe. Although it is clear that all European languages will continue to be somewhat varied, the widespread processes of linguistic homogenisation and dialect death that are currently taking place in many parts of Europe appear to be progressing at an ever increasing rate. It is therefore possible that it will be increasingly less easy for research into distinctive regional dialects to be performed by native-speaking linguists in the future. In particular, it is quite probable that most linguists will find themselves working on koinéised dialects, and that varieties variously known by labels such as *traditional dialects, patois, Mundarten* and so on, will increasingly be lost. If this is the case, we should note that what we may be losing will be distinctive types of language variety which are relatively less affected by dialect and language contact, with less simplification and less regularisation, and with fewer tendencies to rapid but natural linguistic changes (see Trudgill 1996). Research objects of particular value for our understanding of linguistic structure and linguistic change may be lost for ever.

My own research has from time to time focused on the linguistic varieties of the area where I grew up, East Anglia. These dialects, however, are currently very much subject to the dialect death process. The chapters in the present section, although they are on the subject of East Anglian English, are thus motivated not only by a desire 'to find out' but also by a desire to record in some detail certain linguistic facts associated with a traditional dialect which might otherwise not be recorded in spite of the pioneering but necessarily less detailed efforts of the *Survey of English Dialects*. In this section, I discuss a number of linguistic changes which have taken place in my own dialect area over the last 200 years, as well as vestiges of earlier forms of speech. My intention is (a) to see what this can tell us about the linguistic and sociolinguistic processes involved in dedialectalisation; and (b) to record facts about the history of East Anglian English which are well known to older lay people in the area, but which are probably known to very few linguists.

4

TWO HUNDRED YEARS OF DEDIALECTALISATION: THE EAST ANGLIAN SHORT VOWEL SYSTEM

In this chapter, I address the topic of dialect death and the loss of English traditional dialects, in the sense of Wells (1982), by focusing on changes in the short-vowel subsystem of the dialects of East Anglia and the mechanisms involved in these changes for the period 1790–1990. I will be concentrating on the most typically East Anglian of East Anglian dialects, namely those spoken in north-eastern Norfolk, the area of East Anglia most remote from the Home Counties (the counties around London) and the Midlands of England. In this presentation, I shall be relying on a number of different sources, some already referred to in Chapter 2, as follows:

1. Forby (1830)
2. Wright (1905)
3. Ellis (1874)
4. Kökeritz (1932) – a brilliant Uppsala University dissertation.
5. Lowman's records of his fieldwork trip to southern England in the 1930s, copies of which were very kindly made available to me by the late Professor Raven I. McDavid.
6. The publications of the *Survey of English Dialects*, and the detailed notes made by their Norfolk fieldworker Professor W. Nelson Francis during the 1950s, which were very kindly made available to me by the Survey.
7. Trudgill (1974)
8. Local dialect literature.
9. Personal observations of local dialect speakers, including some born as long ago as the 1870s, over the past forty years.

During the course of the twentieth century, a rather large number of developments have occurred in the phonology of the traditional dialect of north-eastern Norfolk. There is some indication that, while some of these developments may have been internally generated, many of them are the result of diffusion from and influence of nonstandard Home Counties varieties (rather than standard or high-prestige varieties – see Trudgill

1999).We consider here developments in that East Anglian phonological subsystem which consists of phonetically short monophthongs phonotactically confined to closed syllables – hence their alternative description as *checked* vowels.

THE VOWEL /ɪ/

One of the most interesting features of the older East Anglian dialect checked vowel system was that, unlike most other varieties, /ɪ/ did not occur at all in unstressed syllables. Unstressed /ə/ continues to be the norm to this day in words such as *wanted, horses, David, naked, hundred*. I have hypothesised (Trudgill 1986) that this feature of East Anglian English may have had some input into the formation of southern hemisphere Englishes such as Australian English, where *schwa* also occurs in such words.

More striking, however, is the fact that /ə/ was the only vowel which could occur in any unstressed syllable in the earlier dialect. This was true not only in the case of word-final syllables in words such as *water, butter*, which of course also have /ə/ in RP, and in words such as *window, barrow*, which are pronounced /wɪndə, bærə/ in very many other forms of English, but also in items such as *very, money, city* which were /vɛrə, mʌnə, sɪtə/. In the modern dialect, dedialectalisation has taken place in that words from the *very* set are now pronounced with final /ɪ/ by older speakers and /iː/ by younger speakers, as is now usual throughout southern England. An interesting question is why dedialectalisation has taken place in the case of *very* etc., but not in the case of *naked* etc. Perhaps the large degree of phonetic contrast between /iː/ and /ə/ has played a role, together with the greater salience of word-final segments.

It is also noteworthy that the vowel /ɪ/ occurred not only in items such as *pit, bid* in the traditional dialect but also in a number of other words such as *get, yet, head*. There is little predictability as to which items have or had the raised vowel, but in all the words concerned the vowel was followed by /t/ or /d/. Most words of this type, however, such as *bet* and *bed*, have not undergone this development. East Anglian dialects are by no means the only varieties of English to demonstrate such raising (see Wyld 1936), but it was certainly a distinctive characteristic of the varieties of this area. The modern dialect has seen increasing dedialectalisation through a process of transfer of these words from /ɪ/ to /ɛ/, although the older pronunciations still survive in a rather smaller set of words.

THE VOWEL /ɛ/

In the older dialect, the vowel /ɛ/ was a rather close vowel approaching [e]. During the course of the twentieth century, it gradually opened until it is now much closer to [ɛ]. I have hypothesised that this close realisation of /ɛ/

may also have had some role to play in the development of the short vowel systems of the southern hemisphere (Trudgill 1986), where all three front checked vowels have closer realisations than in England. In older forms of the dialect, /ɛ/ occurred not only in the expected *bet, help, bed* and so on but also in a number of items which elsewhere have /æ/, such as *catch, have/has/ had*, as well as in at least one word which elsewhere has /ɪ/, namely *sit*. Whether this latter represents some kind of semantic falling together with the word *set*, or whether it implies some kind of hypercorrection due to pronunciations such as *get* /gɪt/, is not clear.

THE VOWEL /æ/

The vowel /æ/ appears to have undergone a certain amount of phonetic change in the last two centuries. At the time when /ɛ/ was [e], it is probable that /æ/ was closer to [ɛ], as in Australian English, while in the modern dialect it is a good deal more open. And at least in Norwich, the largest city of the area, it has also has undergone diphthongisation in some phonological environments: *back* [bæɛk].

It seems probable that in the nineteenth-century dialect, items with following voiceless fricatives such as *laugh, path, grass* had [æː], which was probably at the time simply an allophone of /æ/. The long vowel /aː/ would at that time have been confined to forms such as *part* which had undergone the loss of non-prevocalic /r/ (see below).

Words such as *catch* and *have* (see above) have been transferred to /æ/ in the modern dialect.

THE VOWEL /ʊ/

As we saw in Chapter 2, the vowel /ʊ/ was much more frequent in the older East Anglian dialect than in General English (in the sense of Wells 1982) for a number of reasons. Middle English /ou/ and /ɔː/ remained – and indeed still remain – distinct in the dialects of Norfolk e.g. *road* /ruːd/, *rowed* /rʌud/. However, there has been a strong tendency in East Anglia for the /uː/ descended from Middle English long open 'o' to be shortened to /ʊ/ in closed syllables. Thus *road* can rhyme with *good*, and we find pronunciations such as in *toad, home, stone, coat* /tʊd, hʊm, stʊn, kʊt/. This shortening does not normally occur before /l/, so *coal* is /kuːl/, but otherwise distribution is unpredictable – /ʊ/ does not occur in *foam, load, moan, vote*, for example.

The vowel /ʊ/ also occurs in closed syllables in a number of words such as *spoon, afternoon*, but this is spasmodic, and the vowel does not occur in most words in the set of *moon, soon, boot*. This development may be a relatively recent form of hyperdialectism (see Trudgill 1986). Probably under the influence of other varieties, a large number of words have been transferred from /u:/, the modern reflex of Middle English /o:/, to /u:/, which as we have seen is the modern reflex of Middle English long open 'o'. Thus, items such as *boot, moon* are now frequently homophonous with *boat, moan* /bu:t, mu:n/. This could have led such items to take part in the stylistic alternation between /u:/ and /ʊ/ which we mentioned above.

The vowel /ʊ/ also occurs in *roof, proof, hoof* and their plurals e.g. /rʊfs/; and, in some parts of the region, in *room, broom* (see Chapter 2).

THE VOWEL /ʌ/

As far as the vowel /ʌ/ is concerned, there have been clear phonetic developments, with the vowel moving forward from an earlier fully back [ʌ] to a more recent low-central [ɐ], as in much of the south of England, though the movement has not been nearly so extensive as the actual fronting which has taken place in London.

In most English accents, the number of words such as *blood* in which Middle English long close 'o' was shortened sufficiently early for the resulting /ʊ/ to take part in the change from /ʊ/ to /ʌ/ is relatively small. East Anglian dialects at the beginning of this century had a rather larger number of such lexical items e.g. *soot* /sʌt/, *roof* /rʌf/. Pronunciations of this type have now completely disappeared from the region.

THE VOWEL /ɒ/

The low back vowel of *pot* is unrounded /ɑ/ rather than rounded /ɒ/ in the older Norfolk dialect. This unrounded vowel was formerly common in many areas of England and may have been the source of the unrounded vowel still typical of North American varieties of English (see Chapter 3), although this is controversial (see Wells 1982: 245). This phonetic quality is gradually disappearing from Norfolk under the influence of the rounded vowel found in dialects further south (see Trudgill 1972).

The lexical set associated with this vowel was formerly rather smaller in that, as in most of southern England, the lengthened vowel /ɔ:/ was found before the front voiceless fricatives, as in *off, cloth, lost*. This feature survives to a certain extent, but mostly in working-class speech, and particularly in the word *off*. On the other hand, the forms *un-* and *under* had /ɑn/ rather than /ʌn/ *underneath* /ɑndəni:θ/.

THE VOWEL /ɐ/

A mechanism of obvious importance, then, in the dedialectalisation process, is *transfer* (see Trudgill and Foxcroft 1978) – the transfer of words from a lexical set associated with one vowel to that associated with another. In most cases, the vowel system itself remains intact and the phonetics distinctively regional, but its distribution over lexical items becomes gradually less regional and the variety thus phonologically less distinctive. In at least one case, however, wholesale transfer has led to the complete disappearance of a vowel, and thus a significant restructuring of the whole system. It is generally believed (see Wells 1982) that all varieties of English English have at this point in their vowel systems either – as in the North and Midlands of England – the original Middle English five-vowel subsystem:

/ɪ/ *pit*	/ʊ/ *put, but*
/ɛ/ *pet*	/ɔ/ *pot*
/a/ *pat*	

or – as in RP and the South of England – the newer six-vowel subsystem:

/ɪ/ *pit*	/ʊ/ *put*
/ɛ/ *pet*	/ʌ/ *but*
/æ/ *pat*	/ɒ/ *pot*

However, it is clear that the traditional dialects of East Anglia actually had neither of these systems. One clue to this comes from a series of, on the face of it, rather strange spellings used in local dialect writing. If we examine representations of words which have RP /ɜ:/, we find the following:

RP	**East Anglian**
her	*har*
heard	*hard*
nerves	*narves*
herself	*harself*
service	*sarvice*
earn	*arn*
early	*arly*
concern	*consarn*
sir	*sar*
fur	*far*
dursen't [= daren't]	*dussent*
first	*fust, fasst*
worse	*wuss*
church	*chuch, chatch*
purpose	*pappus*
turnip	*tannip*
further	*futher*
hurl	*hull*
turkey	*takkey*
turn	*tann*
hurting	*hatten*
nightshirt	*niteshat*

shirts	*shats*
girl	*gal*

On the subject of words such as this, Forby (1830: 92) writes:

> To the syllable *ur* (and consequently to *ir* and *or*, which have often the same sound) we give a pronunciation certainly our own.
> Ex. *Third – word – burn – curse*
> *Bird – curd – dirt – worse*
> It is one which can be neither intelligibly described, nor represented by other letters. It must be heard. Of all legitimate English sounds, it seems to come nearest to *open a* [the vowel of *balm*], or rather to the rapid utterance of the *a* in the word *arrow*, supposing it to be caught before it light on the r . . . *Bahd* has been used to convey our sound of *bird*. Certainly this gets rid of the danger of *r*; but the *h* must as certainly be understood to lengthen the sound of *a*; which is quite inconsistent with our snap-short utterance of the syllable. In short it must be heard.

Kökeritz (1932) was clearly puzzled by the behaviour of these word classes, as well as by Forby's remarks, and demonstrates, in his pre-phonemic study, a number of analytical difficulties. He writes (p. 49) the word *church* with [ʌ], [aː] and [æ]. He also somewhat inaccurately interprets Forby's description to indicate [a] (p. 173), and talks of this perhaps being the result of contamination of a: and ʌ (p. 175). He also refers to the [a] vowel which he himself sometimes hears as being 'a variant of ʌ'.

My own observations of speakers suggest that Forby was quite right, although he had no access to phonetic terminology, and that the solution to this problem is as follows: traditional dialects of East Anglian English actually had a checked vowel system consisting of seven vowels, not five or six. The additional item, which I represent here as /ɐ/, was a vowel somewhat more open than half-open, and slightly front of central, which occurred in the lexical set of *church, first*. Dialect literature, as we have seen, generally spells words from this lexical set as either as 'fust' or 'chatch' etc., but the reason for this vacillation was that the vowel was in fact phonetically intermediate between /æ/ and /ʌ/, as Kökeritz also seems to be trying to indicate. (Recall that /ʌ/ was a fully back vowel at this period.) This additional vowel occurred in items descended from Middle English *ur, or* and *ir* in closed syllables. Words ending in open syllables, such as *sir, fur,* had /aː/, as did items descended from ME *er*, such as *earth, her* (as well as items descended from *ar* such as *part, cart*, of course. The word *partner*, often used as a term of address in the older dialect, was an exception to this norm in that it also had /ɐ/.) The vowel /ɜː/ did not exist in the dialect until relatively recently.

During the last fifty years, this vowel has more or less disappeared from the local phonological inventory. In my study of the city dialect of Norwich

(Trudgill 1974) carried out in 1968, the vowel /ɐ/ was recorded a number of times, but the overwhelming majority of words from the relevant lexical set had the originally alien vowel /ɜ:/. The Norwich study showed that only in lower working-class speech was this vowel at all common in 1968, and then only 25 per cent of potential occurrences had the short vowel even in informal speech (p. 113). Note that the disappearance of /ɐ/ must have predated the forward movement of /ʌ/ from [ʌ] to [ɐ] (see above).

We can thus suggest that the short vowel subsystem of the traditional dialect of northern East Anglia was rather unusual, both from a typological point of view and as seen in comparison with other varieties of English. The full short vowel subsystem of the older nineteenth-century East Anglian traditional dialect was as follows:

/ɪ/ *pit, get*		/ʊ/ *put, road, spoon*
/ɛ/ *pet, catch, sit*		/ʌ/ *but, soot*
/æ/ *pat, laugh*	/ɐ/ *church, first*	/ɒ/ *pot, under*

5

NEW-DIALECT FORMATION AND DEDIALECTALISATION: EMBRYONIC AND VESTIGIAL VARIANTS

In Chapter 6, I describe how, in my 1968 sociolinguistic urban dialect study of Norwich (Trudgill 1974), I observed that a very small number, about 5 per cent, of my informants used a labio-dental approximant pronunciation [ʋ] of /r/. I assumed this to be of no significance – that the small number of speakers involved indicated an idiosyncratic speech impediment. When I returned to do a follow-up study in 1983, I observed that the number of informants in my new sample using [ʋ] had increased significantly. Indeed, an apparent-time study matching [ʋ]-use to age-group showed a steady increase in labio-dental approximants across generations. Now, after a further fifteen-year gap, one only has to walk around the streets of Norwich to hear that it has become the majority form amongst younger speakers. Clearly, I was quite wrong in 1968 to ignore this particular pronunciation (see Chapter 6).

Work with the Origins of New Zealand English Project (ONZE) led by Elizabeth Gordon at Canterbury University, Christchurch, New Zealand, has produced what we believe to be a number of similar cases. In Gordon and Trudgill (1999), Elizabeth Gordon has described such features as 'embryonic variants'. Part of our project is based on an unusual and important database. This consists of an archive of recordings, made by the New Zealand National Broadcasting Corporation, of elderly people in the 1940s. Born between 1850 and 1880, the oldest people on these recordings represent the first generation of New Zealand-born anglophones. These recordings were made using a Mobile Disc Recording Unit and were intended to collect pioneer reminiscences. Linguistically, however, they represent a fascinating resource, as I have indicated elsewhere (Trudgill 1998, 1999c). We have already used the data from this archive to solve (in our view) complicated issues concerning the chronology of the development of the New Zealand English short vowel system (see Trudgill et al. 1998).

Embryonic variants that have turned up as part of our research include the following.

1. Most authorities agree that modern NZ English is merging the vowels /ɪə/ and /ɛə/ of NEAR and SQUARE. This merger is of rather recent origin, and older speakers therefore do not have it – except that they do! A small number of the nineteenth century-born ONZE speakers – five out of about sixty, so far – have the merger either variably or categorically. It is probable, then, that this minority feature – very much a minority feature – nevertheless represents the 'seeds' of the later change. One interesting question, of course (see Trudgill *et al.* 2000a) is how and why some such minority variants survive to become majority variants.

2. Another feature which is typical of Modern NZ English, and more strongly established already than the NEAR/SQUARE merger, is the realisation of the NURSE VOWEL /ɜ:/. This is nowadays typically rounded and may also be fronted and/or raised: [ø:, œ:, ɵ:]. Again, our studies show that this was absent from earlier forms of NZ English – except that perhaps as many as 10 per cent of the nineteenth century-born ONZE speakers have at least some tokens of this type. It is not immediately obvious, either, that these speakers inherited such forms from varieties of English or Welsh English which have such variants: most of the speakers involved were of Scottish and/or Irish ancestry, and one had a father from Cheshire and a mother who was a Maori.

3. Another feature very characteristic of modern NZ English is the dis-yllabic pronunciation of past participles such as *sown, grown, known,* so that they rhyme with *Owen.* Current studies show that about a half of all New Zealanders today use this pronunciation, and it is certainly often commented on by outsiders. Again, this appears to be of relatively recent origin. Older speakers do not use this variant, except that, once again, a small number – about 13 per cent – of our ONZE informants do use at least some tokens of this type.

These embryonic variants, then, represent, or may represent, the very earliest stages of linguistic changes in progress. In the case of NZ English, they are also part of the new-dialect formation process (see Trudgill 1986). In the rest of this chapter, I wish to look at the process which is the reverse of new-dialect formation, namely dedialectalisation (see Chapter 4). The point is that during the process of dedialectalisation, including total dedialectalisation, i.e. dialect death, dialect variants disappear at different speeds. Once again, it would be interesting theoretically to know how and why some variants survive longer than others. There are also, as we shall see, methodological implications.

The phenomenon I wish to examine particularly here is thus the reverse of the embryonic variant syndrome. We can perhaps label it the *vestigial variant* syndrome. Let me give two brief East Anglian English examples of what I mean in an attempt to demonstrate why this syndrome can be interesting and even important:

1. Present tense positive forms of the verb *to be* in East Anglian English are for the most part identical with those of Standard English. However, it is still rather common for local dialect speakers, when finding or pointing to something, to say *Here it be!* and *There it be!* On arriving, one can also say *Here I be!* Where does this presentative *be* phenomenon come from? It is not at all clear, but it I believe that it is certainly possible that this may represent the last, fossilised traces of an earlier dialect system when forms such as *I be, you be, it be* were more general, as they still are in many other traditional dialects, notably in western England.

2. Most English dialectologists are familiar with the phenomenon that Ossi Ihalainen (1987) referred to as *pronoun exchange*. In the traditional dialects of the south-west of England, the pronouns *I, he, she, we, they* can occur as objects as well as verbal subjects. That is, one can say:

> Mary saw they.
> John gave it to she.

Similarly, the pronouns *him, her, us* can occur as verbal subjects:

> Us be a-goin.
> Her don't want none.

How these systems work is not entirely clear, but one possibility at least in some dialects is that the 'subject' pronouns occur when the pronoun is emphasised, while the 'object' forms occur in unemphatic position:

> Give it to *she*, not *they*.

It is much less well-known – indeed it was a considerable surprise to me when I learnt about this – that a similar system exists, or existed, in the traditional dialects of Essex, as revealed by the *Survey of English Dialects* materials (see the map in Trudgill 1999b). Essex dialect literature also confirms that pronoun exchange was a typical feature of the traditional dialects of this area. Charles Benham's (1960) *Essex Ballads*, originally published in Colchester in 1895, contain verses such as the following which, incidentally, give some support to the emphatic-position hypothesis (my italics):

> Tha's where they're gooin', are they? Pas the mill,
> Along the fiel' path leadin' tard the woods;
> I'll give *he* what for some däy, that I will,
> For walkin' out 'ith that ere bit of goods.

J'yer hear him call Good arternune to me?
He think he's doin' of it there some tune.
Next time I ketch him out along o' *she*,
Blest if I don't give *he* good arternune.
(From *Jim's New Gal*)

It is interesting that this feature is found in two rather widely separated areas of southern England – the West Country and Essex. I therefore speculatively suggested (Trudgill 1990) that this system might formerly have been much more widespread geographically than it is now, covering large areas of southern England, with a 'wedge', in the terminology of dialectology, emanating from London, having been driven into an originally homogeneous area and producing the two now widely separated areas.

A personal experience which occurred after the publication of this speculation was thus of very considerable interest to me. My maternal uncle, who was born in north Norfolk in 1910, is not a habitual speaker of the basilectal traditional Norfolk dialect but grew up speaking it and, depending on the social situation, may still produce it. One day when we were talking together he came out with a grammatical construction which I had never heard from him before. He was clearly quoting – using the expression as if it were in inverted commas – for humorous purposes. What he said was 'I wouldn't go along o' *he*!'. I have subsequently discussed this with my mother, born in 1918, and she has told me that, as far as she can recall, this is the kind of form that her grandfather, born in the 1860s, might occasionally have used. I had known my uncle for over fifty years and had never heard him quote this sort of form before – he was clearly dredging something up from long ago. But I believe that it is clear evidence that pronoun exchange was formerly part of the Norfolk dialect also. It is therefore not impossible that other areas of southern England also, as I speculated, formerly had this feature.

IMPLICATIONS FOR FUTURE STUDIES

Methodologically, we can say that this sort of evidence is difficult to actually look for, but when it does come our way, it should not be ignored. The message here, too, as with embryonic variants, is that we should not, in diachronic studies, ignore features which are vestigial in the sense that they occur only in a small number of contexts; or in jocular usage; or, as we shall see below, in the speech of a small number of people.

I now offer a preliminary classification of different types of vestigial variant that may be present in dedialectalisation situations. This classification is based on the fact that it is instructive to note that vestigial variants differ considerably in the extent to which native speakers are and are not aware of them. We can relate this phenomenon to Labov's (1966) description of different variables as being indicators, markers or stereotypes depending on the different degrees awareness they have in the speech community, as well as to his notions of change from above and below the level of conscious awareness. We can also note that this distinction applies to vestigial variants both during the dedialectalisation process and after it has been completed. That is, features may also vary in the extent to which people recall them – and therefore from time to time quote them – even after their 'disappearance'.

VESTIGIAL FEATURES ABOVE
THE LEVEL OF CONSCIOUS AWARENESS

In the final stages of dedialectalisation, vestigial variants may, in spite of a relatively low and diminishing level of usage, remain very high in the consciousness of the relevant population approaching the level of Labov's stereotypes. I have reported on such a variant in my work on the vanishing Greek dialect of the village of Chora Sfakion, southern Crete. Typical of this dialect is – or was – a remarkable and interesting allophone of /l/. The linguistic facts are these. Nearly all varieties of Greek have five vowels: /i, e, a, o, u/. In most varieties of Greek, /l/ is realised as a relatively clear [l] before /a, o, u/, with particularly palatalised variants occurring before /i, e/.

In the village of Chora Sfakion, however, a different system occurs: a clear but non-palatalised [l] is used before /i, e/ while in the environment immediately preceding /a, o, u/ a phonetically very different and distinctive allophone is employed. The most distinctive pronunciation, most typical of the local dialect, is a retroflex approximant [ɻ], identical to the pronunciation of /r/ used by English speakers in the south-west of England. For example:

> *kali* kali/ [kɑli] (Different forms of the
> *kales* /kales/ [kɑles] adjective *kalo* 'good')
> *kala* /kala/ [kɑɻɑ]
> *kalo* /kalo/ [kɑɻo]
> *kalous* /kalus/ [kɑɻus].

In Chora Sfakion, the allophone [ɻ] has now acquired vestigial variant status. It has today almost disappeared and, fascinatingly, those speakers who do employ it are exclusively male (see Mansfield and Trudgill 1994). However, it is a feature which remains very high in the conscious awareness of local people. Indeed, the dedialectalisation associated with this feature can be ascribed in part to the fact that this distinctive allophone has become a sociolinguistic stereotype (Labov 1966). It is overtly commented on in the village, it is quoted, it is imitated, and certain younger speakers mock the older men as 'peasants' by teasingly repeating [ɻɻɻ]. We can suppose that since the allophone does not occur in Standard Greek, it has low social status, and its phonetic character, which is acoustically very distinct from standard /l/, attracts sociolinguistic awareness (see Trudgill 1974).

The rarity of the allophone in the dialect of this particular village could have led us to suppose that it was an idiosyncratic feature associated with individual speakers only, and of no consequence. Indeed, when I first heard it I did suppose it to be a speech impediment. However, it actually occurs in other villages in the area, where it is much less moribund, and it has been described in the literature – i.e. it has attracted the attention of linguists a number of times (e.g. Kondosopoulos 1974, 1988; Mansfield [1964] 1992; Newton 1972; Trudgill 1989). The spatial configuration of the areas of western Crete where this feature occurs – a number of different relic areas – also suggests rather strongly that the [ɻ] allophone of /l/ was more wide-spread formerly than now, and a reasonable inference is that it is gradually dying out everywhere. Such is the level of awareness of this feature, however, that we can confidently predict that it will still be being imitated long after it has actually disappeared.

GONE BUT NOT FORGOTTEN

We now direct our attention to a later stage of the same phenomenon, involving a high stereotype-level of awareness of a feature which has totally disappeared from actual usage. In the case of Sfakian /l/, we predict that it will be a feature that will be commented on even after it 'dies.' The extent to which such a thing can indeed happen is revealed by a particular Norfolk dialect feature which is 'remembered' by the local community decades after its actual disappearance. This is the merger of /w/ and /v/ in the traditional dialect of the county. The phonetic facts can no longer be reconstructed (see Trudgill *et al.* forthcoming). What everybody in the area 'knows', however, is that *village* used to be pronounced *willage* and that *very* used to be pronounced *wery*.

This is, of course, a feature of very considerable interest in itself. The *Survey of English Dialects (SED)* materials show sporadic instances of this pronunciation, usually labelled 'older', in many parts of south-eastern England. It is a feature associated with older Cockney (as portrayed, famously, in Dickens' *Pickwick Papers*). And it is a feature which makes an appearance in a number of English-based creoles and lesser-known colonial varieties of English (White Bahamian, St Helena, Tristan da Cunha).

As far as the Norfolk version of the feature is concerned, the longevity of its folk memory is rather remarkable. As a child, I regularly associated with traditional dialect speakers who were born as early as the 1860s. However, I never heard anyone use this feature except as a joke or quotation. Discussions with older Norfolk people suggest that it was in normal unself-conscious use only until the 1920s. The fact that modern dialect writers still use the feature is therefore rather remarkable. For example, Michael Brindred in his local dialect column in the Norwich-based *Eastern Daily* Press of August 26, 1998 writes 'anniversary' <anniwarsary>. This dialect feature remains a stereotype eighty years after its disappearance from actual speech.

VESTIGIAL FEATURES BELOW
THE LEVEL OF CONSCIOUS AWARENESS

Other vestigial features, however, may disappear almost without any comment – below the level of conscious awareness, in Labov's terms. Contrast the above instances with a similar feature in Norwegian which, however, appears to have attracted no attention whatsoever – neither in the local community, nor, for the most part, from linguists. Indeed, specialists in Norwegian dialectology were very surprised when it was drawn to their attention.

Modern forms of eastern Norwegian have a fricative /ʂ/ or /ʃ/ which has a number of historical sources. It has arisen, for example, from combinations of /r/ + /s/, as in *irsk* 'Irish', as well as from combinations of /s/ + /j/, as in *sjø* 'sea'. Many dialects of Norwegian away from the east may lack /ʂ/ altogether or have it only from some of the possible sources. Dialectologists, for instance, often cite southern coastal dialects as retaining the original /sj/ pronunciation. It was a great surprise when work on the Brunlanes peninsula (see Foldvik 1979; Trudgill 1973) showed that a few speakers in this area, many kilometres to the north of the usually cited /ʂ/-less zone, also retained /sj/. Indeed, it was a surprise to my colleague, Arne Kjell Foldvik, who is a native of the area. The survival of this feature in the speech of a few elderly and unusual informants tells us rather clearly that /ʂ/ has made inroads into this area only rather recently, a fact hitherto unsuspected by Norwegian dialectologists and historical linguists.

GONE AND FORGOTTEN

Diachronically speaking, we can say that the interesting question for our purposes is not only why some vestigial features are observed and commented on but also why, later on, some features are remembered, and thus remain in some sense vestigial dialect features, while so many others are forgotten. The answer will presumably be the same in both cases.

Why, for example, is it not remembered, except by dialectologists, that in the traditional dialect of Norfolk, word-initial /θr/ and /ʃr/ used to be – as recently as the 1950s – /tr/ and /sr/ respectively, so that *thread* was /trɪd/ and *shriek* /sriːk/? Why is it that no one imitating the older Norfolk dialect uses clear /l/ in post-vocalic position when as recently as the 1960s this was the traditional dialect pronunciation?

FORGOTTEN BUT NOT GONE

Finally, I would like to finish this chapter with a reference to a rather strange kind of vestigial variant. I conclude by referring to a phenomenon which represents a complete parallel in reverse to the embryonic variant [ʋ] that I began with.

The English of Norfolk is non-rhotic. Indeed, nothing infuriates Norfolk people more than actors supposedly speaking Norfolk dialect on television, radio or in films who pronounce non-prevocalic /r/. People complain that 'they make us sound like we're from the West Country'. The loss of non-prevocalic /r/ in Norfolk must also have occurred some considerable time ago. Lowman (see Trudgill 1974) notes no instances of non-prevocalic /r/ in Norfolk, and it is also absent from the *Survey of English Dialect* records. On the other hand, we should probably not try to push the loss of this feature in Norfolk back too far in terms of time depth. Interestingly, one ONZE speaker whose parents came from Suffolk and who probably speaks a form of English (see Trudgill 1999) representative of that spoken by middle-class Suffolk people born in the 1840s is vestigially rhotic. It is therefore of considerable historical and methodological interest that one of the sixty informants in my 1968 Norwich survey was rhotic. She was born around 1910 and pronounced a high proportion of tokens of the NURSE vowel with /ɜːr/ rather than /ɜː/. Non-prevocalic /r/ occurred in no other phonological context, but in this context it was reasonably consistent. This feature rather bothered me at the time – I did not understand it. I tried during the course of the interview to find out if she had lived for some time in the West Country; or if one of her parents was Irish; or if her husband was American. But all her family were from Norwich, and she herself had lived all her life in the city. I now believe that this was a very vestigial feature which supports the claim by Lass (1997, 281) that /r/-loss in English English was later than many people have believed. In the case of my informant, her rhoticity was so vestigial that she was not aware of it, and no one, she said, had ever mentioned it to her before. Her husband had no idea what I was talking about. So the only person who noticed it and commented on it was a twenty-four-year-old PhD student in linguistics. It is quite possible that, quite by chance, I found the last rhotic East Anglian. Just as with embryonic variants, someone has to be the first, so, with vestigial variants, someone has to be the last.

6

NORWICH REVISITED: RECENT LINGUISTIC CHANGES IN AN ENGLISH URBAN DIALECT

In 1968 I carried out what can by now probably be referred to as a traditional sociolinguistic urban dialect survey, employing Labovian methodology, in the English city of Norwich (see Trudgill 1974). The data obtained were employed, among other things, to investigate and make claims about ongoing phonetic and phonological changes in Norwich English. Analysis showed that some of the phonological variables which were investigated appeared to be involved in different forms of social differentiation but to be stable chronologically and not involved in linguistic changes. Other variables, on the other hand, did seem to be involved in linguistic change, with some variants in the process of being wholly or partially replaced by others. In many cases it was possible to locate the social class and/or sex group which was the focus of a particular linguistic change (see Trudgill 1972).

This investigation of linguistic change in the Norwich data was based on the so-called *apparent-time* methodology (Labov 1966). In the apparent time approach, the speech of older informants is compared with that of younger informants, and, subject to certain safeguards, differences between the speech of older and younger subjects are interpreted as representing linguistic changes, with younger speakers tending to favour newer forms and older speakers tending to favour older forms. The safeguards referred to normally involve comparisons with older records such as those compiled by traditional dialectologists, where these are available, to guard against the possibility that some differences may be due to age-grading. There are, that is, cases where differences between older and younger speakers are repeated in every generation, and we need to guard against this eventuality wherever possible when using the apparent-time methodology. Obviously, there are many advantages to using the apparent-time methodology as opposed to studying linguistic change in real time, the most obvious of which is that one can study results immediately rather than waiting for twenty years or so to see what happens. There are also, however, some obvious pitfalls, one of which is that one cannot predict with absolute certainty which of a number of apparent ongoing changes are going to continue to be successful and which not. One cannot be entirely sure, that is, whether one is dealing with a genuine and long-term linguistic change, or with a temporary, possibly fashionable, but ultimately irrelevant fluctuation in usage. In this paper we contrast changes in apparent time, as portrayed in Trudgill (1974), with changes in real time, as these emerge from a more recent follow-up study of the same city, and discuss some of the lessons which emerge.

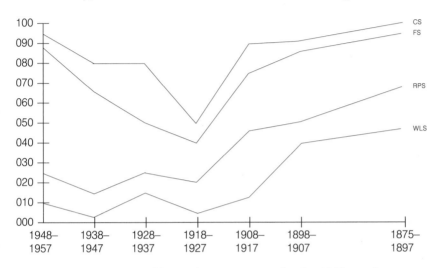

Figure 6.1.   Variable (ng) by age-group and style: 1968 sample

CS= Casual speech
FS= Formal speech
RPS= Reading passage
WLS = Word list

Typical of the stable variables investigated in the 1968 Norwich survey was (ng). This variable deals with the pronunciation of the *-ing* suffix in items such as *walking, running, reading,* etc. and has two variants, the velar nasal and the alveolar nasal. Indices for this variable were computed in such a way that consistent use of [n] would give a score of 100, while consistent use of the velar nasal would give a score of 0. It emerged from the study that this particular variable was not involved in any ongoing change. Figure 6.1, from Trudgill (1974), portrays the correlation of the variable with age-group and style (for a discussion of contextual styles in this type of methodology, see Labov 1966). The fact that the highest scores for this variable were, as can be seen, obtained by the younger and older age-groups, as opposed to the middle-aged groups, appears to be a phenomenon typical of variables which are not undergoing change. We can probably explain this pattern in terms of the lower educational background of older speakers, and in terms of the greater influence of the peer group on younger speakers as opposed to that of the mainstream norm on middle-aged speakers. In any case, we can note that variables not involved in change do not demonstrate an even distribution across age-groups, as might have been supposed, but rather a curvilinear age-graded pattern of the sort that we see in Figure 6.1. Other stable variables of this type from the 1968 survey which have this pattern include (h), which represents the presence or absence of /h/ in the lexical set of *hammer, house* etc.; and (a:), which covers the degree of fronting or backing of the vowel of *cart, last, dance*. Both of these variables correlated with social class, with [h], for instance, being more typical of higher class speakers, and [a:] more typical of lower class speakers. They did not, however, correlate with age. Variables of this type thus contradict claims that variation is always due to ongoing change.

A Norwich variable typical of the other type, namely those involved in change in the 1968 survey, was (e). This refers to the degree of centralisation of the vowel /e/ before /l/ in words such as *bell, well, healthy*. There are three major variants to this variable: [ɛ], [ɜ] and [ʌ]. Scores were calculated in such a way that consistent use of RP-type [ɛ] would give an index of 0, while consistent use of the most extreme local pronunciation [ʌ] would give a score of 200 (see Chambers and Trudgill 1998 for a discussion of this methodology).

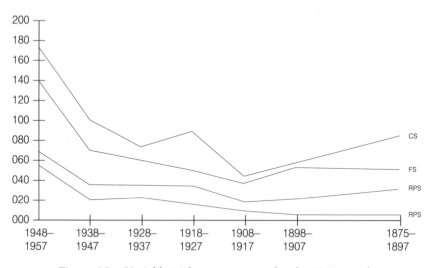

Figure 6.2.   Variable (e) by age-group and style: 1968 sample

As Figure 6.2 demonstrates, a correlation of scores for this variable with age and contextual style shows that it contrasts markedly with (ng) in its patterning, and indeed appears to be involved in a rapid change in progress. Rather than the symmetrical curvilinear pattern associated with (ng), (h) and (a), we can note here a very steep slope of the graph upwards from the middle-aged speakers to the younger speakers from right to left across the graph, indicating a very sharp rise in the use of centralised variants on the part of these younger speakers. (In fact younger working-class male speakers actually scored 198 out of a possible total of 200, that is, nearly all instances of /e/ before /l/ are pronounced [ʌ] by these speakers. See Trudgill 1974). The right-hand side of the graph, on the other hand shows the stable pattern we also saw in the case of (ng), indicating stylistic variation in the pronunciation of (e) by older speakers but no change in progress.

In 1983, I returned to Norwich to carry out a follow-up study in the city and to check on the progress of those linguistic variables which had been involved in linguistic change, as well as to investigate more recent developments. I assumed that the fifteen-year gap would be sufficient for a study of linguistic change in real time, and for predictions arising from the earlier study to be confirmed or disconfirmed. In fact, it emerges that this follow-up study was only one of a number of studies being carried out along similar lines, although it is so far the only one, as far as I am aware, in Britain. The increase in availability of portable tape-recorders in the 1960s, and the rise in secular linguistic research at about the same time, meant that in the 1980s, for the first time ever, large-scale quantitative studies in real time of linguistic changes in particular dialects became feasible. As a consequence, the sociolinguistic literature shows that a number of scholars have seized the opportunity to update and re-evaluate their data in the same way (see for example Cedergren 1990).

In principle, there appear to be two different approaches that one could adopt in returning to the site of one's original research in order to carry out a real-time study, as I did. First, one could seek out one's original informants and reinterview them to investigate whether, how and to what extent their language had changed; this was the approach adopted by Cedergren. There are some obvious difficulties with this approach, particularly the death and other forms of unavailability of some of the informants. The other approach is to return to the fieldwork site and to interview younger informants who were not born or too young to be included in the original sample. This latter was the course of action that was adopted on my return to Norwich. I believe that this decision has been vindicated. We know of course that the speech of even socially and geographically non-mobile adults does change during the course of their lifetimes. However, it is apparent from this study that these changes are in most cases rather small. Most of the more dramatic changes that have recently occurred in the Norwich speech community have not affected at all the speech of those who did not have the features in question by the time they were adults. It is only by studying the speech of the next generation along, it turns out, that we obtain a true picture of the full range of linguistic changes; ideally, however, the two approaches should be combined. In this way we would achieve a better understanding of the relative importance of children, adolescents and adults in the production of different types of linguistic change.

The original Norwich sample consisted of sixty informants who were born between 1875 and 1958 and were thus in 1968 aged between ten and ninety-three (a policy decision having been taken to exclude children under ten; see Trudgill 1974). The sample was a random sample based on the electoral register and on school class-lists. In 1983 I investigated the speech of seventeen additional informants, selected on a quota-sample basis to conform to the social class profile of the earlier sample. These informants were born between 1958 and 1973, and were thus at the time aged between ten and twenty-five. Fifteen extra year-groups were thus added to the sample in line with the fifteen-year gap which had elapsed between the two periods of fieldwork. There is, then, an overall age-range, in the two samples combined, of ninety-eight years.

Some obvious methodological problems presented themselves in the planning of the 1983 fieldwork. The biggest problem was perhaps myself: in 1968 I had been a twenty-four-year-old student only recently removed from my native Norwich speech community. In 1983 I was nearly forty years old and had been away from the speech community for various extended periods of time over a period of twenty years, and my speech had clearly changed. In order, therefore, to secure as far as possible comparability of the two data sets, the decision was taken to employ an interviewer younger than myself who had never left the Norwich speech community.

A further difficulty was involved in the decision that was ultimately taken to keep to the original 1968 methodology in its entirety. Since the late 1960s, of course, many methodological advances have been made in sociolinguistics and we know much more about procedures for securing and recording good data. It was therefore tempting to introduce some methodological innovations into the new fieldwork. This temptation, however, was resisted: none of these advances was actually employed, again because of the problem of the comparability of the data. For example, there was a danger that we might in 1983 succeed in obtaining data that was more genuinely vernacular than that obtained in 1968, which would of course have led to inaccurate conclusions about the direction and speed of linguistic change.

Finally, the reading passage which had been employed during the original fieldwork, and which had been written in a colloquial style designed to provoke relatively informal reading styles, was also now outdated in its content and language. It referred to shops in Norwich which no longer existed, for example, and contained vocabulary typical of the 1960s, such as 'the latest gear'. Once again, however the decision was taken to retain the reading passage as it stood in order to achieve comparability. This decision does not seem to have caused any difficulties.

We can note that the 1983 work produced some interesting non-phonological findings. For instance, it is clear that a considerable amount of lexical attrition has taken place in the local dialect of younger speakers. In both surveys, use and knowledge of a small number of local dialect words were investigated. It emerges that many dialect words such as *dwile* (dish cloth) and *mawther* (girl), which had been used by older speakers in the 1968 sample and were at least known by most middle-aged and younger speakers, were totally unknown in the 1983 sample. The one exception to this was the word *squit* (nonsense) which continues to be both known and used by speakers of all ages.

Second, questions on varieties of language showed that a clear change in linguistic attitudes and awareness has also taken place. To simplify somewhat, we can say that the 1968 middle-class informants tended to make a distinction between the urban dialect of Norwich and the rural Norfolk dialect, and to regard the Norwich dialect as unpleasant and the Norfolk dialect as nice or at least quaint. The working-class informants, on the other hand, tended to have more favourable attitudes towards Norwich speech, and to look down on Norfolk dialect as having unfavourable country yokel connotations. The members of the 1983 sample failed to make such a distinction between the urban and rural dialects, thus reflecting the reality of the rapid spread of speech forms from the city into the surrounding countryside, as well as considerable suburbanisation of the villages surrounding Norwich. They were also altogether more positive about local speech forms. A number of them referred, for example, to the use of locally accented speakers on BBC Radio Norfolk and appeared to regard this as a positive step forward. It is probable that local radio itself has had an effect in influencing evaluations of local speech forms in a positive way. On the other hand, there was also a much greater awareness than there had been in 1968 of the way in which outsiders regard local speech forms. This is most probably to be ascribed to increased geographical mobility, and to a very heavy increase in immigration to Norwich, particularly from the Home Counties, in the past fifteen years. There was, for example, a definite recognition that people from outside the East Anglian region tended to regard all East Anglians, rural and urban, as sounding like farmers. We are thus presented with the interesting paradox of an improved self-image as far as Norwich dialect is concerned combined with an increase in defensiveness with respect to the attitudes of outsiders, particularly Londoners. It is possible that these attitudinal factors have been involved in the development of at least one linguistic change, that involving /θ/ and /ð/ (see below). Because of the methodology adopted, we do not know whether a change of attitudes on the part of the older speakers interviewed in 1968 has occurred or not.

As far as phonetic and phonological change is concerned, a number of changes continue trends that were already apparent in 1968. For example, the use of the vowel /eː/ in the lexical set of *gate* and *face*, which was vestigial in 1968, has now disappeared from the speech of these ten to twenty-five-year-olds, although it can still be heard in the speech of older people. We can therefore predict its total disappearance and replacement by the newer form /æi/ in the next twenty years or so. Clearly, this is also one change which has affected the speech of many adults during the course of their lives. There are certainly many people in the community who used to say /fe:s/ but no longer do so. Similarly, the use of the relic form [ɐ] in *bird*, *turkey* etc. which was also vestigial, has also now totally gone from younger Norwich speech. Moreover, the merger of the vowels of *beer* and *bear* as /ɛ:/ is now complete, with all speakers except those from the UMC failing to make this distinction. On the other hand, the merger between the originally distinct lexical sets of *moan* und *mown,* which in the 1968 sample was confined to a small number of middle-class speakers (see Chapters 2 and 4), is now beginning to expand, and a number of speakers from other social class groups are now beginning variably to adopt this feature. There has also been an increase in the use of variants of /ai/ as in *nice* with a back rounded onset [ɒi]. All these phenomena confirm the 1968 apparent-time findings.

However, we are also presented with some interesting phonetic and phonological cases where certain weaknesses in the apparent-time methodology could be argued to have been revealed. For example, there is at least one feature which we can see in retrospect was involved in 1968 in the beginnings of a linguistic change but which was not perceived or treated as such. This is the change in pronunciation of the consonant /r/. The original pronunciation of this consonant in Norwich English was as a post-alveolar approximate. Now, to an astonishing degree, the younger generation has changed over to employing a labiodental approximant [ʋ]. Figure 6.3 demonstrates the percentages of each of the age groups investigated in the two surveys who have the newer labio-dental pronunciation. In fact, this change in Norwich pronunciation is strikingly apparent even to the casual observer. This feature was already present in Norwich English in 1968, as Figure 6.3 shows. The sample of informants was, however, not large enough to throw up very many speakers who had this feature. I therefore regarded it as an idiosyncratic feature in the speech of those who did have it, assuming it to be simply a speech defect. In a sense, of course, it was a speech defect, at some stage in its development. However, when a speech defect spreads to a majority of the population it is clearly no longer to be regarded as such. Figure 6.3, moreover, suggests very strongly that this pronunciation will be the norm or at least the majority pronunciation within the next few decades. Observations suggest, incidentally, that this will be true of very many other varieties of (at least) southern English English also. However, rather than cite this phenomenon as an example of an inherent weakness in the apparent-time methodology as such, I prefer to ascribe the failure to spot this particular linguistic change in progress to the smallish sample size and/or to the lack of perspicacity on the part of the investigator. Note that this is one feature that would not have been thrown up by a follow-up approach which relied only on recontacting previous informants: no speakers in Norwich appear to have changed their pronunciation of /r/ in this direction in the course of their lifetimes.

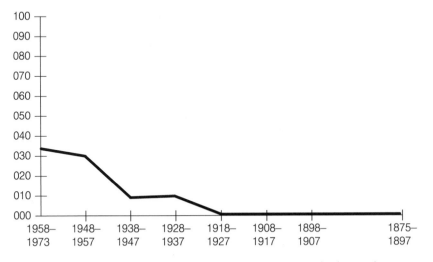

Figure 6.3. Percentage of informants with /r/ = [ʊ]: both samples

In other cases changes have taken place in Norwich English which were not predicted on the basis of the 1968 apparent-time study simply because there was no trace of them in the data. One example of this type is provided by a phonetic change which has affected the vowel /uː/ of the lexical set of *moan, road, rose*. In Trudgill (1974) I described this phonetically as being typically [ʊu], contrasting with the vowel of *mown, rowed, rows* which was [ʌu]. Now, as we have seen, there is an increasing tendency for these two vowels, under the influence of RP and the neighbouring dialects, to merge, as the corresponding front vowels /eː/ as in *made* and /æi/ as in *maid* already for the most part have. With /uː/ and /ʌu/ the merger remains a minority option. However, the actual realisation of /uː/ in the speech of the majority who retain the distinction is clearly changing. In the speech of the ten to twenty-five-year-olds in the new sample there is a very clear, readily audible tendency for the first element of the diphthong to be fronted, giving pronunciations such as *toad* [tʉud]. This vowel has long been typical of neighbouring towns to the south of Norwich, such as Lowestoft, but was totally unknown in Norwich in 1968. Interestingly, this represents a change whose origins can be dated rather precisely. Following my 1968 research, William Labov carried out fieldwork in Norwich in the summer of 1971, exactly three years after my survey. In the course of this work he recorded an eleven-year-old boy who had this feature, and the boy's close friend – who did not. (Labov 1975 shows how this leads the friend to misinterpret utterances such as *toe* /tu:/ as *too* /tʉ:/.) I found this hard to believe at the time, but can now confirm that I have subsequently had trouble in distinguishing between pairs such as *tone* /tu:n/ and *tune* /tʉ:n/ in the speech of Norwich teenagers, although they clearly have no such trouble themselves. The change is occurring in such a way that realisations of /u:/ are moving closer phonetically to /ʉ:/, hence the confusion. If we in future note a corresponding fronting of /ʉ:/, of which there is actually no sign as yet, we will therefore be sure that we have observed a push-chain in progress. This, then, is a change which appears to have started in the speech of Norwich speakers born between 1958 and 1960. It is of course unusual to be able to date the inception of a change so narrowly. It is also a change which current research shows to be spreading into the speech of some adults who formerly had the older pronunciation.

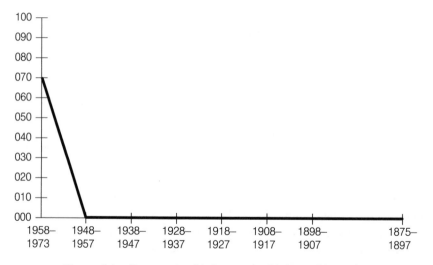

Figure 6.4. Percentage of informants with loss of /θ/ and /ð/

A further and more dramatic example of this type is portrayed in Figure 6.4. Here again we have a change not predicted in 1968; not because of any inadequacies in the sample size or on the part of the investigator, but because at that time there was no sign of it whatsoever. This represents a change which has come completely and dramatically out of the blue. Of course, we do not necessarily mean to suggest that there were no speakers at all who had this, feature in their speech in Norwich in 1968. If our sample had been absolutely massive we might have uncovered a few individuals who had this feature; however, if we had, it is likely that we would have regarded it as an individual idiosyncrasy, and this change has come so rapidly as to suggest that every now and then changes will occur in any speech community which the apparent-time methodology is certain to be unable to detect and predict. The change in question is the merger of /θ/ with /f/ together with the non-word-initial merger of /ð/ with /v/ (/ð/ is always found word-initially in items such as *this, those,* etc.). Not a single speaker in the 1968 sample showed even one instance of this phenomenon. In other words, our random sample suggested that nobody born between 1875 and 1958 has this feature in their speech. But, of people born between 1959 and 1973, as many as 70 per cent have it: 41 per cent have the merger variably; and 29 per cent have a total merger, i.e. /θ/ has been totally lost from their consonantal inventories, while /ð/ is now confined to word-initial position. This is a very surprising phenomenon and one which is not particularly easy to explain. We can note that the loss of interdental fricatives is unsurprising as a linguistic change, these consonants being marked, acquired late by children, and relatively rare in the world's languages; we can also note that it has long been well-known as a feature of the English of London, and we can observe that Norwich is not the only area of southern and central England to be affected by this change: reports and observations suggest that this merger is spreading very rapidly indeed out from London in all directions. What is surprising, however, is the extreme rapidity of this change. Some observers have been inclined to ascribe it to the influence of television programmes that have Cockney heroes popular with young people. This of course fails to explain why it is this feature of London English and not others that has been adopted, and in any case, cannot be correct, for if it were we would expect all areas of the country to be affected simultaneously. This is not in fact what is happening. In spite of the rapidity of the change, we are nevertheless able to detect geographical patterning, with areas close to London being affected before areas further away, and areas in the north of the country being totally unaffected as yet. The pattern of geographical diffusion suggests very strongly that face-to-face contact, as a result of mobility and immigration (see above), must be involved (see Trudgill 1986). The sheer speed of the change, however, may be due to a softening-up process produced by the engendering of favourable attitudes through television programmes, as well as to the salience of this feature (Trudgill 1986) and the naturalness of the change. This is a further example of a change which would not have been revealed by the recontact methodology: current observations suggest that no speaker has lost this contrast in post-adolescent years.

In other cases, we find a reverse kind of phenomenon. That is, we observe that some changes which we would have predicted from the 1968 data to be ongoing appear to have stopped or to be continuing in rather complicated and unpredictable ways. For example, we note in the 1983 data a small continuing increase in the use of the glottal-stop realisation of intervocalic and word-final /t/. The variable (t) deals with the realisation of /t/ in items such as *bet* and *better* as [t], [t?] or [?]. Scores are calculated in such a way as to give speakers who consistently use [?] an index of 200, and speakers who consistently employ the RP variant [t] a score of 0.

Figure 6.5.   Variable (t) by age-group and style: both samples

Figure 6.5 thus shows a small increase in glottal stop usage in casual styles, but it is also apparent that there has actually been a more dramatic increase, if we look at the rise of lines from right to left across the graph, in more formal styles. One reason for this must be that very little increase in glottal-stop usage in casual styles was possible simply because younger speakers were already employing close to 100 per cent anyway. But the increase in formal styles tallies very well with a strong casual impression shared by many older people that younger people in many parts of Britain today no longer feel [?] to be a stigmatised feature to be avoided in certain situations, as older people do. This graph thus provides an interesting example of the way in which a change, having gone almost to completion in casual speech, continues to spread from style to style. We can take this as a vivid example of the way in which linguistic innovations spread not only from person to person, area to area, class to class, and linguistic environment to linguistic environment, but also from contextual style to contextual style. Here is confirmation that most linguistic changes begin in unmonitored, vernacular informal styles and only later spread to more formal varieties of speech. There is, however, one caveat that we should introduce at this point. We have to point out that, methodologically, there is one way in which the two data sets could never have been strictly comparable. In 1983, younger people were much more familiar with cassette recorders and with being recorded than anybody was in 1968. Tape-recorders are now very much a feature of many homes and schools, and no longer regarded as alien and somewhat frightening machines. It could therefore be argued that some of the apparent increase in glottal-stop usage in formal styles might simply be due to the less daunting nature of the tape-recorded interview. However, the fact that other variables, with one exception, do not behave in this way greatly reduces, in my view, the likelihood of this being the correct explanation. Increases in glottaling (Wells 1982) do also appear, impressionistically, to have occurred or to be occurring in the speech of post-adolescents, but this is not supported as yet by research data. Probably, recontact methodology would therefore have been relevant in this case. (Note that in reading Figures 6.5 and 6.6, age-grading has to be allowed for in that both the 1948–57 and 1958–73 groups were aged 10–19 at the time of recording.)

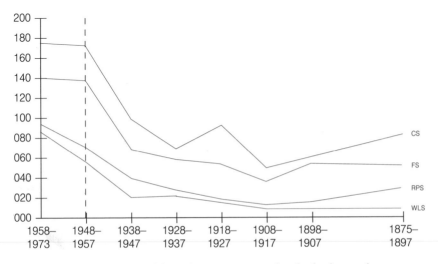

Figure 6.6.   Variable (e) by age-group and style: both samples

The exception, a further somewhat complex example of change, is provided by the variable (e). As we saw above, this variable was a very clear example, probably the clearest example of all in the 1968 data, of a variable involved in linguistic change. This is apparent in Figure 6.2 from the very steep rise between the scores obtained by those born in 1938 and those born in 1958. The 1983 data, however, show, somewhat surprisingly, that this change appears to have halted, except again that the change does continue in the two more formal styles – see Figure 6.6. That is, reading-passage style and word-list style are beginning, as it were, to catch up with the more informal styles. This halting of centralisation was not predictable from the 1968 data. It is, however, quite readily explicable. Note first that the rise in scores in the more formal styles is not due to further actual centralisation of the vowel but rather to a higher proportion of centralised tokens. In other words, the movement in phonetic space has halted and we are now going through a period of consolidation in which older less-centralised variants are becoming less common. There is a clear and interesting phonological explanation for this halting of the phonetic drift. What has happened is that centralisation of /e/ in this environment has now gone so far that tokens of /e/ are now identical with, and presumably therefore are capable of being perceived as, tokens of /ʌ/. That is, total merger of /e/ with /ʌ/ before /l/ has been achieved, so that, for example, *hell* and *hull* are now identical. Notice, however, that for the time being the total merger has been achieved only in informal speech. This is evidence that some phonological changes such as mergers proceed in a stylistically gradual way. Exactly why the phonological merger means the halting of a phonetic change in progress is not entirely clear, but it seems that a change involving /e/ before /l/ is not carrying over to become a change to /ʌ/ before /l/ once surface identity has been achieved. However, we must continue to assume non-identity of underlying forms until the merger has been carried through totally in all styles, and children acquiring the dialect no longer have any reason to suppose that *hell* and *hull* are phonologically distinct.

If we can summarise the findings from our study of linguistic change in real time and the comparison with the earlier apparent-time study, we note that we can differentiate between the changes we have investigated on three different parameters. First, two of the changes studied have been extremely rapid. In the case of the loss of /θ/ and /ð/ we can ascribe this rapidity to multiple causation, with both linguistic and attitudinal factors being involved. The relatively rapid change involving the phonetics of /r/ is less easy to account for, but it is clear that it involves yet another stage in the weakening of the pronunciation of this consonant which, in addition to loss in non-prevocalic position, has also experienced in the last several centuries a progression of changes in the south of England as follows: [r] > [ɾ] > [ɹ] > [ɻ] > [ɻ̥] > [ʋ]. The other changes studied have on the other hand been progressing much more slowly, and represent consolidation of existing trends. Second, it is probable that some of the changes we have dealt with are to be regarded principally as cases of the geographical diffusion of innovations into the Norwich speech community from outside: the loss of /eː/ is a case in point. Other changes appear to be internal to the system, such as the centralisation of /e/ before /l/ and, probably, the fronting of /uː/. Yet others, such as the loss of /θ/ and the development of [ʋ], are more problematical to categorise and may, as we have seen, come into both categories. Third, some of the changes we have observed appear to be due entirely or mainly to developments in the speech of children, while others seem instead or as well to influence the speech of post-adolescents and adults. Thus the change to [ʋ] is not something which happens in the speech of those who have already acquired [ɹ], while the loss of /eː/ in *face* etc., is something which does affect the speech of individuals during the course of their lifetimes. It is tempting to make a connection here and suggest that rapid changes are those that are system-internal and occur in the speech of children, while slower changes are those which are the result of external influence and which occur in the speech of adults. However, as Table 6.1 shows, as ever it is more complicated than that.

It is hoped that continuing research in real time in the Norwich speech community will be able to shed further light on these issues. The apparent-time methodology is an excellent sociolinguistic tool for investigating linguistic changes in progress, but, especially if one can find something else interesting to do in the meantime, the study of linguistic change in real time is in many ways an even more informative experience.

	rapid	children	adults	internal	external
/eː/ in face	−	−	+	?	+
beer / bear	−	+	?	+	−
moan / mown	−	−	+	?	+
/r/ = [ʋ]	+	+	−	?	−
[ʔ]	−	+	?	?	+
/ɛl/	+	+	?	+	−
/f/ > /θ/	+	+	−	?	+

Table 6.1.   Norwich variables involved in linguistic change

III. LANGUAGE CONTACT

INTRODUCTION:
LANGUAGE CONTACT

There is no doubt that current research in linguistic typology is gradually providing us with improving and deepening insights into the range of structures available in human languages. We are also becoming increasingly knowledgeable about constraints on these structures, and about relationships, implicational or of other kinds, between different typological characteristics. However, we do not yet have adequate explanations for why, of all possible structures available to human languages, particular languages avail themselves of particular structures, and not others. It may well be, of course, that ultimately this question will be unanswerable, but it does seem to me to be an interesting and profitable question to ask. Is the distribution of typological characteristics over languages simply random – or can we say something more intelligent about this distribution than just that?

In her controversial, wide-ranging and stimulating book *Linguistic Diversity in Space and Time* (1992), Johanna Nichols addresses this question. In her introduction to the book, she writes that one of her goals is 'to sort out genetic, geographical, and universal determinants of linguistic patterning' (p. 1). With her painstaking research, Nichols has made significant strides in this direction. She has shown that there appear to be linguistic-genetic and geographical factors which, if we look at the languages of the world as a whole, can help us gain some understanding as to why structure selection across languages has the distribution it does.

In some of my own recent work, I have set myself a similar but perhaps more modest and more sociolinguistic goal – to attempt to begin to sort out what might be some of the *social* determinants of linguistic patterning. There seems to me to be a *prima facie* case for examining the hypothesis that certain types of linguistic structures are more commonly associated with certain types of social structure than others. Many scholars, in fact, have attempted to explore links between aspects of societies and aspects of the languages spoken by those societies. No one is surprised to find aspects of physical cultures reflected in the lexicon. More interesting, however, because much less obvious, would appear to be relationships between societal type and aspects of linguistic change (see Grace 1990), and relationships between societal type and linguistic structure. In much of my recent work in this area, I have examined issues to do with language contact. The degree of contact one language community has with another has obvious implications for linguistic structure in terms of increased complexification as a result of borrowing, and in terms of linguistic simplification as a result of pidginisation. It is to this area of study that this section of the book is devoted.

The basic assumptions of this section are the following. Adults and adolescents who are beyond the critical threshold for language learning more or less necessarily subject new languages that they are learning to the process of *pidginisation*. This consists of three major subprocesses (see Chapter 7). The first is *reduction*, or, as it is sometimes called, *impoverishment*. The immediate cause of reduction is restriction in function. Since non-native speakers typically use language for a narrower range of purposes than native speakers, there are large areas of a target language which are simply not present in the usage of non-native speakers. That is to say, a language which has been subject to reduction has, as it were, large areas of itself missing: the vocabulary will be smaller, grammatical devices fewer, and stylistic alternatives less elaborate. Imperfect learning will also play a role here, however: reduction occurs because learners have not (yet) learnt all there is to learn.

The second subcomponent of pidginisation can be labelled *admixture*. As a result of the fact that adults are less than perfect foreign-language learners, a target language will be subject to interference from the learner's native language.

The third component of pidginisation can be labelled *simplification*. Paradoxically, this is a somewhat complex notion, referring for the most part to regularisation and loss of redundancy. It also refers, however, to an increase in *transparency*, by which is meant an increase in forms such as *eye-doctor* as opposed to *optician*, and *did go* as opposed to *went*. Imperfect learning, that is, leads to the removal of irregular and non-transparent forms which naturally cause problems of memory load for adult learners, and to loss of redundant features. This can in turn lead to an often dramatic increase in analytic over synthetic structures.

In some particular sociolinguistic circumstances, pidginisation may lead to the development of a *pidgin language*. What is required for this development is, firstly, for the degree of reduction, admixture and simplification to be rather extensive. Typically, mutual intelligibility with the target language will be lost. Second, the considerably pidginised target language will acquire a relatively stabilised or *focused* form which will eventually be susceptible to learning by future speakers and to description by linguists.

Thus, a pidgin language, relative to the original target language, is reduced, mixed and simplified and has undergone a process of focusing, whereby it has acquired a fixed, stabilised form. As is well known, a pidgin language will not be adequate for all the needs of a native speaker because of the reduction which it has undergone, but, as is also well known, this is of no consequence, since pidgin languages, by definition, do not have native speakers.

Subsequently, in certain rather unusual sociolinguistic circumstances, a further development may take place, that is, a pidgin language may be subjected to creolisation. Creolisation is a process which, as it were, repairs the reduction which a pidgin language has undergone during the course of pidginisation. This repair process can be labelled *expansion*. Expansion may occur, less or more rapidly, when the pidgin language, originally employed simply as a non-native lingua franca, becomes more and more important as a means of communication within a particular community. This is what happened, for example, at least according to one scenario favoured by some creolists, in the case of West African Pidgin English as a result of the transatlantic slave trade. Slaves of West African origin transplanted to the Americas found that West African Pidgin English was the only language that they had in common, and children born into slave communities thus subjected the original pidgin language to expansion in order to render it viable as a means of dealing with all the functions that a native speaker requires of a language. That is to say, the vocabulary was expanded, there was an increase in the grammatical devices available, and stylistic differentiation was increased. A creole language, as a pidgin language which has undergone expansion, is thus a perfectly normal language from the point of view of its native speakers, but it demonstrates admixture and simplification with reference to its historical source language. There are also a number of languages in the world which merit the description *creoloid*. These are languages such as Afrikaans which, as a result of language contact, demonstrate considerable amounts of admixture and simplification as compared to their source language (Dutch in the case of Afrikaans), but which have maintained a continuous native speaker tradition and have never been pidgins (see Chapter 7).

7

DUAL-SOURCE PIDGINS AND REVERSE CREOLOIDS: NORTHERN PERSPECTIVES ON LANGUAGE CONTACT

Most often, language contact does not lead to the development of new (pidgin or creole) languages. In those cases where new varieties do form, however, there appear to be two fundamental mechanisms which are instrumental in their formation:

1. The inability of post-adolescent humans to learn new languages perfectly (see Trudgill 1989); and
2. The process of focusing (see LePage and Tabouret-Keller 1985), which may occur in certain social and linguistic circumstances.

What we might perhaps refer to as the classical model of pidgin and creole formation, which many creolists, particularly those who have worked with the Atlantic creoles, appear to subscribe to – although none of them, as far as I know, have actually formulated it in precisely these terms – can be presented as follows. (Naturally, none of the complexities and subtleties associated with what actually happens in real-life language contact situations can be accurately portrayed in any such model; see Hancock 1986.)

PIDGINISATION

Whenever adults and post-adolescents learn a new language, pidginisation takes place (Trudgill 1989b). Pidginisation consists, as we saw in the introduction to this section, of three related but distinct processes: reduction, admixture and simplification. Reduction, or impoverishment as it is sometimes less happily called, refers to the fact that, in a pidginised version, there is simply less of a language as compared to the form in which it is spoken by native speakers: the vocabulary is smaller, and there are fewer syntactic structures, a narrower range of styles, and so on.

Admixture refers to interference – the transfer of features of pronunciation and grammatical and semantic structure from the native language to the new language, an obvious feature of adult second-language acquisition.

Simplification, as is well known (see Mühlhäusler 1977), is a rather complex phenomenon, but it refers crucially to regularisation of irregularities, to loss of redundancy (such as grammatical gender), and to an increase in analytic structures and transparent forms. Reduction can be considered as being due to incomplete learning and restriction in sociolinguistic function, while admixture and simplification are the result of imperfect learning.

PIDGINS AND PRE-PIDGINS

In some cases, where exposure to the new language is minimal, such pidginisation may be extreme and remain extreme. In certain cases, moreover (see Whinnom 1971), such extremely pidginised forms of language may, in the absence of native speakers of the original language, become important as a lingua franca, a means of communication between two or more groups who have acquired the pidginised forms and who have no native or other language in common. In these cases, focusing may well occur: the pidginised forms of the original language may acquire stability, with widely shared norms of usage, and a new language variety, a pidgin, will have come into being.

Typically, then, a pidgin is a stable language, without native speakers, which is the outcome of reduction, admixture and simplification of some source language, and where, also typically, pidginisation has occurred to such a degree that mutual intelligibility with the source language is no longer possible. We know of at least one such variety from northern latitudes (see below).

The language associated with the chronological stage that occurs before focusing leads to the achievement of stability and the development of shared norms, and where the pidginised forms are still relatively diffuse, can be referred to as a pre-pidgin.

CREOLISATION AND CREOLES

Again according to this model, a further chronological stage may occur. In some circumstances, a pidgin language, as a lingua franca, may become the most important or indeed the only viable shared language of a particular community. The pidgin will therefore be subject to expansion, in some cases rapidly, in other cases more slowly, so that it can be used in an increasingly wide range of functions and come to meet the linguistic needs of native speakers. The result is a creole language. A creole, then, is indeed a pidgin which has acquired native speakers, but most crucially it is a pidgin which has undergone non-contact induced expansion, where the expansion process (as Bickerton has pointed out, one of the most fascinating forms of linguistic change) 'repairs' the results of the reduction process which occurred during pidginisation.

Non-contact induced expansion is known as creolisation, a term which should not be used in a haphazard way for just any form of language mixture (see also Hancock 1996). Nor, indeed, should it be used for just any kind of expansion: if a pidgin comes into renewed or closer contact with its original source language before creolisation occurs, depidginisation may take place. In this case, however, any expansion which occurs will be contact induced and will lead in the direction of the source language rather than being, as with creolisation, internally generated.

A creole language is thus a language which, relative to its source, is simplified (that is, more analytic and regular) and mixed, but not in any way reduced – in other words, creoles are perfectly normal languages with an unusual history.

DECREOLISATION AND POST-CREOLES

The next possible chronological stage that can be experienced by creoles is decreolisation. Like depidginisation, decreolisation is contact induced. However, while depidginisation is clearly the reverse of pidginisation, decreolisation is not the reverse of creolisation, and for that reason it may be that we should develop another term for this process. Hancock (1988) favours the term *metropolitanisation*.

If a creole comes into renewed or intensified contact with its source language and the sociolinguistic conditions are right, it may begin to change in the direction of this source language. Clearly, changes in the direction of the source language will involve processes which reverse the effects of admixture and simplification. We may call these processes purification (the removal of words and forms which are not derived from the source language) and complexification (the reintroduction of irregularity etc.).

Decreolisation may eventually go to completion, so that the creole may become, or become perceived as, a variety of the source language, as may well have happened with African American Vernacular English. Such a variety may be termed a vestigial post-creole. Various intermediate stages are also possible, of course. A well-known phenomenon involving inter-mediate stages is the post-creole continuum, such as that which exists in Jamaica, where a society demonstrates a cline of varieties ranging from a variety of the source language (Jamaican English) at the top of the social scale to increasingly un-decreolised varieties of Jamaican Creole at the bottom. Post-creoles, or partially decreolised creoles, will therefore demon-strate different degrees of simplification and admixture, relative to the source language, although of course less than a totally undecreolised creole such as Sranan.

CREOLOIDS AND NON-NATIVE CREOLOIDS

It now becomes necessary to look beyond the traditional pidgin and creole lifecycle model. We notice first that, interestingly, there are many varieties of language in the world which look like post-creoles but which actually are not. Such varieties demonstrate relatively undramatic admixture and simplification relative to some source language, but are known to have no pidgin history behind them. Such languages, as I have suggested elsewhere (Trudgill 1983: 102) can be called creoloids, and the process which leads to their formation *creoloidisation*.

The process of creoloidisation thus consists of admixture and simplification. Unlike creoles, however, creoloids have not experienced a history of reduction followed or 'repaired' by expansion. Creoloids were never reduced in the first place. The difference between a creoloid and a partially decreolised creole is thus a historical one; it is not apparent from synchronic inspection. Creoloidisation is, of course, the result of the influence of imperfect learning by relatively large numbers of non-native adult speakers. However, creoloids are varieties which have never been reduced because they have maintained a continual native-speaker tradition. A good example of a creoloid is Afrikaans, which is clearly a creoloid relative to Dutch.

Creoloids proper can be distinguished from non-native creoloids, such as Singaporean English (see Platt and Weber 1980). A non-native creoloid may develop when, as in pidgin formation, a pidginised variety of a source language becomes focussed and acquires stability as a result of being employed as a lingua franca by two or more language groups who are not native speakers of the source language, and who have no other language in common. The difference between a non-native creoloid and a pidgin lies in the degree of pidginisation which it has undergone. For example, Singaporean English is a recognisable and rather stable second-language form of English which can be distinguished typologically from foreign-language forms of English such as, say, Japanese English, by its institutionalisation. Relative to metropolitan forms of English, Singaporean English is somewhat mixed and simplified and, because it is not spoken natively, also somewhat reduced. It is nevertheless still clearly a variety of English: the role of English in, for example, the education system and in Singaporean society generally has meant that simplification and admixture have never been extreme, and its use as a primary (as opposed to first) language by many speakers in Singapore means that the reduction is also relatively slight. Unlike Afrikaans, however, it has no native speakers and therefore no native-speaker tradition to maintain.

DUAL-SOURCE PIDGINS

As we said above, the traditional pidgin–creole lifecycle model has been developed, if not always fully articulated, in connection with colonial, usually tropical language contact, especially in the Pacific, and even more especially in the Atlantic Ocean areas. As our discussion of creoloids shows, however, this model needs amending if it is to give us a full and useful typological account of mixed and simplified languages. This requirement has become particularly clear as a result of our study of the less well-known Arctic contact varieties. Our examination over the years of language contact situations, and their outcomes in the Arctic and other northern areas, indicates that the model needs to be supplemented in a number of ways.

In particular, as is illustrated by the case of the best-known Arctic pidgin, Russenorsk, we need to take account of contact varieties that arise from the pidginisation not of one source language but of two. As the terms *language contact* and *admixture* indicate, all pidgin-formation obviously involves more than one language. However, most Atlantic and Pacific pidgin, creole and post-creole languages have a single main source of lexifier language, so that we have no hesitation at all about saying that, say, Sranan and Tok Pisin are both English-based varieties, in spite of the considerable minority input of other languages, e.g. 8 per cent of Sranan lexis is African in origin. Creoloids like Afrikaans and non-native creoloids are also single-source varieties.

Russenorsk, on the other hand, appears to be a pidginised form of Russian and Norwegian in about equal proportions. I suggest here that we need to distinguish such varieties typologically from other pidgins by labelling them dual-source pidgins. These dual-source pidgins are of course linguistically different because their social genesis was different. Broch and Jahr (1984) show convincingly that Russenorsk was a stable, focused variety that had norms of usage which had to be learnt. Unlike the case of those pidgins catered for in the traditional 'Atlantic' model, however, it is clear that this focusing did not take place according to the Whinnomian scenario, that is in the absence of source-language speakers. Russenorsk, although it was also used by native speakers of Finnish and Sami, was mainly spoken by Russian and Norwegian speakers, and must have undergone focusing as a result of interaction between them. Importantly, also, Russenorsk was formed as a result of interaction between two groups of European trading partners rather than in a colonial or pre-colonial situation. (This does not mean to say, of course, that traditional pidgins cannot be found in the Arctic: Taimyr Pidgin Russian, spoken in an area of northern Russia colonised relatively late by Russian speakers, seems to be of this type.)

There must, of course, have been a period, perhaps quite a considerable period, before Russenorsk acquired stability and became a relatively focused, named variety. I suggest here that we refer to this diffuse stage of a dual-source pidgin's development as a jargon. This term has had different uses in the pidgin literature (see the discussion in Mühlhäusler 1986) and is often used as being synonymous with 'pre-pidgin'. If, however, we are making a typological distinction, linguistically and socially, between pidgins proper and dual-source pidgins, it would be useful to be able to distinguish also between their precursors in the same way. A pidgin is therefore preceded chronologically by a pre-pidgin, and dual-source pidgin by a jargon. The Arctic area which gave rise to Russenorsk, perhaps unsurprisingly, seems also to have given rise to a number of relatively unfocussed jargons of this type. For example, the Basque-Algonquian 'pidgin' (Bakker 1996) and the Icelandic-Breton 'pidgin' (Hancock 1996) may have been such jargons.

DUAL-SOURCE CREOLES

In the case of single-source varieties, we saw that there was a potential chronological development of the form:

pre-pidgin > pidgin > creole > post-creole > vestigial post-creole

In our discussion of dual-source varieties, we have so far only noted the following language types:

jargon > dual-source pidgin

This raises the question of whether we can find further parallels: are there examples of the creolisation and perhaps subsequent decreolisation of dual-source pidgins? There seem to be none in the Arctic, and the typical social setting for dual-source pidgin formation – trading between equal partners – would seem to suggest that this would be unlikely: it is difficult to conceive of social situations where such a language would become the only viable language of a community.

However, social situations, albeit highly unusual ones, can arise in which dual-source creoles can develop. One language that clearly merits the label 'dual-source creole' is Pitcairnese (Ross and Moverley 1964). Pitcairnese is the native language of the Pitcairn islanders and does not therefore demonstrate reduction. It is, however, a considerably simplified and mixed form of English and Tahitian. Moreover, its close relative, Norfolk, which has been more heavily influenced by English since the arrival of its speakers on Norfolk Island, can be regarded as a dual-source post-creole. (Naturally, decreolisation of a dual-source creole has to be in the direction of one or the other of the source languages, not both!)

DUAL-SOURCE CREOLOIDS

Our examination of Arctic contact varieties also shows yet another parallel between single-source and dual-source varieties. Copper Island Aleut

(Golovko 1996) is a language which is clearly the historical outcome of a mixture of Russian and Aleut with, for example, Russian verbal inflection and Aleut nominal inflection. There is, however, no reduction – the language is spoken natively. Unlike Pitcairnese, moreover, Copper Island Aleut demonstrates relatively little simplification. Indeed, one could argue that this is an example of language contact involving child rather than adult bilingualism which has therefore in some respects led to complication (cf. Trudgill 1989). The origins of Copper Island Aleut are a matter for dispute and conjecture. It has been argued, for example (see Golovko and Vakhtin 1990), that it was derived from some earlier pidgin. This seems unlikely, however, in view of the vast amounts of synthetic morphology which the language has retained. One possible scenario, therefore, is that there was no prior dual-source pidgin, and that instead the language represents, as it were, a mixture of and compromise between two native-speaker traditions. Two communities, in long and intimate contact, gradually merged to form a single ethnic group, neither abandoning their native language but approximating it to that of the other. There are, that is, some parallels with the language maintenance tradition of, say, Afrikaans, but of course in this case there were two separate native-speaker traditions that were (in part) retained. It may be legitimate, therefore, to refer to Copper Island Aleut and other similar languages such as Metsif as 'dual-source creoloids'.

REVERSE CREOLOIDS

Dual-source pidgins and dual-source creoles are the result of a break in native-speaker tradition followed by new-language formation. Dual-source creoloids, on the other hand, represent a particular kind of result of language contact combined with language maintenance.

There is also, however, a third type of dual-source scenario that we have to consider in this context. There is a type of mixed language, exemplified in northern latitudes but also found elsewhere, which is a particular result of language contact accompanied by language shift.

For example, Shetland Island Scots is clearly a variety of Scots, but one which shows considerable amounts of Scandinavian (Norn) influence, particularly in its lexis. Unlike cases such as Afrikaans, where a language maintains its native-speaker tradition but is subject to considerable influence from non-native speakers, Shetland represents the opposite process, in which a community abandons its native language but takes along with it, as it were, in the process of language shift a considerable amount of influence from its original pre-shift language. A legitimate term for such varieties might therefore be reverse creoles. Other similar languages are Yiddish and Ladino.

It is also possible that we could accurately refer to originally second-language varieties such as Irish English as vestigial reverse creoles.

Ethnolects such as Scandoromani (see Hancock 1996) and Angloromani represent a special case of reverse creoloids, in that, while they do result from language shift, they are specialised codes rather than native varieties which are used for all purposes from childhood.

CONCLUSION

The non-tropical contact varieties discussed here demonstrate the importance of contact varieties formed out of interaction between two languages only, as opposed to the three or more languages in contact associated with the traditional Whinnomian Atlantic pidgins and creoles. We have cited instances of jargons (as defined above), dual-source pidgins, dual-source creoloids, and reverse creoloids, all of which seem to have arisen in bilingual rather than multilingual situations. (We also noted the non-Arctic dual-source creole, Pitcairnese.)

We can argue that the social situations in which these northern varieties were formed were often significantly different from those which obtained in the more tropical regions more frequently investigated by pidgin and creole scholars. We can also suggest, as always with sociolinguistic work, that it is dangerous to draw linguistic generalisations from only one type of linguistic community. Our further understanding of the range of possible outcomes of language contact can only be enhanced by studies of areas such as the Arctic where such contact has so far been relatively less thoroughly investigated.

8

LANGUAGE CONTACT
AND THE FUNCTION OF
LINGUISTIC GENDER

Most functional approaches to linguistics have in common 'the belief that language must be studied in relation to its role in human communication' (Foley and Van Valin 1984: 7). Foley and Van Valin's approach is in particular directed towards explaining grammatical phenomena 'in terms of recurrent discourse patterns in human language' (p. 13). Givón (1979: 49) similarly argues that 'the formal or 'structural' properties of syntax will . . . be shown, to quite a degree, to emanate from the properties of human discourse'; and elsewhere (1984) he argues that the goals of a functionally oriented linguistics include the study of how grammatical devices 'are used in coding and communicating knowledge' (p. 10). The goal of this chapter is not to question such approaches but to suggest that human languages may have rather more grammatical devices than is sometimes thought which, although not dysfunctional (see Lass 1997: 16), may not have any particular function at all in coding and communicating knowledge. There may be, that is, a number of grammatical phenomena that can perhaps be legitimately regarded as being afunctional. We examine this suggestion with particular reference to grammatical gender and to the natural gender of self-reference.

GRAMMATICAL CATEGORIES

Although there is not total agreement about what the major 'grammatical categories' are, or about exact terminology, by relatively common consent (see, for example, Jespersen 1924; Bloomfield 1933; Lyons 1977; Bybee 1985) they would appear to include at least: number, case, tense, aspect, voice, mood, person and gender. Crucially for this chapter, gender can be further subdivided into natural gender and grammatical gender. Natural gender is related to the sex of humans and, often, animals, while grammatical gender is not. Many languages, such as English, have natural gender but not grammatical gender. Note, however, that the distinction between the two types of gender can be a fuzzy one, and that grammatical gender can often be seen as the result of a (perhaps metaphorical) diachronic extension of natural gender down the animacy hierarchy (see Croft 1994). (This view is disputed by Fodor (1959), who also gives an interesting overview of attempts in the nineteenth century and the first half of the twentieth to account for the origins of linguistic gender.)

Some of these categories are more frequent in the world's languages than others. For example, all the languages of the world have the category *person*, but of the other categories some are more and others less common. It is the contention of this chapter, moreover, that these categories may also be of different statuses or degrees of importance, and that their functions may be less or more clear. Some categories, that is, would appear to be more central in some way than other categories. In this chapter it is argued that the category of gender is a strong candidate for the description of 'less central'.

Languages differ, of course, in the extent to which certain of these categories are optional or obligatory. And there are also important differences in how the categories may be expressed, the most obvious difference being between morphological (or synthetic) expression, on the one hand, and lexical and syntactic (or analytic) expression, on the other. As is also well known, the same language at different points in its history can change with regard to which categories it possesses, as well as the way in which they are expressed. Old English, for example, expressed case almost entirely morphologically, whereas modern English expresses it to a considerable extent syntactically.

Language contact is often cited as an important factor leading to a change from the synthetic to the analytic expression of these categories. In Trudgill (1978), for instance, I showed that, in a situation involving language contact, language shift and language death, the Albanian dialects of central Greece (Arvanitika) were undergoing the loss of the morphologically expressed optative mood which was now being expressed instead lexically by the use of the originally Greek word *makari* 'would that'. The point would appear to be that imperfect learning by adults of a language in a contact situation can lead to the loss of features which constitute difficulties for learning, and that analytic structures are in some way easier to learn and/or process than synthetic structures. If we are interested in the centrality or importance of the major grammatical categories in the world's languages, it is therefore revealing to see what happens to them, and their expression, in situations of intense language contact, the most dramatic of which involve pidginisation.

PIDGINS, CREOLES AND GRAMMATICAL CATEGORIES

As a result of simplification and reduction (see Chapter 7), pidgin languages usually lack all morphology: there are usually no cases, numbers, tenses, aspects, moods, voices, persons or genders that are morphologically marked. Person can be signalled by pronouns or nouns; case can be pragmatically deduced or, perhaps, marked by word order; location of events in or through time can be indicated if necessary through adverbs, as can modality. Interestingly, though, there is typically no role at all for grammatical gender – no pidgin language in the world has grammatical gender – and only a very small role, except lexically, for natural gender. Even lexically, the labelling of natural gender is confined to a few basic terms such as *man* and *woman*, and marking is then achieved, if required, on other nouns in a semantically transparent way by compounding, for example Tok Pisin *hosman* 'stallion', *hosmeri* 'mare', where *hos* means 'horse', *man* means 'man', and *meri* means 'woman'. This, then, is a preliminary indication suggesting that in some way gender may be a grammatical category which is less central than most or all others.

Note further, then, what happens during creolisation. The expansion process inherent in creolisation – the 'repair' of the reduction of pidginisation – involves the reintroduction of many of the grammatical categories that have been lost during pidginisation. We have seen that a pidgin is not adequate for all the needs of a native speaker. We can therefore assume that native speakers 'need' some of these grammatical categories and hence reintroduce them. Creole languages thus typically have (optional) aspect and tense markers such as the Sranan particles *ben* 'past' and *de* 'habitual', which are preposed to the main verb. They typically have (optional) plural markers, such as Jamaican Creole *dem* which is postposed to nouns. They continue the pidgin practice of signalling person by pronouns. Case is marked by word order, even for pronouns: Jamaican Creole has *mi* 'I, me'; *im* 'he, him, she, her', *wi* 'we, us', *dem* 'they, them'. Mood can be signalled lexically, as in Arvanitika (see above). And, as far as the active–passive voice distinction is concerned, 'creoles usually express passive voice with constructions that correspond semantically but not syntactically to the passive construction found in varieties of English' (Holm 1997: 71). Thus many Caribbean English-based creoles, for example, permit constructions such as *De chicken eat* which are ambiguous as to whether the chicken is eating or being eaten and where the meaning has to be deduced pragmatically.

However, and vitally for our discussion, there is not a creole language in the world which has reintroduced, during the expansion process, the category of grammatical gender on nouns or verbs. Typical creoles, moreover, do not even demonstrate natural gender. For example, in Sranan, the third-person singular pronoun *en* means 'he, him, his, she, her, hers, it, its'. A very strong inference is that gender is a category that languages and their speakers can more readily do without than many or most other categories. One apparent exception, pointed out to me by Sasha Aikhenvald, is Kituba, which is derived from KiKongo, and which does have noun classes (see Stucky 1978). However, Kituba appears to have arisen out of contact between closely related languages which all have numerous noun classes, and is probably in any case more properly to be described as a creoloid (see Chapter 7). Even here, moreover, we can note that the number of noun classes has been reduced.

GENDER-MARKING SYSTEMS

The way in which both natural and grammatical gender are marked in the world's languages varies considerably. One obvious way is through pronouns. Greenberg showed (1966) that there are hierarchies and implicational universals in the expression of natural gender in pronoun systems. Some languages, like Hungarian and Finnish, have no gender marking on pronouns at all. Others, like English, have gender only in the third-person singular. Others, such as French, have it also in the third-person plural – but there are no languages which express gender in the third-person plural but not in the singular. A smaller number of languages also have gender in the second person, where there may also be complications involving T and V pronouns: Polish, for example, has gender marking for the second-person V quasi-pronouns *pan/pani* (which are actually third-person forms in origin) but not for T pronouns; Spanish has gender marking only in the second-person plural T pronoun but not for the V pronoun, and not at all in the singular. Yet other languages may have gender marking in the first person. Some have this feature only in the first-person plural, such as Spanish *nosotros* versus *nosotras*. Others have it also in the first-person singular (see below). Here again there are implicational universals: if gender is marked in the first person it will also be marked in the second or third, but not necessarily vice versa (Greenberg 1966: 96).

Gender marking can also be effected through articles and adjectival agreement in the noun phrase, as in French. And it can be effected through finite verb forms, as for example in past tense and conditional verb forms in some Slavic languages: Russian, Ukrainian and Belorussian have gender marking in these verb forms in the singular; Polish has it in both the singular and the plural; and modern forms of Kashubian (Stone 1993) also have it in the singular and the plural.

In languages which have both grammatical and natural gender, there may be interesting complications in gender-marking systems concerning the relationship between the two. We can even find interesting differences between two forms of the same language. Norwegian Nynorsk, for example, uses the pronouns *han, hon* and *det* for all nouns which are respectively grammatically masculine, feminine and neuter, in the manner of German. Norwegian Bokmål, on the other hand, uses the equivalent forms *han* and *hun* only for natural gender – for animates, especially humans – while *den* is used for grammatical gender, to pronominalise nouns which are grammatically masculine or feminine but not animate. Thus Nynorsk *han* can be translated as 'he' and 'it', while Bokmål *han* can be translated only as 'he'. There is similarly the interesting fact about Polish (see below) that in both nouns and verbs male humans form a distinct gender in the plural only, while female humans are grouped together with non-humans and inanimates. And there are other well-known problems of gender resolution, such as the clash between grammatical and natural gender in cases such as German *das Mädchen* 'the girl', which is grammatically neuter but semantically feminine. For a full survey of these issues, see Corbett (1991).

THE FUNCTION OF NATURAL GENDER

It is the thesis of this chapter that the function of linguistic gender is to a considerable extent obscure. However, it must be conceded that the function of natural gender is a good deal less puzzling than that of grammatical gender (see below). It is much less surprising that human languages have gender distinctions for human beings than that they have grammatical gender, since the distinction between male and female is the most fundamental one there is between human beings, and it is therefore presumably often important to know if a man or a woman is being talked about; perhaps we can make the same point about non-human animate beings.

Three functions for natural gender have been discussed in the literature:

1. The primary function of natural gender is presumably that it can be helpful in making clear the sex of a third person where this has not been previously established. This may be particularly useful (or on some occasions problematical!) in cases where nouns such as *friend, person, teacher* are not marked for gender. Compare the following examples:

    (a) *Meine Freundin ist gestern angekommen. Sie ist glücklich.*
    [my(f.) friend(f.) is yesterday arrived. She is happy]

    (b) *My friend arrived yesterday. She is happy.*

    (c) *Ystäväni saapui eilen. Hän on onnellinen.*
    [friend-my arrived yesterday. S/he is happy]

In the first, German, example, we know from the very beginning that the friend is female. The noun *Freundin* bears the female morphological marker *-in*, and the possessive pronoun *meine* is also feminine in form. The pronoun *sie* 'she' is thus superfluous. In example (b), on the other hand, it is not clear in English what sex the friend is until we get to the pronoun *she*. And in (c), Finnish, it is never clear what sex the friend is. Other languages of course have yet other ways of doing this.

(d) *I   fili   mou eftase   xtes.   Ine eftixismeni.*
   [the(f.) friend(f.) my   arrived yesterday. Is happy(f.)]

(e) *Moja   kolezanka przyjechala wczoraj.   Jest szczesliwa.*
   [my(f.)   friend(f.) arrived(f.) yesterday. Is happy(f.).

In (d), modern Greek, which is a pro-drop language, does not employ a pronoun at all but signals feminine gender from the very first definite article. In (e), Polish, there is additional information in that gender is also marked on the verb.

2. The other important function would appear to be the disambiguation and reference-tracking function which operates in certain constructions, as in sentences such as *John kissed Mary and then he ran away*, as opposed to *John kissed Mary and then she ran away* (cf. Comrie 1988).

> Human referents are by far the most frequent in text frequency studies. For this reason, humans are further subclassified in order to aid in identification and tracking of multiple human referents in discourse. The primary salient distinction among human beings is sex. This is manifested . . . in the very common distinction of masculine and feminine genders in noun class systems. (Croft 1994: 162)

Many languages, however, such as Hungarian, Turkish and Finnish and most creoles, have no gender in their pronominal systems and manage perfectly well without. What do languages such as Finnish do in these cases? The answer is blindingly obvious. They do the same as English does in the case of sentences such as *John kissed Bill and then he ran away*, where the tracking function is of no help at all and where, in the absence of a switch-reference system (see Foley and Van Valin 1984), one has to say, if one wants to be clear, *John kissed Bill and then Bill ran away*. In Finnish, for example, these two sentences would run as follows:

Jussi suuteli Marjaa ja   juoksi sitten pois
[John kissed Mary   and ran   then away]

Jussi suuteli Marjaa ja   sitten Marja juoksi pois
[John kissed Mary   and then Mary ran   away]

Other strategies can also be employed in such languages, such as Hungarian:

János megcsókolta Marit és   elfutott
[John kissed   Mary and ran-away]

János megcsókolta Marit, aki   elfutott
[John kissed   Mary, who ran-away]

81

3. Corbett also tells us that gender systems can have the function of indicating speaker attitudes. Rothstein (1993: 697) confirms that in Polish 'most personal nouns can be "depersonalised" [e.g. masculines can be made neuter] for emotional effect, usually pejorative' (see also Dressler *et al.* 1998; Lewandowska-Tomaszczyk 1992). This is presumably, however, a relatively minor and derivative sociolinguistic function.

The widespread though not universal expression of natural gender in the third person in the world's languages is thus unsurprising. If someone is not present, it may often be useful to know if they are male or female.

THE FUNCTION OF GRAMMATICAL GENDER

Much more puzzling is the function of grammatical gender. It is very interesting indeed to observe that, of the 323 pages of text in Corbett's enormously erudite and stimulating book *Gender* (1991), 321 are devoted to the origins, nature and workings of gender systems, and only two to the function of grammatical gender. This is not surprising: it is not at all clear what gender is for. As Hickey (forthcoming) says: 'Grammatical gender . . . is largely semantically redundant'. The function of noun classes in general and of grammatical gender in particular in human languages is actually largely obscure.

Corbett asks: 'Why do languages have gender systems?' From a Chomskyan perspective, Alice Davison (pers. comm.) suggests that since gender is spread out over syntactic constituents such as noun phrases, gender agreement may aid in processing strings of words into syntactically coherent phrases, thereby aiding interpretation; features such as gender may also be crucial in cross-referencing predicates with subjects: 'If you can identify what is linked by the agreement relation, you have solved a number of computations about what the structure of the sentence is'. A similar point is made by Fodor (1959: 206), who points to the function of gender (and other forms of) concord in helping with parsing in languages with free word order, particularly in literary style, as in the classical Latin of Ovid: *lurida terribiles miscent aconita novercae*. On the other hand, gender still clearly constitutes an additional complication at the level of production.

Aikhenvald (1998) has also shown that in languages – and there are many such – like Manambu (East Sepik Province, Papua New Guinea) in which gender is related in non-humans to size and/or shape, gender can have a minor semantic function. In Manambu, gender assignment to non-human animates is based on their size, so that ' large animals belong to the masculine gender, and smaller animals belong to the feminine gender', while in inanimates it is based on their size and shape, so that 'long and/or large objects are treated as masculine, and small and/or round ones as feminine'. There are, however a number of cases in which the same noun can be either masculine or feminine, depending on its size or other

82

characteristics.Thus *val* 'canoe' 'is masculine if big, feminine if small'. Lyle Campbell (pers. comm.) has speculated that this type of phenomenon, like the unusual Polish plural gender differentiation system already mentioned, may ultimately be linked in some way to animacy and agentivity: just as animates make 'better agents' than inanimates, so large objects may have been perceived as making better agents than small, and, in a sexist society, men make better agents than women.

Another minor function is identified by Fodor (1959: 206), who suggests that gender 'lends itself to the purposes of animation, sexualisation and personification in literature' and cites a Russian folk song where a rowan tree *r'abina* (feminine) is yearning for an oak tree *dub* (masculine).

The most common answer that has been given, however, as Corbett points out, is that, as with natural gender marking, gender systems help with disambiguation and reference tracking. Foley and Van Valin (1984) give extensive evidence showing the importance of gender in languages in which 'gender functions as the dominant system of discourse cohesion' (p. 326). Heath (1975) argues that there is an inverse relationship between the number of verbal means – such as switch-reference, passive and anti-passive – for reference tracking in a particular language and the number of nominal gender classes, the point being that the more you have of the one, the less you need of the other. And Lyons (1977: 288) also writes 'it is clearly the pronominal function of gender which is of primary importance in communication'. Thus, for example, the German sentence (Zubin and Köpcke1981) *Der Krug fiel in die Schale, aber er zerbrach nicht* is not ambiguous (as the corresponding English translation *The jug fell into the bowl but it didn't break* would be) because the two nouns are of different genders. One cannot help wondering, however, whether this function is, as it were, 'worth it'. After all, as with the solution to the 'problem' of the absence of natural gender marking in Finnish, it is not an enormous effort to say, in English, *The jug fell into the bowl but the jug didn't break*. In what sense does the (one has to assume) occasional German sentence such as the above 'justify' the wealth of morphological complexity demonstrated by the German gender system, particularly in view of the fact that the disambiguation only works anyway if the two nouns involved just happen to be of different genders. It seems likely that the reference tracking role of gender can only be seriously important if there are many more than the three genders which German has. Foley and Van Valin themselves convincingly demonstrate (p. 326) the very important reference-tracking role gender plays in the New Guinea language Yimas which, however, has about sixteen different noun classes (!), and say that reference tracking of this type only works if 'there is only one noun from each class in a discourse' (p. 324).

Further problems with this interpretation can also be noted:

1. Gender marking can in some cases lead to tracking failure and ambiguity: in German, *Katze* 'cat' is feminine and *Hund* 'dog' is masculine, so that in a household with a male cat and a female dog, conflict between natural and grammatical gender can lead to considerable pronominal confusion.
2. There is also the the important point made by Croft (1994: 162) that 'people talk about people more than about anything else' and that, therefore, reference tracking is most important for human referents – which is precisely where we find natural as opposed to grammatical gender.
3. We also have to consider the perplexing fact, pointed out by Fodor (1959), that languages with gender often do not employ it in an efficient, functional way. He observes, for example, that German distinguishes between male and female horses lexically (*Hengst* versus *Stute*) rather than by means of grammatical gender; and that the French for a female elephant is not *une éléphant* or *une éléphante* but *un éléphant femelle*, just as it is *nóstényelefánt* (literally 'female elephant' in Hungarian, a language without gender).

A further possible psycholinguistic role, to do with processing, has been suggested to me by Paul Fletcher (pers. comm.). Given that most adults know several thousand nouns, and given that the time available for the recognition of a word can be measured in milliseconds, listeners need all the help that they can get in finding the right item in the lexical store. Anything which might cut down the range of possibilites for identification of an upcoming noun might be functional in this sense (see also Grosjean *et al.* 1994). Once again, however, this seems likely to be of most benefit in languages which have large numbers of genders or very extensive classifier systems.

As we have seen, case, number, tense, aspect, person, mood and voice are all, like gender, grammatical categories that can be morphologically manifest in languages. Unlike grammatical gender, however, which appears to be of relatively little benefit for purely communicative purposes, especially if a language has only two or three genders, it is much easier to see intuitively what these other categories are 'for' in the sense, in Givón's terms, of the knowledge they communicate. We have also established that grammatical gender is perhaps somewhat different from other grammatical categories – and, perhaps we can say, relatively afunctional – by its non-reappearance during creolisation. Indeed, we can even suggest that its relative lack of importance makes its appearance in languages where it does occur somewhat mysterious. Pidgins can manage without most of these grammatical categories. Creoles need all of them – except grammatical gender. There is therefore a case for suggesting that grammatical gender is a rather perplexing category. Our first question then is: why, unless like Yimas they are going to have enough noun classes to do an important job of reference tracking, do languages have grammatical gender?

NATURAL GENDER AGAIN

There is also another important question we have to face up to. We have distinguished between grammatical and natural gender, and suggested that the function of the former is more puzzling than the function of the latter. Even natural gender, however, is not without its enigmas. We have agreed that natural gender marking in the third person may tell us something that we did not already know, as well as sometimes help with reference tracking. But what of natural gender marking in the second and first persons? This, like grammatical gender generally, most often tells us very little indeed that we do not already know. It is very unlikely to help us with reference tracking: all of Foley and Van Valin's crucial examples involve the importance of gender as a reference tracking device in the third person. There can by definition be no reference-tracking problems in the case of the first-person singular, and such problems are also highly unlikely to occur very often in the first-person plural or in the second person.

It is possible that some disambiguation may occur from time to time with second-person pronouns. For example, a question such as *How are you* [sing.]? addressed to one person in the presence of another might be ambiguous as to the addressee unless one is male and one female and the language in question distinguishes between male and female second-person pronouns (or, in pro-drop languages, verb forms). The same may also be true with first person plural pronouns – making it precisely clear who 'we' are if there are different groups of people involved that are distinguished by sex.

But what can possibly be the function of gender distinctions in the first-person singular? This form of gender marking is particularly puzzling. It is true that there is the secondary function that written narratives in languages which have such marking reveal the sex of the narrator in a way which is not possible in other languages. But except in the written language – and the masculine/feminine first-person distinctions we see in some of the world's languages cannot be assumed to have arisen as a result of the advent of writing (or crackly telephone lines!) – this form of gender marking gives us no 'information' as such at all. It communicates no knowledge to us that we do not already have. It is quite normal to be able to tell whether a speaker is male or female – we seldom need distinct pronouns or other forms of grammatical marking to tell us this. (Didier Maillat has pointed out to me (pers. comm.) that there may be a useful disambiguating function here when it is not clear whether a speaker is using indirect or reported speech, as in 'He said I love you'.)

Our second question is therefore: why do languages have natural gender other than for third-person pronouns?

THE GENDER OF SELF-REFERENCE

If gender is a relatively marginal grammatical category, this makes the gender of self-reference an even more remarkable phenomenon. All human languages would appear to allow speakers to refer to their own status as being male or female. Given that, as we have already remarked, the difference between male and female is the most fundamental difference there is between human beings, and undoubtedly therefore a semantic universal, it is hardly surprising that this difference is universally lexicalised and that all languages distinguish between lexical categories of the type *man–woman, boy–girl*. This then permits – indeed often requires – individual speakers to signal not only the sex of others but also their own sex lexically: *I am a happy woman* and *I am a sick man* and their equivalents are thus likely to be unremarkable sentences in all the languages of the world.

Languages, however, do differ considerably in the extent to which sex differences are lexicalised. This can be true of kinship terms, where for example 'cousin' is not marked for gender in English but is in many other languages. It can also be true of occupational descriptions where, for example, languages may or may not distinguish between *actor–actress, manager–manageress*, and so on. This issue has of course been the subject of much controversy recently – witness discussions in the English-speaking world as to whether a woman may be a chairman or not, and in the French-speaking world as to whether a female firefighter should be called a *pompière* or not.

This is an interesting and important topic. More interesting for our purposes, however, is the extent to which the sex of speakers is signalled grammatically. In the languages of the world there seem to be a number of possibilities for how the expression of self-referential natural gender may occur grammatically:

1. It may not occur at all – as in English and Hungarian. This appears to be linked to the fact that such languages do not have grammatical gender.
2. It may occur through the use of adjectival gender marking, as in French *je suis heureuse* versus *je suis heureux,* 'I am happy'. In European languages this appears to occur only in those which also have grammatical gender, although of course it is not inevitable in such languages – witness many languages including, for example, German, where it does not occur except, as Theo Vennemann (pers. comm.) has pointed out to me, in appositional deadjectival nominal predicates such as *Ich unglückliche(r)!* 'poor me! f(m). In many Slavic and Romance languages, verbal past participles also behave like adjectives as far as gender marking is concerned. Interestingly, this gives rise in Portuguese to gender marking in the word for 'thank you': *obrigado* versus *obrigada*.

3. It may occur through the use of distinct gender-marked verb forms in the first-person singular, as in Polish past tense and conditional verb forms. This also appears to be true, at least in Europe, only of languages which also have grammatical gender.
4. It may occur through the use of distinct gender-marked first-person singular pronouns. Laycock (1965:133) reports, for example, that the New Guinea language Ngala has the forms /wn/ 'I (m.)' and /ɲən/ 'I (f.)'.

The second question we posed above concerned the function of the gender of self-reference: what is it for? This question is not an easy one to answer. What is clear is that we do not receive any additional information as a result of first-person singular gender marking. In Givón's terms, no knowledge is communicated to us:

(a) if a Ngala man says /wn/ while a Ngala woman says /ɲən/; nor
(b) if an Italian man says *sono stanco* while an Italian woman says *sono stanca* 'I am tired'; nor
(c) if a Polish man says *przyjechałem* while a Polish woman says *przyjechałam* 'I arrived'.

So how can we explain the existence of such self-referential gender-marking in the world's languages? Does it have any function? If so, what is it?

POSSIBLE FUNCTIONS

One interesting issue we should perhaps consider in this connection is whether there are any psycholinguistic consequences or even 'benefits' to such gender marking. Let us approach this issue in the following way. Corbett points out that in many languages grammatical gender has to be maintained even when there is no disambiguating function possible at all, for example when an object is being pointed to or is in some other way the obvious topic. Corbett discusses this interesting phenomenon and points out that it is of considerable semantic and psycholinguistic interest at what level of classification pronominalisation is decided: for instance do French speakers pointing to, say, a car and exclaiming the equivalent of 'It's dirty!' use a pronoun translating *it* appropriate for pronominalising 'thing' or 'vehicle' or 'car' or 'Peugeot'?

It was a source of great psycholinguistic surprise to me, when I was learning Norwegian as a young adult, to be told when somebody passed something to me and I exclaimed *Det er tungt* – 'It's heavy' – that I had made a mistake because the thing I had been passed, a hammer, was grammatically masculine, while I had used a neuter pronoun and adjectival form – I should have said *Den er tung*. I protested that I was not thinking of it as a hammer but just as, well, something – but to no avail! Can this mean that speakers of languages which have grammatical gender are doing something which speakers of other languages do not? Do Norwegians constantly think when they are picking something up what it is in a way English speakers do not? If so, can this also apply to natural gender? Does it mean that French speakers are more aware of the sex of the person they are talking to than English speakers? Does this mean that speakers of languages which extend natural gender into the first and second persons are also doing something which speakers of other languages do not do? If so, what is it? Can it possibly be that Russian or Ngala speakers are more aware, in some sense, of their own sex than speakers of English? In what sense could it be? Does it make any difference that French speakers have to learn as infants to say *heureux* rather than *heureuse* – or vice versa? In the absence of any psycholinguistic evidence, this all seems rather improbable.

Another possibility in our search for a function is to remind ourselves of work, particularly on American Indian languages, which has dealt with the issue of separate men and women's 'languages'. The well-known data from Haas' study (1944) of the American language Koasati, for instance, shows that men and women employed different verb morphology (see also Foley 1997: 300). In Trudgill (1974) I tentatively suggested that it was perhaps not a coincidence that such sex-exclusive differences were maintained (see Crystal 1971 for other instances) in societies with rather rigid and institutionalised gender-role differentiation. We can also remind ourselves of the issue of 'appropriateness' (see Trudgill 1982) as an explanation for linguistic sex differences as revealed in sociolinguistic studies of Western societies, which typically have sex-preferential tendencies in language use, such as the well-known tendency for men, on average, to use prestige forms less often than women. It is not clear, however, where reminding ourselves of such phenomena will get us. Can there be a connection between societal structure, or social roles and the grammatical signalling of one's own sex? Again this seems unlikely. As Corbett (1991) is forced to concede:

> When we consider work with sociolinguists and sociologists, where the concern is the link between language and society, we find the problems are more challenging than expected . . . it is not at all straightforward to establish links between grammatical gender and the relative status of those classified by the different genders . . . In Polish we find a distinction male human versus all other in the plural, which appears to be a particularly sexist division. Russian, which is related to Polish, has no such feature: however, this does not reflect any obvious difference in the relative status of Polish and Russian women and men. (p. 323)

The point about the inherent sexism of Polish is made less tentatively by Sullivan (1981). However, it does not seem to me immediately obvious that, for example, the Polish distinction between *oni* (they, masculine personal) and *one* (they, masculine impersonal, feminine, neuter) is necessarily structurally sexist. It is just as likely that we are dealing with a case of polysemy. Polish recognises, we could say, five categories of nominals in the plural: (1) masculine personal; (2) masculine impersonal; (3) feminine personal; (4) feminine impersonal; (5) neuter. It just so happens that while, in the singular, to simplify somewhat, forms for (1) and (2), as well as for (3) and (4), are homophonous, in the plural it is 2–5 that are all homophonous. That is to say, the collapse of the formal distinction in the plural is not necessarily accompanied by any semantic collapse between these categories that is recognised by or has any cognitive effect on native speakers.

Wierzbicka (1992: 323) does however make the interesting observation, concerning unsuccesful attempts by the Polish Communist government to encourage the use of the second-person plural T pronoun *wy*, that 'Polish courtesy stresses respect for every individual and is highly sex conscious. The collectivist and genderless ring of the form *wy* was jarring in that tradition'. See also the comments above about animacy and agents; Jaworski (1986, 1989); and Herbert and Nykiel-Herbert (1986), who argue rather convincingly that Polish is in some respects structurally sexist.

One further point to consider, however, is the possibility suggested by Wierzbicka (1992: 394) that certain linguistic features may be a reflection of aspects of culture from 'the past, possibly the remote past' rather than from the present. (On the supposed sexism of Indo-European society, and its role in the development of the feminine gender in proto-Indo-European, see Miller 1977, as well as other references cited there.)

In any case, it is clear that in Ngala society it is considered appropriate for men and women to use different first-person singular pronouns, perhaps in rather the same way in which it has traditionally been considered appropriate in many Western societies for women to swear less than men. But it is not clear why this is so, nor where this notion of appropriateness came from. And it is not clear, in particular, why failure to observe this distinction would be not only inappropriate but also ungrammatical.

NON-FUNCTIONALITY

One further explanation that we should consider seriously is that self-referential gender marking is not really functional at all, but that it occurs as a natural consequence of gender marking where it is useful, namely in the third person. Note that it is not very surprising that gender is marked on adjectives or verbs in pro-drop languages such as Italian or Polish where third person pronouns meaning 'he' and 'she' are likely to be absent. The distinction between *e stanco* 'he is tired' and *e stanca* 'she is tired' is a helpful distinction. Similarly the Polish distinction between *przyjechał* 'he arrived' and *przyjechała* 'she arrived' is also very functional.

It could therefore be argued that grammatical systems being the regular systems that they are, it is only natural to extend adjectival and verbal agreement to other persons. It would be unsystematic to have agreement for third-person adjectives but not for the other persons. (This patterning also explains how children eventually acquire correct gender marking, even where, for instance, boys are mostly exposed to the speech of women or girls. There is anecdotal evidence that initially boys in this situation may use, for example, feminine verb forms in Polish, but that this state of affairs does not last long.)

This explanation will clearly not work, however, in the case of non-pro-drop languages such as French, where the adjectival distinction between *il est heureux* versus *elle est heureuse* tells us nothing additional. And it does not work either for the existence of gender-marked first-person singular pronouns.

Let us consider further, however, the notion of non-functionality. One conclusion we may be able to draw from the evidence cited above is the following. Natural gender marking in the third person does indeed have a number of functions. So does grammatical gender marking in those languages which have large numbers of gender classes. However, grammatical gender marking such as those in European languages which have only two or three genders seems to be almost totally non-functional. And, as Hickey (forthcoming) says, grammatical gender is a category which is 'not guided by semantic needs'; if it were, he asks, why would we find languages such as modern Swedish and Danish which do not distinguish between masculine and feminine grammatical gender at all but simply between neuter and 'common' gender (historical masculine and feminine combined)? Similarly, natural gender marking in the second and first-persons – particularly the first person singular – has little or no function at all. We are used to the idea that human languages contain and indeed need redundancy to aid with processing. But do not these particular forms of gender marking represent redundancy on a somewhat non-functional scale?

The only way we can explain these phenomena satisfactorily would appear to be historically. We know that languages drag along with them a certain amount of, as it were, unnecessary historical baggage. This is most obvious in the case of grammatical irregularities which all languages appear to be able to tolerate up to a point. If the plural of *foot* in English is *feet* rather than *foots*, native learners can cope with this, and linguists can explain why it is so on historical grounds. But it may well be that in languages, or at least in some languages, there is much more of this afunctional historical baggage than has sometimes been thought. For example, the presence of different declensions for nominal forms and different conjugations for verbal forms in inflecting languages would appear to provide good evidence that languages can demonstrate large amounts of complex and non-functional differentiation which provide afunctionally large amounts of redundancy and whose presence in such languages can again, presumably, only be explained satisfactorily in historical terms.

Corbett (1991: 310) tells us that 'we are still some way from understanding how gender systems arise'. Nevertheless, he argues that a likely origin for noun classes in general is to be found in nouns themselves and in particular in 'nouns with classificatory possibilities such as "woman", "man", "animal"'. We then have to suppose diachronic processes involving the grammaticalisation of such nouns as classifiers (see also Lee 1988), which are well known to occur in languages such as Chinese. Classifiers can then in turn either come to be used anaphorically and turn into demonstratives – and subsequently pronouns and other gender markers – or they can be repeated within the noun phrase and give rise to gender agreement in that way (see also Harris and Campbell 1995: 341–2).

Other, probably secondary, forms of gender marking can also be explained historically. For instance, Slavic gender-marked verb forms derived originally from compound tenses which consisted of the verb 'be' plus a past participle which, like adjectives (see above), agreed in gender. Then developments such as that which occured in Russian took over: 'the present tense of the verb "be" in Modern Russian [became] the null form, which has left the original participle as the only verb element present' (Corbett 1991: 126).

When we say 'explained,' of course, it should be clear what manner of explanation we are talking about. These gender phenomena are 'linguistic male nipples', in the sense of Lass (1997: 13). They came into being for a reason, but with no purpose. The reason was a series of grammaticalisation processes, as suggested by Corbett, which would appear to be 'invisible hand' phenomena, in the sense of Keller (1994), in that they occur for reasons which have nothing to do with the ultimate outcome. Lyle Campbell (pers. comm.) points out that the gendered Polish forms *pan/pani* and the gendered Spanish forms *vosotros/vosotras, nosotros/nosotras* are also the result of – rather different – grammaticalisation processes: they are phenomena which, as biologists would say, have an explanation but no function. Whether or not it is clear why such grammaticalisation processes take place, it is clear that their motivation is not originally to divide nouns into agreement classes, or to aid with reference tracking or disambiguation. The possibility of reference tracking and disambiguation using gender differentiation in the third person of the type described by Foley and Van Valin is, as it were, a bonus (that is, an example of exaptation, in the sense of Lass 1990). And it is a bonus which is scarcely operative in languages with few genders, or in gender marking in the second-person and the first-person plural, and which is not operative at all in gender marking in the first-person singular.

Gender marking occurs with a very high degree of frequency indeed in those languages which have it, and is thus a feature with a very high degree of *entrenchment,* in the sense of Langacker (1987: 59). It is thus very readily maintained in the speech of individuals; and because of the amazing language learning abilities of the human infant, languages readily maintain this type of complex historical baggage from one generation to another even though it represents a complication and/or an excess of redundancy, and even though it may have no particular or very important function. Indeed, Weist *et al.* (1991) have demonstrated, in connection with child language acquisition of tense and aspect marking in Polish, that a well-differentiated and regular set of paradigms may facilitate early learning, although it is not at all clear that we can generalise from this to gender. And this does not mean to say that languages cannot demonstrate considerable dialectal or idiolectal variation in gender assignment – see Fisiak (1975) and Kryk-Kastovsky (1998).

Gender marking of the afunctional type disappears only when adults start playing an influential role in language learning in contact situations such as those which give rise to the development of pidgins, creoles and creoloids (see above). This disappearance also occurs in the development of koinés, by which is meant varieties which arise in dialect contact situations and which result from dialect mixture, levelling and simplification (see Trudgill 1986): for instance, the standard forms of Swedish and Danish have only two genders, while many nonstandard dialects of these languages still have three. Given that language contact is becoming an increasingly important fact in the modern world, this opens up an intriguing possibility. In Trudgill (1992), I argued that it was interesting to consider the title of Labov's influential (1975) paper 'On the use of the present to explain the past'. While totally supporting the Labovian enterprise, I suggested that, increasingly, the present is going to be unlike the past in demographic and social network terms, and that this might well lead to differences in the direction of linguistic change and in the distribution of structures over the world's languages. I also suggested that increasing language and dialect contact means that creoles, creoloids and koinés are on the increase, and that languages spoken in small, isolated, communities with tightly-knit social networks – which I hypothesised were the types of language most likely to produce complexity and redundancy and to transmit them to descending generations (for fuller argumentation, see also Trudgill 1998) – were becoming less and less common. It is therefore not unlikely that languages with large numbers of afunctional grammatical devices will become less numerous, and indeed it is not entirely impossible that linguistic gender, except perhaps for natural gender in the third person, will one day disappear from the languages of the world, never to return. If this is so, we should, like Foley and Van Valin, do as much as we can, as quickly as we can, to investigate languages with complex gender systems before it is too late.

9

THIRD-PERSON SINGULAR ZERO:
AFRICAN AMERICAN VERNACULAR
ENGLISH, EAST ANGLIAN DIALECTS
AND SPANISH PERSECUTION
IN THE LOW COUNTRIES

AFRICAN AMERICAN VERNACULAR ENGLISH

East Anglian dialects of English English had their brief moment of international academic glory in the 1960s and 1970s when the big sociolinguistic issue was the historical origins of American Nonstandard
Negro English, as it was then called. To simplify rather considerably, there
were two major groups of American academic linguists in competition on
this issue (see Chapters 1 and 3). One group, the Creolists, argued that, to
the extent that American Black Vernacular English (BVE) was linguistically
different from White varieties of English, this was due to the fact that BVE
had its origins in an earlier creole similar to Gullah and to the other English-
based Atlantic creoles (Bailey 1965). The other group, who we can perhaps
call the Dialectologists, argued that, without denying that Black and White
varieties of American English differed, it was not necessary to postulate a
creole history. They argued instead that differences were due to differential
loss and retention of original features of British Isles English, together with
subsequent independent developments (see the presentations in Dillard
1970; Burling 1973).

A number of features of African American Vernacular English (AAVE)
were advanced as evidence for and against these hypotheses. As is well
known, one of these was the absence from verb forms in these varieties of
third-person singular present-tense -s (see Fasold 1972). The Creolists
pointed out that loss of -s represented a typical case of regularisation or
simplification of the sort which often happens in language-contact situations, and that the Caribbean and other Atlantic English-based creoles also
demonstrated this feature. If White American speech had -s and vernacular
Black varieties had zero, then this was not surprising in view of the large-
scale processes of language shift, pidginisation and creolisation that the
speech of the ancestors of modern Black Americans had been subject to as a
result of their enforced transplantation from West Africa to slavery in the
Americas (see Dillard 1972).

The Dialectologists' view (see Kurath 1928) was that third-person singular present-tense zero was a feature of certain British Isles dialects, and the obvious explanation was that Black varieties had acquired and retained this original British Isles feature, while White dialects for the most part had not. The British Isles dialects in question were those of the English region of East Anglia, where forms such as the following are the norm (see Trudgill 1974; 1990):

> He like it, do he?
> That go ever so fast.
> She buy some every day.

The creole or non-creole history of AAVE continues to be discussed in the sociolinguistic literature today, though these more recent discussions tend to be based on more sophisticated data and argumentation from historical linguistics and variation theory. The antiquity, status and grammatical function of third-person singular zero in AAVE have also been called into question, as has the role of s-marking on persons other than the third-person singular (see Schneider 1983; Poplack and Tagliamonte 1989; Winford 1992; McElhinny 1993; Montgomery *et al.* 1994).

However, there was one obvious question which nobody in the 1960s and 1970s ever thought to ask and which has never been asked since: why is it that the dialects of *East Anglia* lack present-tense -s?

EAST ANGLIA DIALECTS

Third-person singular present-tense zero is a well-known feature of the traditional dialects of Norfolk, Suffolk and northern Essex (see Chapter 10). In Norfolk and Suffolk, at least, the feature also continues to be very much a feature of modern dialects. In the city of Norwich, for example, working-class speakers use forms without -s most of the time. Percentage of usage correlates with social-class background, but zero predominates in informal colloquial speech (see Trudgill 1974). The same is true for other urban areas such as Ipswich and Great Yarmouth. Interestingly, hypercorrect forms with -s, on verbs other than third-person singular, do not occur (see Chapter 10).

ENGLISH PRESENT-TENSE VERB SYSTEMS

The modern Standard English system is often held to be typologically unusual among the world's languages. Among present-tense verb forms, only the third-person singular shows morphological marking. Typologists are of the opinion, however, that this is precisely the verb form which is *least* likely to receive special marking, and that English is unusual in this respect (see Chapter 10).

It is therefore not at all surprising that many dialects of English do not share this characteristic of Standard English. Certain forms of English have, like East Anglian dialects, regularised this unexpected and irregular system by having zero marking for all persons. These varieties are rather considerable in number, but all of them except East Anglian English are spoken outside the British Isles. We have already mentioned AAVE in the United States, together with the English-based creoles and post-creoles of the Caribbean and West Africa. Other varieties of which this is true include the South Pacific pidgin and creole varieties Tok Pisin, Bislama, and Solomon Islands pidgin; the language spoken on Pitcairn and its sister language on Norfolk Island; the English of St Helena; and the institutionalised second-language varieties of Singapore, Malaya and elsewhere. In Pitcairnese, for example, we find utterances such as the following (Ross and Moverley 1964: 127):

If any want one melon, first up *get* it.
[If anyone wants a watermelon, the first up there gets it.]
It *make* I think its lost ball.
[It makes me think it's a lost ball = a ship not going to stop.]

What all these non-British Isles varieties have in common, of course, is that they are varieties with a history of considerable language contact. Adult language contact is well known to lead to simplification and regularisation (Thomason and Kaufman 1988; Trudgill 1992), and loss of -*s* in these varieties is therefore not surprising.

East Anglian English would therefore appear to be the odd one out here: it is the only British Isles, as opposed to overseas, variety which demonstrates third-person singular zero. This lining up of East Anglian dialects, alone of all British varieties, with the overseas contact varieties on this point therefore leads us to ask the following question: is it possible that third-person singular zero is a contact feature in East Anglian English also?

THE CHRONOLOGY OF EAST ANGLIAN VERB FORMS

What evidence we have from the Middle English of East Anglia shows that, from the eleventh to the fifteenth centuries, it shared the fully inflected present-tense verb systems of other Middle English dialects. The regional location of East Anglia, moreover, would lead one to expect that geographical diffusion would have led to the replacement of southern -*th* by the originally northern -*s* form at about the same time as in London, namely during the 1500s in colloquial speech and during the 1600s in more formal prose (see Baugh and Cable 1993). Indeed, the Paston letters up to 1509, written in colloquial style by natives of the county of Norfolk, show *-th* throughout.

On the other hand, it is certainly clear that zero has been a feature typical of East Anglian English since at least 1700. This is apparent, for instance, from the work of the Revd R. Forby, who was probably born in 1732 and died in 1825. In Forby (1830) he describes the East Anglian dialect 'as it existed in the last twenty years of the eighteenth century', that is from 1780–1800. He writes of East Anglian speakers that "we so stubbornly maintain that the first and third persons are of the very same forms 'I love, he love' " (p. 142). We can, indeed, be reasonably confident that it was typical of Norfolk English even well before that: a number of zero forms occur in the correspondence of Katherine Paston from the period 1603–27 (Hughey 1941).

If we then want to consider a contact-based explanation for why modern East Anglian dialects have zero, then we must consider sociolinguistic factors that date from the hundred years between, say, 1510 and 1610. We can also note that there are presumably two historical linguistic scenarios: (a) either East Anglian English arrived at the modern zero-marking system via an intermediate *s*-marking system, in between the early Paston letters and Katherine Paston/the Revd Forby, as it were; or (b) there was no intermediate stage, and East Anglian dialects lack *-s* because they never acquired it in the first place:

(a) *-eth* > *-es* > *-Ø*
(b) *-eth* > *-Ø*

What, then, are the relevant sociolinguistic factors, and which is the correct scenario?

SPANISH PERSECUTION IN THE LOW COUNTRIES

I now present historical sociolinguistic evidence which suggests, first, that third-person singular present-tense zero in East Anglian dialects is indeed a contact feature and, second, that it is the second scenario which is the correct one.

There are two important historical factors to consider. First, today the greater urban area of Norwich has a population of about 250,000 and is by no means one of the largest cities in England. In medieval times, however, and up until the seventeenth century, Norwich was the largest city in England apart from London, with the possible exception of Bristol and York. Green and Young (1964) give a population for Norwich in 1662 of 29,200 and say that 'Norwich was then probably the largest provincial town in England'. It was certainly therefore by a very long way the dominant urban area of East Anglia, and we can imagine that social and cultural developments taking place in sixteenth- and seventeenth-century Norwich would have had a very good chance of diffusing geographically to other areas of East Anglia.

Second, there were important events overseas which eventually had significant repercussions in England. In 1567, King Philip of Spain sent the Duke of Alva with an army of 20,000 Spaniards to the Low Countries – modern Belgium and The Netherlands – which at that time were under Spanish control, to quell an anti-Spanish, anti-Catholic revolt. Many prominent people were executed, estates were confiscated and opposition was ruthlessly suppressed. In particular, penal edicts against 'heresy' led to considerable persecution, including torture, of Protestants (see Chapter 10 for a more detailed history).

Not surprisingly, thousands of inhabitants of the Low Countries, at that time probably the wealthiest and most civilised part of Europe, fled abroad. Equally unsurprisingly, very large numbers indeed of these fled across the North Sea to independent, Protestant England. And a very large number of those who fled to England fled to the largest city of eastern England, Norwich. The population of Norwich in 1579 was 16,236. Of that number, approximately 6000 – about 37 per cent – were Dutch- and French-speaking aliens. Norwich at the turn of the sixteenth century was the scene of very considerable language contact indeed.

CONTACT AND CHANGE

The Dutch and French languages survived in Norwich for a long time. According to Moens (1888), 'in the first half of the seventeenth century, as much Dutch and French was spoken in Norwich as English'. The first books ever to be printed in Norwich were in Dutch, and orders for the conduct of the 'Strangers', as they were called, were written in French in 1659. Then, 'slowly but inevitably the Strangers became merged into the surrounding population and the community lost its separate identity' (Ketton-Cremer 1957). French and Dutch continued to survive, but by 1742 the congregations attending church services in these languages were small, and the churches decayed. I conclude that the Dutch and French languages, having arrived in the period 1565–70, finally died out of use as native languages in Norwich during the 1700s. Norwich was a trilingual city for perhaps as long as 200 years.

I suggest, then that East Anglian third-person singular present-tense zero is in origin a contact feature which developed as a result of the presence of large numbers of non-native speakers in Norwich who, in using English as a lingua franca among themselves and with the native population, failed to master, as non-native speakers often do, the non-natural person-marking system of English verbs. This feature then spread out from Norwich as the dominant central place, in the well-known pattern of geographical diffusion of linguistic innovations (see Trudgill 1983: 57–87), until it covered the whole area of East Anglia.

We nevertheless have to provide an explanation for why language contact resulted in the simplification of this one particular feature and of no others. We have already pointed, of course, to the typological oddity and highly marked nature of marking only third-person singular verb forms in the present tense: such an unusual system must be more susceptible to simplification than most. However, by far the most important explanatory factor for this development in East Anglia must be precisely the timing of the arrival of the Strangers in Norwich. That is, these immigrants arrived exactly at the time when the present-tense system of verbs in English was in a state of flux in Norwich, with considerable variability between *-th* and *-s* forms. In other words, at any other time in history, competition between minority non-native zero forms and majority native forms with third-person marking would not have led to the replacement of native by non-native forms. In the late sixteenth century, however, competition was *not* between zero and a single native form. On the contrary, competition was between zero and *-th* and *-s*. It was, that is, a much more equal struggle, as it were, and one in which the non-native form had the advantage of linguistic naturalness and simplicity. (It is also possible that the zero form received further support from present-tense subjunctive forms, given the weakening of the grammatical and semantic distinction between subjunctive and indicative during at this period.)

We can imagine a situation, then, where, as far as this feature was concerned, the non-natives were not outnumbered 2-to-1. If the native population were varying between *-s* and *-th* endings, there must have been a crucial decade or so, to simplify enormously, when each of the three forms had approximately one-third of the population supporting it, so to speak, with the indigenous citizens divided 50–50 as to their usage of the older and newer forms:

Non-natives	Natives	
	older	newer
-Ø	-th	-s
(100% = 33% of total)	(50% = 33% of total)	(50% = 33% of total)
Linguistically favoured		
by being unmarked		

The originally non-native forms eventually won out.

Although we are supposing that the developments we are discussing are the result of language contact, we can also conceive of the situation, as far as third-person singular present-tense verb forms are concerned, as being one of dialect contact: that is, contact between the original Norwich English dialect with *-th*, the newer indigenous dialect with *-s*, and the form of

English spoken by the Strangers with zero. As often happens in dialect contact situations, other things being equal – and for this particular feature alone they were equal – natural forms tend to win out over non-natural ones (see Trudgill 1986: ch. 3).

It was also of very considerable importance that there were at this time not one but two foreign language communities in Norwich. The fact is that English was not only used by the Strangers to communicate with the indigenous population; it was also used as a lingua franca for communication between French speakers and Dutch speakers. This, as per the Whinnom (1971) three-language model of pidginisation (see Chapter 7), would have further reinforced the non-native morphology and encouraged focusing (see Le Page and Tabouret-Keller 1985) on the zero form.

I conclude that the explanation for the absence of third-person singular *-s* in East Anglian English is similar to the explanation for its absence from other varieties, including AAVE. The explanation lies in language contact. My thesis is that Norwich English has had zero marking ever since the more or less simultaneous arrival in the city of (a) third-person singular *-s* from the north of England and (b) the Strangers from the Low Countries.

10

LANGUAGE CONTACT AND INHERENT VARIABILITY: THE ABSENCE OF HYPERCORRECTION IN EAST ANGLIAN PRESENT-TENSE VERB FORMS

HYPERADAPTATION

It is a matter of common linguistic knowledge that contact between different languages and different dialects not infrequently leads to relatively straightforward influence of one variety on another. Phenomena resulting from such influence are typically described by labels such as *interference, transfer* and *borrowing*. It has also been observed, however, that such contact also often results in more complex changes which cannot be explained straightforwardly in terms of influence, and which produce forms which were not originally present in any of the dialects or languages in contact. Labels used to describe such phenomena include *interlanguage* (Selinker 1972) and *interdialect* (Trudgill 1986). Interdialectal forms may include: (a) forms which are phonetically or in some other way intermediate between forms used in the original dialects; and (b) hyperadaptations. Hyperadaptive forms result from speakers' faulty analysis of the structure of one dialect in relation to the structure of another, together with subsequent overgeneralisation. Such forms include both hypercorrections and hyperdialectisms (ibid.).

In this chapter, I examine a situation of apparent dialect contact which could have been expected to lead to the production of hypercorrect forms, but which has not in fact done so. I then attempt an explanation for this absence of hypercorrection.

EAST ANGLIAN VERB FORMS

As we saw in Chapter 9, the traditional dialects of East Anglia lack third-person singular present-tense -*s*. The publications of the *Survey of English Dialects* show zero marking for this verb form in northern Essex, all of Suffolk, and all of Norfolk except the Fens. According to David Britain (pers. comm.), who is an expert on the sociolinguistics of the area (see Britain 1991), the non-Fenland Norfolk town of Downham Market has zero while the Cambridgeshire Fenland town of Wisbech has -*s*. Emneth, which is a suburb of Wisbech but is administratively in Norfolk, also has -*s*.

Local dialect literature confirms that third-person zero is a typical feature of the traditional dialects. For example, Charles Benham's *Essex Ballads*, originally published in Colchester in 1895, contain verses such as:

> I loike to watch har in the Parson's pew
> A Sundays, me a-settin' in the choir;
> She *look* jest wholly be'tiful, she *do*.
> That fairly *seem* to set my heart a-fire.
>
> That *seem* ridic'lous nons'nse this, I doubt,
> A-tellin' on yer how she *make* me feel,
> But who's to help it when she *walk* about
> More like a angel than a gal a deal.
> ('Miss Julia: the Parson's Daughter')

Similarly, the Norfolk dialect poet John Kett in more recent writings uses forms such as:

> That *seem* as though, whenever I sow seeds
> They fare t'come up slow, or not a'tall.
> An' them there hollahocks agin that wall
> In't haaf as big as them untidy weeds.
>
> But I'll say one thing, bor, an' that in't tew –
> Now Winter's come, an' that ole North wind *blow*,
> My garden's buried und'ra foot o' snow . . .
> That *look* like all the others now, that *dew*!
> ('My Garden')

This zero form also survives in the more modern dialects of at least the northern and central parts of the area, as in the urban dialects of Norwich, Great Yarmouth and Ipswich. However, it is clear that in these varieties the usage of zero forms is variable. In the modern dialect of Norwich, forms with zero alternate with forms with -*s*. This variability correlates with social class background, and with formality of style. Trudgill (1974) shows the following extent of zero-form usage:

	% -*s*	
Speakers	Informal	Formal
Lower working-class	3	13
Middle working-class	19	36
Upper working-class	25	62
Lower middle-class	71	95
Upper middle-class	100	100

An obvious explanation for this variability would appear to lie in contact between the original traditional dialect forms, which lacked -*s*, and the prestigious Standard English of the education system and the media, which of course does have -*s*. This explanation also appears to be favoured by the strong and obvious correlation of percentage of usage of standard forms with social class and formality of situation.

ABSENCE OF HYPERCORRECTION

If contact between the local dialect and Standard English lies at the root of the variability we find in modern East Anglian English, we would then expect to find at least spasmodic, individual occurrences of hypercorrect forms on the part of East Anglian speakers, especially perhaps those with less education. We would imagine that, in attempting to speak in a more statusful or 'correct' manner, they would employ standard -*s* but, because of a faulty analysis of the Standard English system, they would also from time to time add -*s* to persons other than the third-person singular. There are many examples in the literature of similar forms of contact between standard and nonstandard varieties leading to instances of hypercorrection. For example, hypercorrect -*s* occurs in the speech of native speakers of forms of Caribbean English which lack third-person -*s* in their basilectal form (see Edwards 1979). Similar hypercorrect forms are reported in some varieties of AAVE (Schneider 1983).

The focus of this chapter is on the interesting and perplexing fact that in East Anglian English, hypercorrection does not in fact occur for this feature. It is always difficult to argue for the total absence of a phenomenon, and some sociolinguists will doubtless find this assertion difficult to accept. The absence does, however, seem to be genuinely total. There are, for example, no hypercorrect present-tense forms at all in the data from the Trudgill (1974) Norwich study; and in a lifetime of observation of speakers in the area, I have never heard a single example of -*s* being added to persons other than the third singular. When East Anglian speakers use more standard or formal styles, it is true that they do variably add -*s* to third-person singular forms, but they always get it right and never append it to other persons.

I argue here that the correct explanation for this rather surprising lack of hypercorrection in East Anglian English lies in the historical sociolinguistics of the area, and is intimately connected with the way in which the local dialects acquired zero forms in the first place.

THE HISTORY OF -*S* IN ENGLISH

Any explanation for the absence of third-person singular -*s* from East Anglia must necessarily look at the history of the development of -*s* in modern English itself. Middle English present-tense verb forms had a regional distribution as follows, illustrated from the verb *to thank* (see Fisiak 1968):

	South	Midlands	North
1st-person singular	thank**e**	thank**e**	thank**e**
2nd-person singular	thank**est**	thank**es(t)**	thank**es**
3rd-person singular	thank**eth**	thank**eth/es**	thank**es**
plural	thank**eth**	thank**en**	thank**es**

The Midland plural form *-en* was borrowed from the subjunctive, and provided a singular/plural distinction not available in the other dialects. During the Middle English period, this form gradually spread to the other dialects, and the *-n* was increasingly lost. With eventual loss of final /ə/, only the second- and third-person singular forms retained inflectional endings. With the loss of the singular second-person *thou* forms in favour of plural *you* forms, this left the third-person singular forms as the only ones distinct from the base.

As can be seen, and as is well known, the third-person singular ending in the south was *-(e)th*, in the north *-(e)s*. The origin of the northern *-es* form is somewhat controversial. Hogg (1993: 306) writes:

> In Northumbrian only, final /θ/ in [the third-person singular and in the plural present indicative] is often spelled as (s) . . . The morphological restriction on these forms indicates that the shift could take place only under favourable morphological conditions, but its spread to the plural shows that the stimulus cannot solely have been an analogy with Scandinavian.

Whatever its origins, the originally northern form spread gradually south. According to Brook (1958) 'The forms in *-es* spread from the north to the East Midlands and the North-West Midlands in Middle English, and by the fifteenth century spread to London English'. Baugh and Cable (1993) claim that the spread of *-es* forms to the south is 'difficult to account for, since it is not easy to see how the Northern dialect, where they were normal, could have exerted so important an influence on the language of London and the South'. Nevertheless, spread they did. The general consensus is that this spread was gradual and affected colloquial speech first, and that there was a long period in the London area when both forms were available to differing extents. It is often pointed out that Shakespeare, for instance, was able to use both *-th* and *-s* forms depending on the needs of style and metre. According to Baugh and Cable, *-s* forms predominated in the London area by 1600. The geographical spreading did not, of course, end in London, and forms in *-th* are known not to have been replaced by *-s* in traditional dialects in the far south-west of England (Devon and Cornwall) until the early years of this century (see Wakelin 1972).

A number of third-person zero forms occurred from the fifteenth century onward (Holmqvist 1922), but these were very infrequent: Kytö (1993) reports 7 (= 1.5 per cent) examples out of a total of 461 third-person singular present-tense verb forms in the Helsinki corpus for 1500–70.

TYPOLOGY

As we saw in Chapter 9, typologists are agreed (see Croft 1990) that Standard English is unusual among the languages of the world in having marking in the present-tense only on the third-person singular, which is typologically the form least likely to have person marking. It is therefore not at all surprising that many dialects of English do not share this characteristic of Standard English. Many dialects of British Isles English, for example, have a system in which present-tense -s occurs with all persons. In north of England dialects where it occurs, it is likely that this represents a survival of the original Middle English system. There is, however, the further complication that many north of England varieties, like Scottish and northern Ireland varieties, have a subject agreement rule such that third-person present-tense plural verb forms take -s unless they are governed by the pronoun *they*. This constraint has also been found in some American varieties (see for example Wolfram and Christian 1976) and elsewhere (Poplack and Tagliamonte 1989), and has been argued by Bailey *et al.* (1989) to have been present at earlier periods at least in parts of the south of England also. The generalised -s system, however, is also very prevalent in large areas of southwestern England and south Wales (see Hughes and Trudgill 1995), where it must represent a more recent regularisation.

Conversely, there are many other varieties of English which have achieved regularisation by having no person marking at all for any person in the present tense. In Chapter 9, I argue that it is not a coincidence that all these varieties, such as Pitcairnese (Ross and Moverley 1964) and Caribbean English, are forms of English which have been involved in language contact. I suggest that the loss of an irregular and typologically unusual form of personal marking is a typical example of the kind of simplification which takes place in contact situations involving adults. I also argue that East Anglian English is no exception, and that here too contact provides the correct explanation for the origins of zero forms.

CONTACT AND CHANGE

Histories of the English language, having dealt with the influence of Norman French and Old Norse on English, rarely thereafter comment on language contact or multilingualism in England at all, with the possible exception of a brief mention of the shift from Cornish to English in Cornwall, which was completed in the eighteenth century. A consideration of the earlier history of English, however, suggests that language contact of different types has frequently occurred not just in Ireland, Scotland and Wales, but also in England. Consider the linguistic history of East Anglia itself.

After the gradual replacement between the fifth and seventh centuries of the ancestor of modern Welsh – and what little Latin there was – by the Anglo-Saxon spoken by the invading Angles and Frisians, East Anglia must have remained fairly monolingual for a century or so until the arrival of the Danes in the ninth century. For the next few hundred years, however, multilingualism must have been a frequent feature. After the Norman conquest, for instance, Norwich itself in the twelfth century must have had, in addition to the original speakers of English and Danish, speakers of the newly arrived Norman French, as well as the Breton and Flemish spoken by many of the Normans' followers. Large numbers of Jews also arrived with the Normans, and they may have been speakers of Ladino (Judaeo-Spanish). Later, during the fourteenth century, there were also numerous Flemish-speaking weavers who arrived in the city. It is very unlikely, however, that these particular instances of language contact had any kind of effect on the present-tense verb system of East Anglian English.

Historical events which do appear to be relevant are the following. From 1348 onwards, the different provinces of the Low Countries, for the most part modern Belgium and The Netherlands, came gradually under the control of the Dukes of Burgundy. Mary, the daughter of Charles the Bold, Duke of Burgundy, married Emperor Maximilian of Austria. Their son Philip married Joanna, the daughter of Ferdinand of Aragon and Isabella of Castile, and thus control of the Low Countries ultimately passed to their son, who as Charles V was Holy Roman Emperor as well as being King Charles I of Spain. When he abdicated in 1556, the imperial office went to his brother, Emperor Ferdinand I. The crown of Spain, however, together with control over the Low Countries and other colonies such as Naples and Milan, went to his son, King Philip II.

Although Charles had been educated in the Low Countries, his son Philip had been brought up in Spain. Philip was also a devout Catholic, and most of his domestic, colonial and foreign policies were focused on stamping out Protestantism. It was therefore inevitable that there would be friction in the Low Countries where, in the northern provinces (now The Netherlands), Calvinism had taken deep root. Under the control of Philip's sister, Margaret of Parma, the stationing of Spanish troops in the Low Counties, the prosecution of 'heretics' and the Spanish Inquisition led to an insurrection against Spanish domination even in the mainly Catholic south (modern Belgium), where loss of autonomy was resented.

Dutch, Flemish and Walloon refugees fleeing to England from this Spanish persecution settled in Sandwich (Kent), London and Colchester, but the biggest group of refugees by far found its way to Norwich, probably attracted at least in part by an already established group of invited weavers.

In 1565, the mayor and Aldermen of Norwich had invited thirty 'Dutch-men' and their families – no household was to exceed ten persons – to Norwich in an attempt to modernise the local textile industry, which was of great economic importance to the region, but which had been lagging behind in terms of technology, design and skills. In the event, twenty-four Flemish and ten Walloon master textile makers arrived and settled in Norwich (Rickwood 1984; Vane 1984).The refugees themselves, although predominantly also textile workers, included ministers, doctors, teachers, merchants and craftsmen. They were mostly from Flanders and Brabant, but there were also many Walloons from Armentieres, Namur and Va-lenciennes (note that at this period, the border with France was further south than it is today), and even some German speakers from Lorraine. The very high proportion of 'Strangers' (see Chapter 9), as they were called, in the city did lead to a certain amount of friction, and there was at least one attempted revolt against them; but generally, the absorption of a very large number of refugees into the population, while it undoubtedly caused overcrowding, seems to have been relatively trouble free. The economic benefits of the reinvigorated textile trade were plain for all to see.

By 1579, as we saw in the previous chapter, 37 per cent of the population of Norwich, which at that time was 16,236, were native speakers of Dutch or French. Some of the Flemish community returned to the Low Countries as a result of religious persecution during the 1600s, but the foreign community was further strengthened by the arrival of some French Hu-guenots after the edict of Nantes in 1685. According to Ketton-Cremer (1957), church services in Dutch and French were maintained in the churches that had been given over to the immigrant communities 'for many decades', and the congregations seem to have remained vigorous until 1700 or so. The last French-language service in Norwich was in 1832, and the last in Dutch in the 1890s, but by then the languages had attained the status of liturgical languages only. Now only surnames survive, and most of those in anglicised form. It is clear, however, that Norwich remained a trilingual city for 200 years or so, well into the eighteenth century.

The argument, given in detail in Chapter 9, is that the zero form, typical of the kind of simplification that takes place in language-contact situations as a result of imperfect learning by adults, was introduced into Norwich English by the Strangers. This is not to say, however, that East Anglian English was or is as a whole a contact variety like, say, Pitcairnese. Clearly it is not. The modern dialect of Norwich contains no other interlanguage features which can be described as the result of contact-induced simplifica-tion, nor indeed any phonological or grammatical features which appear to be the result of direct interference of or borrowing from Dutch or French. (There are, it is true, some probable lexical items, such as *lucam* 'attic window' from French *lucarne* 'skylight', and *dwile* 'floorcloth' from Dutch *dweil* 'floorcloth'.)

As far as crucial grammatical features are concerned, however, Norwich English, like other forms of East Anglian English, bears no resemblance to a creoloid, by which term is meant a variety which, when compared with some source variety, resembles a post-creole in that it shows some features of simplification as a result of the influence of imperfect learning by non-native-speaker adults, but which has maintained a continuous native-speaker tradition, unlike pidgin-derived creoles and post-creoles (see Chapter 7). Indeed, we would not expect Norwich English to resemble a creoloid like Afrikaans, for example, because the degree of language contact was not nearly so great nor as prolonged. At all times, in spite of the large numbers of foreigners in the city, native speakers outnumbered non-natives by at least two to one.

It is apparent (see Chapter 9) that, under normal circumstances, given that the Strangers were in a minority, albeit a large one, the zero form would never have won out. Circumstances were not normal, however. The point is that the Strangers must have arrived in Norwich from the Low Countries at more or less the same time as the new -*s* form arrived from the north and Midlands of England. It was in a situation of three-way competition between the older -*th* form, the newer -*s* form and the foreigners' zero form that the typologically simpler zero form was successful (see Chapter 9), leading to the situation that we find in the dialect today.

INHERENT VARIABILITY

As far as the absence of hypercorrection is concerned, we can say the following. It had always seemed probable that the current social and stylistic variability involving -*ø* and -*s* in the English of Norwich and other parts of East Anglia, as outlined above, was a relatively recent phenomenon resulting from twentieth-century and perhaps nineteenth-century interaction between the local dialect, on the one hand, and Standard English, on the other. The absence of hypercorrection seems, however, to detract from the probable validity of this scenario. I now hypothesise that this variability, totally free from hyperadaptation as it is, may be the direct and continuing result of the way in which zero forms were introduced into Norwich English in the first place.

The zero ending, as we have seen, appeared in the English of Norwich, the capital city and central place of East Anglia, simultaneously with the new -*s* form which had spread geographically from the north of England. The two new forms, however, must have been differentially influential in replacing the original -*th* in different sections of the community. A large number of the Strangers, although they brought wealth to the city, remained among the poorer sections of the population, as is often the case with immigrants and refugees (Rickwood 1984). It is probable, therefore, that their non-native English had a greater influence in the city on the developing English of the lower classes, of whom many of them became a part, than on that of the upper classes, who would have been subject to greater influence from the fashionable new -s forms that was also taking over in London and elsewhere in the south.

In my work on dialect contact (Trudgill 1986), I have shown that, in a dialect mixture situation, it is usual, if new-dialect formation takes place, for only one variant of a given feature from the mixture to survive. However, where, unusually, more than one variant survives, these variants are usually subject to *reallocation*. A phonological example of this is provided by the fact that the modern Norwich dialect has three variant pronunciations of the vowel of words from the lexical set of *broom, room*: /ʊ/, /ʉː/ and /uː/ (see Chapter 4). It is clear from rural dialect studies that each of these pronunciations is to be found in the immediate rural hinterland of Norwich, /ʊ/ to the south, /ʉː/ to the north and east, and /uː/ to the west (see Trudgill 1986: 112–19). In the urban dialect, however, with the involvement of in-migration in the development of the urban dialect followed by dialect-mixture and reallocation, /uː/ is now the middle-class variant, /ʊ/ the upper working-class variant, and /ʉː/ the lower working-class variant.

If we conceive of language contact in sixteenth-century Norwich as leading to a situation of contact between three dialects as far as third-person verb forms were concerned – the older indigenous dialect with -*th*, the newer indigenous dialect with -*s*, and the Strangers' more regular but lower-status dialect with zero – then we can see the current situation as resulting from a process of reallocation that took place 400 years ago. The reallocation of variants in a dialect mixture may result in the redistribution of variants according to social class dialect, as with Norwich *broom, room*, or formality of style (see examples in Trudgill 1986). In the case of East Anglian -*s* versus zero, however, the reallocation of variants was according to both style and social class. In the three-way competition between the different third-person present-tense singular forms, -*th* was lost forever, but both -*s* and zero survived because they were allocated different functions in the local dialect. The ability of native-speakers of Norwich and East Anglian English generally to switch stylistically between zero and -*s* without hypercorrection may thus be the result of centuries of familiarity with a system that originated in language contact and dialect mixture, and which produced, as a result of reallocation of variants from different dialects – native -*s* and non-native zero – long-term and thus genuinely inherent variability.

IV. LANGUAGE CREATION
AND LANGUAGE DEATH

INTRODUCTION: LANGUAGE CREATION AND LANGUAGE DEATH

The chapters in this section have to do in part, as was discussed in the General Introduction, with the application of sociolinguistics to the solution of real-world problems. The first major thesis of this section is as follows. Linguists are in many respects no better placed than professionals in any other field to actually do anything about solving the problems faced by linguistic minorities in Europe or anywhere else. Linguists do tend to be better informed than most about the situations in which linguistic minority groups find themselves, as well as about the social, political and educational problems they face. But we have no special qualifications which assist us in obtaining funds for minority schooling. We have no special political skills which might enable us to move governmental bodies to improve the lot of minority language communities. And we are no more proficient than any other academic group at networking and obtaining the support of journalists in an attempt to obtain favourable publicity.

There are two respects, however, in which linguists are much better equipped for analysing the situations in which minority languages are spoken and for defending the rights of minority groups than other professionals. First, and paradoxically, since linguists seem to be the only people who are fully aware of the extent to which the question of whether a linguistic variety is a language or not (as opposed to a dialect) is not a truly linguistic matter at all, we are very well placed to defend linguistic minorities against attacks which are aimed at – and to help with problems and misconceptions that are associated with – the linguistic status of their mother-tongue. These are of course not the worst problems that linguistic minorities experience. But they are significant, and the international linguistics community can help.

Sociolinguists know that most European languages are, in Kloss' (1967) terms, *Ausbau* languages – 'languages by extension'. These are varieties which form part of geographical dialect continua and which are constituted as separate languages for political, social, cultural and historical reasons as much as, if not more so than, for linguistic reasons. We are aware that

111

dialects like Luxemburgish and Slavomacedonian can become languages without anything happening to their linguistic characteristics, and languages like Scots and Provencal and Low German can become dialects without anything in the language changing at all. The very same dialects can be dialects of one language at one time and dialects of another language at another time, as in the case of the Swedish but formerly Danish dialects of Scania. On purely non-linguistic grounds one language can become three, as in the case of Croatian, Serbian and Bosnian. The mention of Luxemburgish reminds us too that 'some languages are more languages than others'. Crucially, sociolinguists know that these phenomena have very little to do with language as such, and we can talk knowledgeably and persuasively about these issues.

Second, in discussing language status and in formulating language policies for minorities, it is often very important to look specifically at the language varieties themselves, in terms of their linguistic characteristics, in an analytical way. Sociolinguists can help in this respect because we are professionally skilled in describing languages. This is relevant because some languages, such as Basque, are, again in Kloss' terms, so-called *Abstand* languages – 'languages by distance' – languages in their own right solely on linguistic grounds. Basque is so different from all other languages in terms of its linguistic characteristics that no one could even begin to suggest that it was a dialect of something else. There are also relationships and interactions between Abstand and Ausbau status – which only linguists seem to have genuine insights into – which mean that language minority policies need to be based not only on an examination of political, cultural and economic considerations but also of the language varieties themselves. That is, in developing our minority policies we do need to look at vowels, consonants, lexis and syntax.

The second major thesis of this section has to do with respect for variety in language. The regrettable truth for those of us who work in linguistics is that, in spite of a century or more of scientific research in linguistics, there is still in the world as a whole, and perhaps especially in Europe, a lack of respect for language in its entirety. Even more sadly, this seems to be most prevalent where one would expect it least: among certain members of the intelligentsia, the literati, the journalists, the politicians, the opinion-makers. They value great literature, abhor illiteracy and are fanatical about the preservation of what they call 'standards' in speaking and writing. They support the fallacy that appears everywhere in every generation that their own language, whatever it is, is in decline – that the young do not write or speak as well as the old. But a closer examination shows that what respect they have for language is confined to varieties spoken by a very small proportion of the population. The only languages which they deem worthy of respect, and which they recognise as valid, are the major languages, those with millions of speakers. And the only varieties of those languages which they respect are the standard, written varieties. In other words, we are presented with a phenomenon amongst intelligentsia which we can call: the denigration of vernacular varieties. That is, there is a widespread view that some varieties of language are somehow more worthy, more valid, in some mysterious way simply better than others. Linguists know that this view is wrong, and worse, pernicious. But we, as experts on language, ought to do more to combat it than we currently do because it can have disastrous consequences. The second major theme of this section, then, is language death.

11

AUSBAU SOCIOLINGUISTICS AND THE PERCEPTION OF LANGUAGE STATUS IN CONTEMPORARY EUROPE

With the expansion of the European Union and the liberalisation of Eastern Europe, language is once again becoming an important political topic on the European scene, especially insofar as linguistic minorities and their ethnolinguistic vitality are concerned. Speakers of minority languages may, depending on their circumstances, face a number of different problems. Not the least of these problems may be that the majority in the nation-state in which they find themselves deny that their language is actually a language at all. This is not true for all language minorities, however. This chapter outlines a typology of minority languages and discusses the extent to which these different types of language are susceptible to this form of attack. This sociolinguistic typology focuses on macro-sociopsychological strategies which governments and other bodies may adopt when making non-liberal responses to linguistic minority situations. Obviously, different linguistic and geopolitical situations produce different responses. As this typology shows, however, it is not only the social and economic circumstances surrounding language varieties which are of political importance, but also their linguistic characteristics.

In any discussion of the problems faced by speakers of minority languages, it is important to recognise the sociolinguistic problems associated with distinguishing between a *language* and a *dialect*. As is well known, the concept of a *language* is in many cases as much a political, cultural and historical concept as it is a linguistic concept. Whether a linguistic variety is to be perceived as a language or not may have to do with many other factors in addition to its purely linguistic characteristics.

AUSBAU AND ABSTAND LANGUAGES

This becomes clearer if we consider the distinction, mentioned in the introduction to this section, between Abstand languages and Ausbau languages (Kloss 1967). In the case of Abstand languages, we do not need to consider anything other than linguistic characteristics. Abstand is the

114

German for 'distance'. An Abstand language is thus a linguistic variety which is perceived as being a language in its own right by virtue of its linguistic distance from all other linguistic varieties. A very clear example of an Abstand language in Europe is Basque. All varieties of Basque are at least reasonably mutually intelligible. More importantly, they are all so utterly unlike any other language that there can be no doubt that Basque is a separate language: there is no possibility of claiming that it might be a dialect of some other language. Basque, which has not been convincingly shown to be historically related to an other language anywhere, is thus a language by reason of its linguistic distance from all other languages. Basque, of course, is also a true minority language: it is not a majority language in any nation-state, and its speakers constitute minorities in both the nation-states where it is spoken – Spain and France. One of the problems it does not have, however, is that of non-Basques attempting to deny it status as a language. As we shall see later, there are different degrees of linguistic Abstand.

Ausbau languages, on the other hand, are in a very different and, in many parts of the world, much more usual situation. Ausbau is the German for extension. An Ausbau language is thus a linguistic variety which is considered to constitute a language in its own right for cultural and political as well linguistic reasons. Crucial to an understanding of the nature of Ausbau languages is the concept of the geographical dialect continuum (see Chambers and Trudgill 1997). As is well known, on such a continuum, dialects – or at least, conservative rural dialects – change gradually from place to place, with neighbouring dialects being very similar to one another. There are many such dialect continua in Europe. For example, the West Germanic dialect continuum includes dialects of what we normally refer to as German and Dutch. The Romance continuum covers dialects of French, Italian, Catalan, Spanish, Galician and Portuguese. The North Slavic continuum includes dialects of Russian, Belorussian, Ukrainian, Polish, Slovak and Czech. And the Scandinavian continuum incorporates Norwegian, Swedish and Danish.

On the West Germanic dialect continuum, the Dutch dialects of Belgium are linked to the German dialects of Austria by a chain of mutual intelligibility: a dialectologist's journey from Bruges to Vienna would reveal dialects changing gradually from west to east, with no clear linguistic break anywhere on the continuum. Nevertheless, the dialects of Bruges and Vienna are not mutually intelligible: the cumulative effect of the gradation of small linguistic differences between one village dialect and the next is, after a distance of several hundred kilometres, sufficient to make communication impossible. As far as this particular continuum is concerned, it is usual to refer to some of the dialects as Dutch and others as German. We are also in no doubt as to where the geographical boundary between Dutch and German dialects lies: it lies on the frontier between The Netherlands and Germany. The distinction between Dutch and German dialects has very little to do with the linguistic characteristics of the dialects. The dialects on either side of the Netherlands–German frontier are very similar indeed and are much more similar to each other than to dialects of Dutch and German, respectively, which are spoken in areas further away. Obviously, the reasons why we refer to some of these border-area dialects as Dutch and to others as German are non-linguistic. Speakers of dialects on the Dutch side of the border will look to Standard Dutch as the standard variety that naturally corresponds to their vernaculars, and they will read and write in Dutch; any standardising tendencies in their dialects will be in the direction of Standard Dutch; and any new technical vocabulary will be taken from Dutch. On the other side of the border, speakers will receive their education through the medium of Standard German; they will watch German television and read German newspapers.

AUTONOMY AND HETERONOMY

It is usual in sociolinguistics to say that these two standard varieties, which are enshrined in grammar books and dictionaries and have bodies of literature written in them, are, like other standard varieties, autonomous: they have, as it were, an independent existence. The nonstandard local dialects, on the other hand, are heteronomous or dependent: the dialects as spoken on the one side of the frontier are heteronomous with respect to Standard Dutch and on the other side to Standard German. A reasonable definition of an Ausbau language is thus that it consists of an autonomous standard variety together with all the nonstandard varieties from the dialect continuum which are heteronomous with respect to it.

Because autonomy and heteronomy are political and cultural as well as linguistic characteristics, they are subject to change and conflict. Autonomy can be lost or acquired: languages can become dialects, and dialects can become languages. Autonomy and heteronomy can also be disputed. Examples of languages which have lost autonomy and have come to be perceived as dialects of other languages include Scots (now most usually thought of as a dialect of English), Provençal (French) and Plattdeutsch (German). Conversely, dialects which acquired autonomy during the course of the twentieth century and which have come to be perceived as independent languages include Afrikaans (formerly Dutch), and Macedonian (Serbian/Bulgarian – see further below). A typology of minority languages, and of potential attacks on their perception as having language status, is presented in Table 11.1. A distinction is made there between two types of minority language: true (also known as endogenous) minority languages, which are not spoken by a majority in any nation-state; and situational (or exogenous) minority languages, which are majority languages in at least one nation-state but minority languages elsewhere. There is also a distinction between two different types of Abstand status.

116

One would imagine that, other things being equal, the most vulnerable languages would be those of the type listed at 1A: languages which have neither majority demographic status anywhere nor linguistic Abstand status to protect them. Correspondingly, again other things being equal, one would suppose that languages of type 3B would be the least threatened as far as their status as languages is concerned.

	A	**B**
	True minority languages	*Situational minority languages*
1. Ausbau languages	Catalan Frisian Friulian	French in Italy German in Belgium Polish in Czechia
2. Geographical Abstand languages	Sorbian Ladino Yiddish	Swedish in Finland Dutch in France Danish in Germany
3. Absolute Abstand languages	Basque Romany Welsh	Hungarian in Austria Finnish in Sweden Albanian in Greece

Attacks on language status
1A 'Catalan is a dialect of Spanish'
2A 'Ladino is a form of Spanish'
3A 'Romany is just a dialect'
1B 'It's not Polish, it's Czech'
2B 'It's not Dutch, it's Flemish'
3B 'It's not Albanian, it's Arvanitika'

Heteronomy and autonomy
1A denial of autonomy; assertion of heteronomy
2A denial of autonomy; assertion of heteronomy
3A denial of autonomy
1B assertion of heteronomy
2B denial of heteronomy
3B assertion of autonomy

Table 11.1. Potential attacks on language status

1A: TRUE MINORITY AUSBAU LANGUAGES

There are many minority languages in Europe whose speakers have suffered and/or continue to suffer problems because their vernacular lies on a dialect continuum; the independent status of their language is therefore based on an Ausbau-type autonomy which can be lost, attacked or disputed. Most European countries suffer from sociolinguistic problems which have to do with linguistic Ausbau, the preservation (or otherwise) of autonomy, and the direction of heteronomy.

The West Romance continuum

In Spain, for example, extensive efforts were made under the Franco dictatorship to extinguish the autonomy of Catalan, but since the restoration of democracy, Catalan once again has undisputed status as a language – except that there is now disagreement as to whether Valencian is a variety of Catalan or a language in its own right. Galician, which resembles Portuguese more than it does Spanish, has also been afforded official recognition in Spain, and hence autonomy.

In France, the once-distinct language Provençal has lost its autonomy to French, as mentioned above, but efforts are under way in the south of France to encourage the use of Occitan, as it is now called, in a wider range of situations. The status of Corsican is also controversial: is it Italian, or an independent language? In Italy, it is now accepted that Ladin and Friulian are distinct from Italian, but there is some discussion as to whether, together with the Swiss language Romansch, they constitute one, two or three languages. The position of Sardinian as a language separate from Italian is also a controversial issue, as is that of a number of other 'dialects' of Italian: the linguistic distance between Lombard and Standard Italian has been used as a propaganda weapon by the right-wing northern Italian separatist movement.

The West Germanic continuum

In Belgium it has been decided that the Germanic dialects of the north of the country should be heteronomous with respect to Standard Dutch rather than any attempt being made to establish Flemish as a distinct Ausbau language. In The Netherlands, West Frisian now has official recognition as a language distinct from Dutch. North Frisian also has some recognition as an independent language in Germany.

The situation of Plattdeutsch or Low German is very similar to that Provençal – it was clearly at one time an independent language, but in modern times it has become heteronomous with respect to High or Standard German. However, attempts are being undertaken to restore at least some of its autonomy: it has been spoken in the Schleswig-Holstein Land parliament, it is used in broadcasting, and a certain amount of literature is appearing in Plattdeutsch.

In Luxemburg, the government has declared that Letzeburgisch is to be regarded as an independent language rather than a dialect of German. In Switzerland, however, where the Germanic dialects are radically different from Standard German and where there would therefore be a good case for establishing a separate language on Abstand grounds, Swiss German continues for the most part to be regarded as heteronomous with respect to German.

The North Slavic continuum

Ukrainian and, in particular, Belorussian have at times had difficulties maintaining their status as languages distinct from Russian. In Poland Kashubian (or Cassubian) has a long tradition as a separate language but it is now widely regarded as a dialect of Polish. Also in Poland, there is a question as to whether Lemko is a dialect of Ukrainian or a language in its own right (although there is no suggestion that Ukrainian is a variety of Polish).

In ex-Czechoslovakia, Czech and Slovak were linguistically very similar, but differences between them were institutionalised, and the status of minority Slovak as a separate, albeit mutually intelligible, language was not challenged: distinct orthographies, grammars and dictionaries were important devices in the maintenance of autonomy. Ukrainian in eastern Slovakia is sometimes known as Ruthenian, and of course the distinct name also brings with it a suggestion of autonomy and separate status.

The languages of the Balkans are particularly interesting for the problems they pose when it comes to Ausbau and Abstand, heteronomy and autonomy. Of the Slavic varieties, one of the languages with official recognition in the Vojvodina (formerly) autonomous region of Serbia in Yugoslavia is known as Rusyn, but it may not be distinct from Ukrainian and/or Ruthenian and/or Lemko.

The South Slavic continuum

Slovene, although part of the same south Slavonic dialect continuum as Serbo-Croat, Macedonian and Bulgarian, has successfully established an independent status as the language of the ex-Yugoslavian republic of Slovenia (it is also spoken in neighbouring areas of Austria, Hungary and Italy and in parts of Romania).

For Serbo-Croat, the major language of former Yugoslavia, the main question has been whether it is one language or two. Serbian and Croatian are perhaps less different from one another than Czech and Slovak in terms of lexis and phonology – in other words, they are very similar. They are, however, written in the Cyrillic and Latin alphabets respectively, and among emigrant communities, such as in Australia, they are widely regarded as separate languages, reflecting the religious (Orthodox versus

Catholic) and traditional ethnic separation. The foundation of Yugoslavia as a nation-state, however, led to a drive for national unity and a down-playing of the Ausbau-type differences between the two, especially under Tito. More recent political developments, on the other hand, have led once again to an insistence that the languages are distinct. The amount of Abstand between the dialects of, say, Split and Belgrade make this a not entirely unreasonable claim. It is equally clear, however, that speakers in some geographically intermediate areas have no such linguistic Abstand to rely on and thus claim to speak Serbian or Croatian according to their ethnic identity rather than because of linguistic realities. Speakers of mixed or unclear ethnic origin who come from geographically intermediate areas of the dialect continuum therefore have generally felt more comfortable claiming Serbo-Croat as their native tongue: they had no way of choosing between Serbian and Croatian. In the most recent climate of 'lexical cleansing' activities on the part of Serbian and Croatian governments in an attempt to increase the amount of at least symbolic Abstand between their two varieties, it is not at all surprising that the Bosnian government has now announced that its official language is to be called Bosnian.

The most controversial of the issues among the Slavic languages of the Balkans, however, concerns the status of Macedonian, the official language of the ex-Yugoslavian republic of Macedonia (see Chapter 12). It is a recently developed Ausbau language based on and constructed out of dialects from the south of the (at that time) Yugoslavian part of the south Slavic dialect continuum. In order to underline its character as a specifically Yugoslavian language, the standard variety of Macedonian was based on those dialects which were most unlike Bulgarian: part of the Ausbau process was to make the most of what relatively little Abstand there was on the dialect continuum. In the years immediately after the Second World War, Macedonian was accepted as an independent language not only in Yugo-slavia but also by Bulgaria, to the extent that Macedonian was taught as the mother tongue in the south-western area of Bulgaria immediately adjacent to Yugoslavian Macedonia. As relations between the two countries cooled, however, this changed, and Bulgaria currently does not accept the inde-pendent language status of Macedonian; it regards the Slavic varieties of this part of the dialect continuum as being dialects of Bulgarian. (Similarly, some Serb nationalists want to claim them for Serbia.) However, outside Greece, where the name of the language has been objected to (see Chapter 12), and Bulgaria, Macedonian's status as a language is generally accepted and it is now the national language of the Former Yugoslav Republic of Macedonia (FYROM). An interesting consequence of this dispute is that it is not clear how to refer to the south Slavic dialects of northern Greece (which have in any case been mostly repressed or simply ignored by most Greek governments). One does not know whether to refer to the Slavic dialects of Greece as dialects of Bulgarian or dialects of Macedonian, although, of course, the western varieties are more like Standard Macedonian, the eastern varieties more like Standard Bulgarian.

IB: SITUATIONAL MINORITY AUSBAU LANGUAGES

Languages at IB in the Table are distinguished from those at IA by being situational as opposed to true minority languages, and their autonomy is therefore more difficult to attack. Because such Ausbau languages are protected by their status as majority languages elsewhere, the only form of attack is to suggest that the dialects in question have, as it were, been wrongly classified. It would not be possible, for example, to claim, with reference to the Polish-speaking communities in northern Czechia, that 'Polish is not a language'. Rather, what has to be attacked, if such an attack is desired, is the direction of the heteronomy: 'This is not Polish, it is Czech'. This form of attack is possible, of course, because in any situation where the varieties are geographically contiguous, the degree of linguistic Abstand is not very great.

2A: TRUE MINORITY
GEOGRAPHICAL ABSTAND LANGUAGES

The minority languages classified in the Table as 2A are Abstand languages, but Abstand languages of a particular sort. They owe their Abstand status to their geographical situation as isolated linguistic islands as much as to linguistic considerations. Basque, as we saw, is linguistically distant from all known language varieties. Certain other Abstand languages, however, are simply linguistically distant from neighbouring language varieties: the autonomy of the northern Slavic language Sorbian, for instance, might be disputed if it were spoken in Poland rather than in eastern Germany; the Jewish language Ladino would almost certainly be regarded as a variety of Spanish if it were spoken in Spain rather than in Turkey, Greece and elsewhere; and the Jewish language Yiddish, which is closely related to German, could also suffer from similar perceptions. In these cases, attacks on autonomy are certainly possible – it is not too difficult, for example, to argue that Yiddish is a German dialect – but such attacks are less convincing and carry less weight because of the geographical separation involved.

3A: TRUE MINORITY ABSOLUTE ABSTAND LANGUAGES

As we have seen, absolute Abstand languages (3A) are not, and cannot be, subject to the kind of assault that focuses on autonomy. As mentioned above, the status of Basque as a language separate from French and Spanish is clear, and not even the Franco regime in Spain was able to suggest otherwise. Certain other European minority languages are equally protected from at least this form of attack by their Abstand status: Irish in Ireland; Gaelic in Scotland; Welsh in Wales; Breton in France; Sami in Scandinavia; Turkish in Bulgaria and Greece; and the Gypsy language Romany.

Attacks do occur, of course, but they generally have to take the rather lame and linguistically ill-informed but also potentially damaging line that 'it's not a language, it's only a dialect'. Such claims are baseless and ignorant, of course, and rest on the erroneous assumption that 'dialects' do not actually have to be dialects of any particular language. These arguments, unfortunately, may be accepted by journalists and politicians, particularly if the degree of literacy in the language in question, as with Romany, is not very high.

Note, however, that unlike Basque, even some Abstand languages do have problems of an Ausbau type: Irish and Gaelic have at times been regarded as the same language; how many Sami languages there are is not entirely clear; and there is disagreement about whether Sorbian (also known as Lusatian) is one language or two.

2B/3B: SITUATIONAL MINORITY LANGUAGES – GEOGRAPHICAL AND ABSOLUTE ABSTAND LANGUAGES

Finally, and perhaps most interestingly, we move on to languages of the type cited as 2B and 3B, which we will examine together. These are languages which are protected from attack by Abstand status, as are types 3A and to a lesser extent 2A. However, these types of situational minority languages are, at least theoretically, even stronger, by reason of their majority status elsewhere. First, there are those where the linguistic characteristics of the majority and minority languages are such that the minority Ausbau language has Abstand status within the country in question (2B). Examples include: Swedish in Finland; Danish in Germany; Dutch in France; Slovene in Austria and Italy; German in France, Italy, Serbia, Czechia, Slovakia, Hungary, Poland and Romania; and Rumanian in Yugoslavia, Bulgaria, Albania and Greece. Second, and theoretically in an even stronger position, are absolute Abstand languages (3B): Finnish in Sweden; Hungarian in Austria, Slovakia, Slovenia, Serbia, Ukraine and Romania; Albanian in Yugoslavia, Italy and Greece; Greek in Albania, Macedonia (FYROM), Bulgaria, Turkey and Italy; and Turkish in Bulgaria, Macedonia and Greece. In both sets of cases, no attack on the linguistic minority can take the form of an attack on the language's autonomy.

This does not mean, of course, that such languages do not come under attack. Some attacks, for example, may – again in a linguistically ill-informed way – focus on language-contact phenomena and suggest that such language varieties are 'bastardised' or not 'pure'. More interesting for the purposes of this chapter, however, are a number of fascinating cases where attacks do indeed focus on autonomy and heteronomy but have of necessity to be of a type which is the complete reverse of those we have met in all other cases. They take the form of an assertion of the language variety's autonomy. Rumanian, for example, has acquired a number of Ausbau-type problems. In the former Soviet republic of Moldavia, now Moldova, the Rumanian language was written in the Cyrillic alphabet from 1945 in order to increase the apparent amount of Abstand between it and the Rumanian of Romania, and a new standard form has been devised which is based on local dialects. The aim, in other words, was to establish Moldavian as a language separate from Rumanian (in the same way Macedonian was separated from Bulgarian) in order to promote the legitimacy of the separation of this area from Romania and its inclusion in the Soviet Union. Moldavian's autonomy was asserted, and its heteronomy with respect to Rumanian was denied. Forms of Rumanian are also spoken elsewhere in the Balkans – in Serbia, Macedonia, Bulgaria, Albania and Greece. These varieties are linguistically considerably different from Standard Rumanian, and mutual intelligibility is not always possible: (linguists generally refer to southern Balkan forms of Rumanian as Arumanian.) Earlier this century, Romanian governments established Rumanian-medium schools in some of the relevant areas of Greece and argued, with some linguistic justification, that these dialects were varieties of Rumanian. Since the 1920s, however, Greek governments have not allowed this practice to continue. The common practice in Greece is to refer to this language as *Vlachika*. The political situation in the Balkans, that is, has led to an interesting Ausbau-linked phenomenon. No Greek government could attempt to argue that Arumanian was a dialect of Greek, for obvious Abstand reasons. What they have done instead, in order (as they would see it) to forestall any threats to the territorial integrity of Greece (in spite of the lack of a common border with Romania), is to attempt to deny the heteronomy of these varieties with respect to Standard Rumanian and to assert – with some linguistic justification – that, on the contrary, they constitute an autonomous language. Vlachika is thus not Greek, but it is 'a Greek language' (see Chapter 12).

A similar policy is adopted in Greece with respect to the varieties of Albanian which are widely spoken in many parts of Greece, especially in Biotia and Attica. Again, Abstand prevents any attempt from being made to argue that they are dialects of Greek, which would be absurd. What has happened instead is that they have come to be known in Greece by the term *Arvanitika*, while the Albanian of Albania is known in Greek as *Alvanika* (see Chapter 12). The implication, of course, is that they are not the same language. Once again, as with Vlachika, since it is impossible to categorise these dialects as Greek, it is important to argue that they are not Albanian. There is some linguistic justification for this in Abstand terms, although less so than in the case of Vlachika, because Arvanitika has acquired considerable amounts of Greek lexis which is unknown in Albanian. Mutual intelligibility is still generally achievable, however, and there is equal linguistic justification for calling these dialects Albanian, as most non-Greeks generally do. As has been reported elsewhere (Trudgill 1983: ch. 7), Greek policy has been very successful: Albanian speakers in the Attica and Biotia areas of Greece show little consciousness of ethnic links with Albania or Albanian, and ethnolinguistic vitality is very low.

CONCLUSION

All minority languages are potentially open to attacks on their linguistic status. The most obviously vulnerable are those minority languages, especially true minority languages, which, like Catalan or Kashubian, stand in a clear Ausbau relationship with the majority language. However, even situational minority languages, as we have just seen, can be vulnerable to attack, even or perhaps especially when they stand in a clear Abstand relationship with the majority language. In these cases, attacks will take a very different form. All attacks on the status of languages and dialects, however, share the common feature that they remind us that all language varieties are just as much cultural and political constructs as they are purely linguistic entities.

12
AUSBAU SOCIOLINGUISTICS AND IDENTITY IN GREECE

In this chapter, as an illustration of some of the issues concerning Ausbau and Abstand sociolinguistics discussed in Chapter 11, we examine the sociolinguistics of four of the ethnolinguistic groups found in modern Greece.

ELLINIKA

Greek is the only surviving member of the Hellenic branch of the Indo-European language family. Indeed, it is not known if there ever were any other members. Scholars have variously speculated that the original language of the ancient Macedonians, before they became assimilated into mainstream ancient Greek culture, was (a) a dialect of Ancient Greek; (b) a Hellenic language related to but distinct from Ancient Greek; or (c) not Hellenic at all but some other language altogether, such as Illyrian (which in turn may or may not have been the ancestor of modern Albanian). As is well known, the Ancient Greek dialects were in historical times for the most part subject to levelling, leading to the formation of the interdialectal koiné, and modern Greek varieties are almost all descended from this koiné (Browning 1969). Unlike Latin, however, Ancient Greek did not give rise to a number of different daughter languages. The only descendant of Ancient Greek is Modern Greek. This has had the consequence that the Greek language today is one of only a relatively small number of European languages that have the sociolinguistic status of Abstand languages, in the sense of Kloss (1967). This means that Greek can be considered an independent and separate language for purely linguistic reasons without having to resort also to cultural, political and historical factors, as has to be done with Ausbau languages. Greek has no close linguistic relatives, and it is not part of a dialect continuum which includes other languages in the manner of, say, Dutch and German.

The status of Modern Greek as an Abstand language is not without its significance for Greek identity. For most native speakers of Greek today, ethnicity is an unproblematic concept. Greeks are those whose mother tongue is Greek, whether they are citizens of Greece or are part of overseas communities, such as the long-established ones in Cyprus, Italy, the Balkans, Syria, Egypt, Turkey, Ukraine and Georgia, or the more recently established communities in areas such as Australasia and North America. It is difficult for many Greeks to conceive of situations where language and ethnicity might be problematical or indeterminate. The unique Greek alphabet is also a factor in strengthening Greeks' perception of themselves and their language as being clearly and unambiguously distinct from all other peoples and languages.

This unambiguous identification of ethnicity is not necessarily shared by linguistic minorities in Greece (see below). It is also of relatively recent origin. When Crete, certain other islands, and parts of Macedonia were incorporated into Greece in 1913, many native Greek speakers voluntarily left the country for Turkey, together with Turkish speakers and others, because they were Muslims (about 475,000 Muslims left altogether); religion was a more important factor for them in their subjective perception of their ethnic identity than their mother tongue.

As far as the language itself is concerned, there are two varieties of Greek that are sufficiently different from all others – that have a sufficient degree of Abstand – that linguists might want to suggest that they are actually different languages. The first is Tsakonian (see Newton 1972), a Hellenic variety spoken in the eastern Peloponnese which is descended from ancient Greek but *not* by way of the koiné. Although Tsakonian is reported to be dying out, some schools in the area have acknowledged the degree of difference between it and other forms of Greek by providing pupils with teaching materials written in this variety. The second is Pontic. Although the term 'Pontic' originally applied only to the Black Sea varieties of Greek spoken in Georgia and northern Turkey, it is now also sometimes used to refer to varieties of Greek originating in central areas of Turkey such as Cappadocia (see Dawkins 1916; Mirambel 1965; Sikkenga 1992). These varieties are very different from other dialects of Greek because of the long period of separation and in some cases because of considerable influence from other languages, notably Turkish. Both Tsakonian speakers and Pontics, however, regard themselves and are regarded as Greeks, and, although Pontics who have recently arrived in Greece do complain of discrimination, this ethnic identification appears to be uncontroversial.

When Greece eventually achieved independence from the Ottoman Empire in 1832, a number of competing solutions were advanced to solve the problem of what form the standard written language of the nation should take. Language conflict of a kind had already been a feature in the Greek-speaking world for many centuries. In the progression from classical Ancient Greek to the hellenistic Attic koiné through New Testament Greek and on to Byzantine Greek, an ever-increasing gap had grown up between spoken and written forms of Greek. The written language, which to varying extents harked back to Classical Greek, lagged further and further behind the spoken language, which quite naturally underwent many internal changes and also borrowed extensively from Italian and Turkish.

With the first stirrings of Greek independence movements in the late eighteenth century, and with the publication of educational and non-religious texts in Greek under the influence of the western European Enlightenment, the fact that contemporary vernacular Greek had hitherto been relegated to the status of a spoken language only (with the exception of some popular verse) came to be perceived as a problem. With the benefit of hindsight, it is possible to discern four different solutions that were advocated to this problem. First, there was the reponse of the conservatives who had been members of the Phanariot Greek élite in Istanbul and who advocated the continuing use of the archaic, Byzantine Greek that had been in written use at the Sultan's court whenever Greek rather than Turkish was employed. Second, inspired by the renewal of awareness of links with ancient Greece, there were a small number of intellectuals who advocated a complete return to Ancient Greek. They believed that it would be possible to persuade the population of Greece not only to write but also to speak the classical language. Naturally, they had no success.

The third approach was that of the compromisers or purisers. Led by the Paris-based Adamantios Korais (1743–1833), who despised the Byzantine Orthodox tradition and who was greatly influenced by the French intelligentsia, they recommended that a modern Greek national language should be formed gradually by taking the current spoken vernacular and 'cleansing' it of Turkish loans and regional dialect features at all linguistic levels. The result of this approach was a form of Greek known as the 'purifying' or *Katharevousa* language. This variety of Greek was not then and never has been codified, but there were already many people who were employing a somewhat haphazard mixture of Ancient, New Testamant, Byzantine and modern vernacular Greek in their writings while trying to avoid the use of loan words, particularly borrowings from Turkish.

The fourth approach represented a populist or vulgarist tendency which advocated the use of the ordinary everyday vernacular as the national language, as in western European countries. Poets in the Ionian islands of western Greece, which had remained for the most part outside the Ottoman Empire, were already writing in the vernacular. And in 1814, Yannis Vilaris, a scholar based in Epirus, published a *Romaic Grammar* (for the term 'Romaic' see below) in which he laid down norms for a normalised Greek based on spoken dialects. Vilaris' grammar made little impact. Especially important for the populist approach, however, was the work of Yannis Psicharis (1854–1929) whose intention was to make a codified version of vernacular spoken, demotic Greek the only national language of Greece; this came to be known as *Dhimotiki*. He himself carried out no codification, but his famous novel *To Taxidhi Mou* ('My Journey') (1888) was the first literary prose work to be published in *Dhimotiki* and was extremely influential. The language he used was a vernacular form which had developed as a result of dialect mixing in the Peloponnese, the first area of Greece to be liberated, and especially in Nafplion, the first Greek capital, as people from all over the Greek-speaking world flocked to this area to fight the Turks and enjoy independence (see Jahr and Trudgill 1993). This koiné also became the dominant form of Greek in Athens as it expanded from a small town to become the national capital, replacing the original local dialect, insofar as the inhabitants were Greek-speaking at all.

Although much of the fighting in the War of Independence took place in the Peloponnese and a majority of the fighters were from there, élite conservative Greeks from Istanbul soon took control of the new government. This group was disconcerted by, as they saw it, the dangerous notion of using the language of the people as a national language, and Korais' purising movement was therefore favoured by the government, although in fact in a more extreme form than he had ever intended. Thus, during the course of the nineteenth century, *Katharevousa* became institutionalised as the language of education, government and the press. Linguistically, it underwent considerable focussing and stabilisation, but it remained an artificial form of language, full of hypercorrections and false archaisms.

In the meantime, Psicharis' approach received considerable support, particularly from the 1880s onwards, from intellectuals who were becoming very disenchanted with the artificial and difficult *Katharevousa*, especially in view of the educational difficulties it caused and the lack of success of any literature written in this variety. Following the publication of Psicharis' novel, there was therefore a very rapid move to the use of *Dhimotiki* in the writing of nearly all novels, poems and plays. Because of its close association with the deeply unpopular and enormously discredited military junta that was overthrown in 1974, Katharevousa has now more or less completely disappeared from the Greek scene, not, however, without having exerted a considerable amount of linguistic influence on the actual linguistic form of *Dhimotiki* as it is spoken and written today.

Of considerable interest is the fact that the struggle between the two language forms was often conducted on the basis of issues intimately connected with nationalism and identity (see Tsiouris 1989). *Katharevousa*, which harked back to the great days of the classical Greek past and which had attempted to remove all lexical signs of the humiliating period of Turkish colonial rule, was associated symbolically in the minds of many Greeks with Hellenism, the monarchy, Orthodox Christianity and right-wing politics. *Dhimotiki*, on the other hand, was associated with republicanism, democracy and left-wing politics.

The conflict in modern Greece between two competing perceptions of Greek identity and nationality, *Ellinismos* and *Romiosini* (a reference to the fact that the Byzantine Empire was the successor to the empire of Rome), is

128

especially interesting (see the discussion in Leigh-Fermor 1966), and has a definite though complex link to the language question. Briefly, we can say that a focus on Hellenic identity is one which stresses the Classical Greek past and the Ancient Greek contribution to modern Western civilisation, order and logic. A remarkable manifestation of this was the decision taken after Greek independence to move the capital from Nafplion to Athens, at the time an unimportant and rather scruffy small town inhabited mostly by Albanian speakers. A focus on Romaic identity, on the other hand, is one which stresses the Byzantine heritage and the heroism of the struggles against the Turks; it has a greater association with Greek peasant culture as well as with Orthodox mysticism. The European Philhellenes who were so influential in fighting for Greek independence from Turkey both politically and militarily were primarily motivated by Hellenism and their admiration for Ancient Greece and certainly not by Romiosini.

THE MINORITY LANGUAGES

Modern Greece has always been a multilingual country. Unfortunately, accurate information on how multilingual it has been and continues to be is very difficult to obtain. This is partly the result of the fact that no Greek census since 1951 has included a question about language. It is also a result of the distortion of some of the academic research on this topic by anti-minority Greek nationalism. This all has to be seen in the context of modern Greek history. The nation-state of Greece has been in existence for only 160 years or so, but its development as a nation has not been a peaceful one. Indeed, 'few countries in Europe have had such a harrowing and strife-torn recent history' (Clogg 1979: vii), and an examination of this history suggests that it is not at all surprising that issues connected with nationalism and language can still arouse passionate argument and debate – not all of it entirely rational – in certain sections of Greek society today (see Woodhouse 1984). Much of the history of Greece since 1832 has to do with the fact that the borders of the newly liberated Greece contained none of the major Ottoman Greek centres of culture and commerce such as Alexandria, Istanbul, Thessaloniki and Izmir (Smyrna), and that a majority of ethnic Greeks still remained unliberated in areas under Ottoman (or, in the case of the Ionian islands, British) rule. The population of the new state was about 750,000. Some 1,250,000 ethnic Greeks, however, still remained outside the country. One of the major themes of modern Greek history has been the *Megali Idea* or 'Great Idea': that the borders of Greece should be expanded so that it might include all ethnic Greeks.

It is probable that many Greeks outside Greece were initially not at all interested in this 'idea'. Many of the Asia Minor Greeks had become Greek only in name – they might have been Christians, but they had become Turkish-speaking. Elsewhere, in Macedonia and Crete especially, there were

Greek-speakers who, as a result of conversion on the part of their ancestors, were Muslims. In 1881, as a result of various diplomatic and military events, Thessaly and southern Epirus – areas which were inhabited predominantly by ethnic Greeks – became incorporated into Greece. In 1913 Greece obtained Crete and most of the other predominantly Greek islands of the Aegean which had so far remained outside its control; most, but not all, of the rest of Epirus (the newly formed state of Albania was given the far north of this area); and a large area of Macedonia, which was now divided between Albania, Serbia, Bulgaria and Greece. For the first time, however, large numbers of people who were not ethnic Greeks were included within its frontiers. The newly Greek Macedonia had very large populations of Slavs and Turks in particular, as well as Greek-speaking Muslims whose ethnic loyalties were not at all clear. At the same time, many ethnic Greeks still remained outside Greece, notably in northern Epirus (Albania), especially in Agii Saranda (Sarandë), Argirokastro (Gjirokastër) and Koritsa (Korcë); in Thrace and Constantinople (European Turkey); and especially in Anatolia (Asian Turkey), where there were between 1 and 1.5 million Greeks, although, as we have seen, some of them were more Greek than others.

SLAVIKA

The problem of wresting Macedonia from the Turks, and of whether control of this area would ultimately pass to Serbia, Bulgaria or Greece, had a clear linguistic component. Most of the population of this area was originally mixed, with Greeks predominating only in the coastal areas. In 1912, Greeks constituted only 43 per cent of the population of the newly Greek part of Macedonia (Clogg 1979: 121). Probably as a consequence, of all the linguistic minorities in Greece, it is the Slavs who have been regarded with the greatest suspicion by centralising and Hellenising Greek governments. In 1994, the International Helsinki Federation for Human Rights issued a report extremely critical of the Greek state's treatment of minorities (see *The Guardian* 12 May 1994). It cites harassment of Slavs in the northwest of the country; the refusal of Greek authorities to co-operate with European and other international bodies concerned with minority rights; and the prosecution six times in the space of four years of a Greek Slav for claiming that Greece has a Slavic minority. Approaches by Slavic-speakers to the European Community have been met by personal reprisals on the part of the Greek civil service (Karakasidou 1993: 13).The fact is that modern slavophone Greeks occupy an area that was incorporated into Greece only as recently as 1912, and in spite of the fact that under the Ottoman Empire many of them thought of themselves as 'Greeks' (at a time when that term could be taken to mean simply 'Orthodox Christians'), their residence in areas bordering on other countries has been perceived as providing a threat to the territorial integrity of Greece.

The Macedonian dispute, interestingly, had implications for the Greek language also. In laying claim to Macedonia, the Serbs and Bulgarians could not, of course, base any claims on ancestry or direct descent from the Ancient Greeks. They could quite legitimately, however, lay claim to the inheritance of Byzantium, of which they had been a part. Anything which stressed the descent of the modern Greeks from *pre*-Byzantine Ancient Greece, such as *Katharevousa*, was therefore favoured by all Greeks who espoused the 'Great Idea'. Particular controversy was also aroused in Greece by the well-publicised claim of the Austrian right-wing politician and doubtless racist historian Jakob Fallmerayer, who argued that modern Greeks 'did not have a drop of genuine and pure Greek blood' in their veins and that they were instead descended from Slavs, Albanians, Turks, Rumanians and others. Genetically, of course, this is obviously not without some truth, but its effect on Greek public opinion was enormous, not least because it seemed to directly contradict all the positive sentiments associated with Hellenism. Support for *Dhimotiki* was thus often seen, particularly by those on the political right, as representing support for the Slavs and constituting anti-nationalistic subversion.

The Greek Orthodox Church also had an important part to play. During the centuries of Muslim Turkish occupation, the church had played a leading role as the only organised body which could act as a symbol of Greek identity and resistance, and as a guardian of Greek culture and nationality. *Katharevousa* was much more similar to the language of the Scriptures and church services than was *Dhimotiki*, and any attack on *Katharevousa* could be construed as an attack on the church. Thus, support for *Dhimotiki* could be perceived as hostility to Christianity, treachery to the nation and support for pan-Slavism. When a demotic translation of the gospels was published in 1901, there were riots in the streets of Athens in which eight people were killed. And in 1903 there were further riots leading to one death following a performance of Aeschylus's *Orestia* in a demotic translation. Mobs marched through the streets of Athens shouting, among other things, 'death to the Slavs'.

Slavic has a long history in the area which is now Greece. During the course of the sixth and seventh centuries, southern Slavic peoples penetrated and overran large areas of what is now modern Greece as part of a general southward movement which saw them enter also into parts of Asia Minor. Some Slavs reached as far as Crete, but the areas which saw heaviest in-migration were Macedonia, Thrace and the Peloponnese. In most parts of Greece, these Slavic peoples were gradually assimilated into the original populations. Large areas of northern Greece, however, remained predominantly Slavic speaking for 1200 years or so, until the present century. For example, the first Slavic literary language, Old Church Slavonic – the language used by the Apostles Cyril and Methodius for translating the Scriptures from Greek into Slavic – was based on the Slavic dialects spoken in the region of Thessaloniki. Under the Ottoman Empire, Slavic continued to predominate in northern Greece. For instance, as recently as 1892, schools in Kastoria (Slavic *Kostur*) prepared teaching materials in the local Slavic dialect for use with pupils.

After the Balkan Wars, it is estimated that in 1913, on the Greek side of the border, there were somewhere between 300,000 and 500,000 Slavic speakers (see Breatnach 1991), including a sizeable Slavic-speaking minority in Thessaloniki. According to the Treaty of Neuilly, Greece undertook to defend the rights of the national minorities within its borders and, in the 1920 Treaty of Sèvres (which was never ratified), promised to open schools for minority language pupils. In 1925, the government of Greece submitted copies of a school primer, which was written in Slavic for use with Slavic minority pupils and published by the Greek Ministry of Education, to the League of Nations as evidence that they were carrying out these obligations. During the 1930s, however, under the totalitarian dictatorship of Metaxas, education in Slavic was made illegal, as indeed was the use of Slavic for any purpose whatsoever, including in the home. Slavic family names were also compulsorily changed to Greek ones (Hill 1992). Karakasidou (1993) shows that Slavic-speaking villages are still to be found in many areas of Greek Macedonia, and towns such as Florina, Kastoria, Edessa and even Verria certainly contain sizeable numbers of Slavic speakers, although they tend to conceal their ability to speak Slavic in public situations. Current estimates (see Lunden 1993) suggest a Slavic-speaking population in Greek Macedonia of about 50,000.

There is also a community of Slavic speakers in Greek Thrace. This is a Muslim community known as the Pomaks, 20,000 strong in 1951, perhaps 10,000 today (some estimates suggest as many as 40,000), who live in the area around Xanthi. (There are also Pomaks in Bulgaria.) As Muslims, they receive their education in Turkish and tend to send their children to Turkey for their higher education (Lunden 1993). There are also Gypsies who are native Slavic speakers, as indicated above. In 1913, a much bigger proportion of the Slavic-speaking population of northern Greece were Muslims. During the resettlements that took place between 1913 and 1922, however, most of these left for Turkey, religion being, as for Greek-speaking Muslims, a more important feature in their subjective ethnicity than language.

So far, I have used the imprecise term 'Slavic' to refer to the language spoken by these minorities in northern Greece. There is, however the very interesting Ausbau sociolinguistic question as to whether the language they speak is Macedonian or Bulgarian, given that both these languages have developed out of the South Slavic dialect continuum that embraces also Serbian, Croatian and Slovenian (see Chapter 11). In ex-Yugoslavian Macedonia and Bulgaria there is no problem, of course. Bulgarians are considered to speak Bulgarian and Macedonians Macedonian, although, as we saw in Chapter 11, there was a short period in the 1940s when the Bulgarian government recognised the existence of Macedonian speakers within the borders of Bulgaria. The Slavic dialects of Greece, however, are 'roofless' dialects whose speakers have no access to education in the standard languages. Greek non-linguists, when they acknowledge the existence of these dialects, frequently refer to them by the label *Slavika*, which has the Ausabu-sociolinguistic implication of denying that they have any connection with the languages of the neighbouring countries. It seems most sensible, in fact, to refer to the language of the Pomaks as Bulgarian and to that of the Christian Slavic-speakers in Greek Macedonia as (Slavo-) Macedonian.

Of course, in Greece itself, particularly in the 1990s since the achievement of independence by the former Yugoslavian republic of Macedonia, the name 'Macedonian' for the language, as well as 'Macedonia' for the country itself, has given rise to a certain amount of nationalist controversy (see Chapter 11). Greek linguists have sensibly for the most part adopted the disambiguating practice when writing in Greek of referring to the language as *Slavomakedhonika*, since, quite properly, the most obvious meaning of *Makedhonika* is 'the dialect of Greek spoken in Greek Macedonia'. Certain non-linguists, on the other hand, including politicians, have recently taken to arguing that, given the recent Ausbau development of Macedonian, there 'is no such language' and that Slavic-speakers in Skopja, as they refer to the Former Yugoslav Republic of Macedonia, are really speakers of Bulgarian (or Serbian). It is therefore interesting to note that, at earlier periods, different Greek governments have been at pains to distinguish between Macedonian and Bulgarian. The 1928 census gave figures for speakers of Bulgarian and Macedonian-Slav separately, and the 1925 Slavic primer referred to above was written in a variety of South Slavic quite distinct from Bulgarian – that is, it more closely resembled the modern standard Slavo-Macedonian language – and was, interestingly, written in the Latin alphabet, both steps obviously taken in an attempt to stress the lack of connection between Bulgaria and the Slavic population of Greece. Ironically, during the course of the nineteenth century, printers and publishers in Thessaloniki played a very important role in developments that were eventually to lead to the standardisation of Macedonian in the 1940s.

VLACHIKA

As we noted in Chapter 11, varieties of Balkan Romance spoken in the southern Balkans are generally referred to by linguists as *Arumanian*. In more careful usage, however (see Mallinson 1988), this term is reserved for those varieties found in the Pindus mountains of Greece and in Thessaly, and the term *Megleno-Rumanian* is employed for those varieties spoken in Greek Macedonia. Speakers of these varieties, as we have seen, are known as *Vlachs* and are to be found in Albania, ex-Yugoslavia and Bulgaria as well as Greece (Nandris 1987; Scarlatiou 1992). There are also small communities in Romania and Turkey, as well as emigrant communities in North America and Australia. The origins of the Vlachs remain mysterious (see Winnifrith 1987), particularly since it is known that, under the Roman Empire, the boundary between the Greek-speaking areas and Latin-speaking areas lay to the north of modern Greece. Obviously, then, they must be either direct descendants of Roman garrisons stationed in the mountainous areas of central Greece or, as seems more likely, Romanised descendants of some original Balkan population group, perhaps Albanians, who resisted Slavicisation and who have migrated south during the intervening period.

In historical times, they have traditionally been transhumant shepherds in relatively remote areas, which would explain their resistance to Slavicisation, with the largest concentration in Greece today lying in the Pindus mountains, focusing on Metsovo, today the only major town which is Vlach speaking. The number of speakers of *Vlachika*, as it is called in Greek, is difficult to determine for the reasons outlined above and because of their migratory lifestyle. Census returns and other sources suggest a population in Greece today of at least 50,000.

Most Vlachs, whether in Greece or outside, have a relatively weakly developed – or perhaps deeply concealed – notion of their own ethnic identity, tending to assume, at least for public consumption, the ethnicity of those around them. Winnifrith (1993) describes them as a 'minority which never achieved ethnic identity', although he also suggests that it may have been mainly wealthy Vlachs who identified with Greece, and on whom Greece relied for support – for example, in Macedonia in the nineteenth century – and poorer Vlachs who were more inclined to be 'pro-Vlach'. Certainly, many Vlachs were very active on the Greek side in the wars of independence from Turkey, and some are regarded as national heroes by Greeks today who do not necessarily know that they were Vlachs. Rigas Velestinlis, also know as Pheraios, who was executed by the Turks for his role in promoting the struggle for Greek independence in the late eighteenth century, was a Vlach. The wealthy Vlach Georgios Averoff donated large sums of money for the purchase of a Greek battleship in the 1890s. Yannis Kolettis, the first Prime Minister of Greece, who played a very important part in the struggle against the Turks and in the revolutionary governments of the 1820s as well as in post-independence governments, and who was a passionate advocate of the Greater Greece 'Great Idea', was a Vlach. And Andreas Tzimas, one of the leaders of the left-wing anti-German guerrilla army during the Second World War, was also a Vlach. Many of the Greek merchants in eighteenth-century Europe were also actually Vlachs. Vlach speakers have not traditionally been regarded by Greek governments with the same degree of suspicion as Slavic speakers, although as Exarchos

(1992) says in connection with the lack of linguistic support given to the Vlach minority in Greece, 'here in Greece, if you speak about something like [the preservation of the minority language Romansch in Switzerland], people will accuse you of stirring up trouble and will want to know which hostile power you are acting as a secret agent for' [my translation].

The submerged nature of Vlach ethnicity has also led to a number of misunderstandings. It is often reported in Greece, for example, that the town of Bitola (Greek *Monastiri*) in the former Yugoslav Macedonia has or had a sizeable Greek population. The vast majority of them, however, turn out to have been Vlachs (Winnifrith 1993). This submerged ethnicity has also led to increasing language shift in modern times, and many younger Vlachs now have only passive competence in the language. The Vlach headteacher of the High School in Metsovo reports (pers.comm.) that no attempt is being made there to save the language and that he has no interest in doing so. The extent of this language shift should not be exaggerated, though. A majority of the inhabitants of Metsovo still speak Vlachika, and in nearby Anelio the children are mostly fluent native speakers (Winnifrith, 1993). Interestingly, some Meglen Vlach villages on the Greek side of the border with ex-Yugoslavia have become linguistically Slavicised rather than Hellenised (ibid. 1993).

From a sociolinguistic point of view there is the interesting Ausbau linguistic problem of whether Arumanian and Megleno-Rumanian are dialects of Rumanian or not (see Lazarou 1986; Trudgill 1992). We argued in Chapter 11 that the Greek practice of referring to the language as Vlachika has the Ausbau-sociolinguistic effect of implying that they are not Rumanian, which is of course something which certain Greek nationalists would want to stress. This linguistic problem naturally has parallels with the ethnic question of whether Vlachs are 'really' Rumanians or not. Certainly, earlier in this century, the Romanian government, who of course had some interest in claiming this identity, established Rumanian-medium schools in some areas of what is now Greece, as mentioned before. Since the 1920s, however, there have been no such schools, except for one which survived more or less by accident in Ano Grammatiko (Greek Macedonia) until 1945 (Winnifrith 1993), and most of the Pindus Vlachs, at least, would not today support the idea that they are ethnically Rumanian. This was not always so, however, particularly in the Meglen. In the period of population movements after the First World War, a large number of Meglen Vlachs emigrated to Romania, less or more willingly, and the Greek government was particularly keen to remove from Greece those Vlachs who did identify with Romania (and to replace them with Pontic Greek refugees). Some Meglen Vlach villages were forcibly evacuated during the Second World War, which also resulted in considerable population movement. In addition, some Meglen Vlachs were Muslims and left for Turkey in 1924.

ARVANITIKA

The position of the Albanian-speaking minority in Greece is in some ways very similar to that of the Vlachs, in that their sense of separate identity is weak, as we have seen, and their feelings of connection with Albania for the most part are non-existent. They are all Christians – at least 20,000 Muslim Albanians, mostly from northern Greece, have left the country since the 1920s – and this, too, aids their sense of identification with Greek culture and society. Indeed, many Albanian-Greeks have played a prominent role in modern Greek life. George Koundouriotis, for example, was an Albanian-Greek from the island of Hydra who was president of one of the revolutionary governments established in the 1820s during the war of liberation from the Turks. Admiral Koundouriotis, from the same family, was President of Greece in the 1920s.

The Arvanites have been in what is now Greece since medieval times (see Trudgill and Tzavaras 1977), and the biggest concentration of Arvanites today is in the areas where they were formerly the dominant element in the population, in Attica, Biotia and much of the Peloponnese – the well-known authority on Albanian, Eric Hamp (pers. comm.) knows of at least sixty traditionally Arvanitika-speaking villages in the Peloponnese (see also Williams 1992). And indeed many of the suburbs of Athens are, or were until recently, Arvanitika speaking. The number of Athenians with at least some Arvanitis ancestry is very large indeed. The number of speakers is, once again, difficult to determine. The 1951 census gives a figure of 23,000, but this is certainly too small. There are, of course, complications due to the fact that nearly all Arvanites are now bilingual and that many younger members of the community no longer speak the language (Tsitsipis 1983). But my own research in the 1970s in the villages of Attica and Biotia alone indicated a figure of at least 30,000 speakers (see Trudgill and Tzavaras 1975, 1977). Lunden (1993) suggests 50,000 for Greece as a whole.

Linguistically, there is no doubt that their language is a variety of Albanian; the degree of linguistic Abstand between it and the dialects of southern Albania is so relatively small that mutual intelligibility is usually possible – problems are caused mainly by the usage of Greek loanwords – and the identification is much less controversial than that of Vlachika. Nevertheless, all Greeks have adopted the interesting practice of referring to the language of this minority not as Alvanika ('Albanian') but as Arvanitika, and the people themselves not as Albanians but as Arvanites (singular Arvanitis). (Writers in English sometimes use the term *Arberol*.) This, as in the case of Vlachika, has the effect of implying that Arvanitka is an autonomous language – a language which though not Greek is a 'language of Greece' – rather than a dialect of Albanian, the national language of a neighbouring country, as we saw in the previous chapter.

13

LANGUAGE MAINTENANCE AND LANGUAGE SHIFT: PRESERVATION VERSUS EXTINCTION

Labov (1982) has argued, in discussing the famous US court case in Ann Arbor, Michigan involving dialect and education, that linguists have certain duties towards communities from which they have obtained data, especially in terms of combatting linguistic misconceptions and attacking linguistic injustices: it is not enough, and it is certainly not ethical, just to take one's language data and leave. It was this stance of Labov's, of course, which led to his involvement in the Ann Arbor case in the first place, and, like many other sociolinguists, Labov has been involved, both before and since, in many other debates which have involved the application of linguistic knowledge to the solution of problems concerning language and education, language and the law, and so on, in particular communities, especially disadvantaged communities in urbanised Western societies.

As a contribution to the argument that linguistics can and should be applied to the solution of many more real-world problems than just the teaching of foreign languages, I want to suggest in this chapter that there are in fact thousands of communities in the world, outside urbanised Western communities, which currently need the help, direct or indirect, of language scientists. I also want to point out that, as a number of linguists have already acknowledged, we have a duty as experts on language not only to these communities, but also to ourselves and to the human population of the planet as a whole, to apply our linguistic knowledge to the solution of a particular and growing real-world problem.

As experts on language, we are often asked questions about how many languages there are in the world. It is very difficult to answer such questions because of our ignorance of the linguistic situation in some parts of the world, and more especially because of the impossibility of enumerating discrete languages in sociolinguistically diffuse situations where there are dialect continua without superposed autonomous varieties. One thing that we can be very sure about, however, is that whatever the total number of languages in the world may be, it is less than it used to be and is getting smaller all the time. In these first years of the twenty-first century, languages are dying out at an increasingly catastrophic rate, without being replaced.

There is a tendency among linguists to retain the impression, perhaps from their student days, that there is continuous growth in the number of the world's languages. Such an impression is due to their familiarity with the Stammbaum theory of linguistic change, whereby an ever-increasing number of language varieties come into being as languages split into dialects and then into further languages. This picture, however, is not one that has any obvious validity in most parts of the world today. Of course, languages have been dying out for centuries. What is different about the twenty-first century is the speed with which languages are dying out and the extreme improbability of their being replaced in the traditional Stammbaum manner because of modern demographic and communications conditions. It is true, of course, that new languages have been created in relatively recent times: in the last 400 years or so, numerous creole languages have developed, especially as a result of colonialism in the Atlantic and Pacific areas. Generally speaking, however, the trend is overwhelmingly the other way. (It is also true, as we saw in Chapter 11, that some formerly heteronomous dialects, such as Afrikaans and Macedonian, acquired the status of autonomous languages in the twentith century, but this of course has not increased the number of extant language varieties.)

Sociolinguists have employed two terms to describe the phenomena which lead to the loss of language varieties. One is *language shift*. As is well known, this is the process by which a community more or less gradually abandons its original language and, via an intermediate stage of bilingualism, adopts another. In 1700, for instance, all – or nearly all – the inhabitants of Ireland spoke Irish; now nearly all of them are effectively monolingual in English. The other term is *language murder* (see Aitchison 1981). This is the linguistic concomitant of genocide, referring to situations where an entire community is massacred and its language is lost with it, as happened in Tasmania.

In actual fact, of course, there is no clear dividing line between language shift and language murder. The Gaelic-speaking Highland Scots, for instance, were not the victims of genocide as such, but they were certainly victims of oppression, and speaking Gaelic was made a crime by the British government. Indians in El Salvador were not actually sent to death camps, but in the 1930s people who were heard speaking Indian languages were sometimes shot on the spot (Dorian 1989). Language shift normally occurs as the result of some form of social, cultural, political, economic and/or military pressure. What varies from one situation to another is simply the degree of the pressure. Both language shift and language murder lead, obviously, to language death. Equally obviously, if all the speakers of a particular language are involved in the process, then we are faced with the *death of a language* – the total and, under normal circumstances, totally permanent and irrevocable loss of a language from the face of the earth. To clarify this point: Albanian is currently undergoing language death in Greece, as we saw in Chapter 12. This, however, is not the death of a language, since Albanian survives strongly in Albania and Kosovo.

A consideration of the death of languages in the 1990s shows that a large number of even very well-known languages are under more or less severe threat. In most parts of the world, this is part of a larger picture of galloping linguistic homogenisation. Even in Europe, where some languages have been lost in relatively recent times – Cornish, Dalmatian, Livonian and Manx, for instance – many more must be considered to be in a precarious situation: Irish, Scots Gaelic, Breton, Welsh, Basque, North Frisian, East Frisian, North Sami, Central Sami, South Sami, Sorbian, Kashubian, Romansch, Ladin, Romany, Yiddish and Ladino, to name but some. Less dramatic, but part of the same overall picture of homogenisation, is the large number of language varieties which, although the total death of a language is not involved, are under threat through language death in locations where they are minority languages: German in France, Denmark and Italy; Catalan in France; French in Italy; Dutch in France; Turkish in Bulgaria and Greece; Greek in Albania, Bulgaria, and Turkey; Bulgarian in Greece – and so on. We can also mention as part of the same trend the dramatic reduction in regional dialect variation in most parts of Europe as a result of urbanisation and standardisation, accompanied by dialect death and lexical attrition of dialect vocabulary.

In other continents, the picture is much bleaker even than in Europe. In the Americas, for example, probably around 1000 different languages were spoken between Alaska and Tierra del Fuego in the sixteenth century (Ruhlen 1987). In the last 400 years, at least 300 have disappeared. Of the remaining 700, only seventeen have more than 100,000 speakers, of which only one, Navaho, is spoken in North America. There is clearly some danger, then, of losing a further 680 or so. In the United States alone, more than fifty languages have been killed off since European contact: this is approximately numerically equivalent to all of the languages of modern Europe having been wiped off the face of the earth. In the whole of North America, perhaps 150 indigenous languages still remain, but most of them are thought to be likely to disappear within a generation. To give just three examples, figures suggest that Kutenai has 200 speakers, Ritwan ten and Chinakuan ten (Ruhlen 1987). Only 300 out of 2000 Haida can speak the language, and only 2000 out of 8000 Tlingit retain Tlingit. There are even 20,000 out of 150,000 Navaho who can speak only English. The Inuit (Eskimo) languages, moreover, are under threat in Alaska and Canada; and only 700 out of 2200 Aleuts can speak Aleutian.

Probably the most worrying area of the world as far as language loss is concerned is the Pacific. According to some authorities, as many as one-quarter of the world's languages may be spoken in this area. Australia, for instance, had at least 200 languages at the time of European contact. Fifty of these have died out already, and another 100 are very close to extinction (Dixon 1980). Australian linguists constantly revise in a downward direction the number they believe will survive into the twenty-first century, but it is currently thought that maybe 30–50 will do so. Some of the approximately forty Polynesian and fifty Micronesian languages are also threatened by language shift, with Hawaiian and Maori, which are both involved in bilingual situations with English, being especially vulnerable. And we cannot be at all confident about the future of all the 700 languages of Papua New Guinea, or the 800 languages of the Solomons, Vanuatu, New Caledonia and Fiji. Most of these languages, of course, have always been spoken by small groups of people, but they are now exposed as never before to rapid social and technological change.

Languages around the world which are involved in replacing and thereby killing off other languages in a major way are mostly, but by no means exclusively, European languages. English is an obvious 'killer language' – we have mentioned the plight of Hawaiian and Maori, to cite but two examples – but Spanish is a very clear threat to hundreds of languages in Central and South America, and to the Polynesian language of Easter Island. Portuguese is a severe danger in Brazil: Hecht and Cockburn (1989) report that between the years 1900 and 1957, approximately 80 Indian tribes were exterminated in the Amazon area as a whole, and the number of Indians went down in the same period from a million to 200,000. Moreover, reports continue to surface in the media of events which appear to represent or be close to genocide and language murder.

Elsewhere in the world, language shift to Russian has been occurring quite rapidly in a number of areas of the Soviet Union, while Arabic is producing shift in North Africa, as are Swahili in East Africa, and Chinese in China and Taiwan. Perhaps we should be most concerned about Indonesian: reports by Survival International suggest a scenario closely resembling language murder in parts of Indonesia, notably Irian Jaya, and there has apparently been far more shift to Bahasa Indonesia than there ever was to the former colonial language Dutch.

Any language, however, has the capacity to be a killer language. In a geographical dialect continuum situation, for instance, any elevation of one particular variety from the continuum to higher social, economic or religious status may eventually kill off the other neighbouring varieties. For example, the elevation of Tahitian by the European colonial power to higher cultural and political status within French Polynesia is leading to the gradual replacement of Tuamotuan, a closely related Polynesian language, by Tahitian in the Tuamotu Islands (see Mühlhäusler 1987). Similar developments can be expected in many parts of Africa, where nations which may be transferring to their indigenous languages some of the attention and finance that were formerly accorded colonial languages, nevertheless may have the resources to encourage education and literacy only in those local languages which are spoken by the most demographically numerous or otherwise favoured groups in their populations, thereby weakening the position of all the other languages.

Some estimates (see Ruhlen 1987) suggest that the five languages in the world with the highest number of native speakers (Mandarin Chinese, English, Hindi, Spanish, and Russian) between them cover 45 per cent of the world's population as their native speakers, and that the demographically top 100 languages of the world account for 95 per cent of the world's population. If, for the sake of argument, we estimate the number of languages in the world to be 5000, this leaves 4900 languages spoken by 5 per cent of the planet's human population. None of these languages can be regarded as having a secure future. In most parts of the world, modern conditions are leading to dialect death, linguistic uniformity, codification, homogenisation, standardisation, loss of diversity, and, worst of all, the death of languages.

Linguists should note at this point that the existence of many languages in the world is widely perceived by non-linguists as posing difficulties for communication. The curse of the Tower of Babel is seen as hampering understanding and slowing down progress to world peace. At a more mundane level, people whose main contact with languages other than their own has been with irregular verbs in the classroom are inclined to regard linguistic diversity as a nuisance. There is a widespread belief that everything would be much better if we all spoke the same language, or at least that the rapid disappearance of languages as barriers to communication would be no bad thing. People who share this view will shed no tears at all over the current rapid loss of languages from the world. The main objective of this chapter is therefore not only to argue against this perception, but to suggest – to return to Labov's Ann Arbor argument – that all linguists have a duty to argue against this perception wherever they encounter it.

To argue for the preservation of language diversity, however, is no easy matter in the face of widespread indifference and even hostility in the non-linguistic community. There is, for instance, an important and powerful case that many linguists can be heard to argue for, if only informally, along the lines that each human language is a unique creation of the human brain (and, sociolinguists would add, of human societies), and that each one helps us to shed a somewhat different light on the puzzle of the nature of the human language faculty. Of course, previous generations of linguists have rather weakened our case here by arguing that one could in principle find out more or less everything important there was to discover about human language by concentrating in depth on one variety of a single language (usually, of course, the linguist's own native language), the implication therefore being that any one language would do as well as any other (see Newmeyer 1986 on this point). Most of us, however, whether we are typologists or universal grammarians, are much less likely to argue in this way today. A more common and surely more tenable view is that it is essential that linguists should know as much about as many languages as possible. A good example of this point from a typological perspective, and one that has the advantage of being readily comprehensible to lay people, is the 'discovery' by linguists only in the 1970s of Hixkaryana and other object-initial languages (Derbyshire 1977). These languages are spoken by small groups of speakers in Amazonia and may not survive for very long into the twenty-first century. If these languages had undergone language death before they had come to the attention of linguists, perhaps linguistic science would never have known that object-initial human languages were possible.

This argument, however, can unfortunately be very readily interpreted by non-linguists as arising out of nothing more than self-interest on the part of linguists. After all, they might say, it is no wonder that linguists should argue in this way since, if all languages except a few were to die out, where would linguists and linguistics be then? It is therefore important that we should acknowledge amongst ourselves as well as before wider audiences that there may be many other reasons for wishing to preserve linguistic diversity, and that at least some of these reasons may have less to do with intellectual inquiry and perhaps more to do with issues that might even be as important as the future of the human species.

One such argument is outlined in Mühlhäusler (1987). He argues that it is important that those of us – the vast majority – who speak one of the world's major languages should give ourselves the possibility of learning from the world-views encapsulated in the world's minority languages. The relationship between language and thought is well known to be a controversial one, and the Sapir–Whorf hypothesis is very far from being accepted or shown to be of undoubted validity, but Whorf's discussion of Standard Average European languages does provide us with a powerful concept that is worth considering. Mühlhäusler argues that the languages of Papua New Guinea, Amerindian languages, Australian languages, and others may possibly reflect realities that are somewhat different from those reflected by European languages. If they do – if Whorf is (perhaps only partly) right – then these languages may have the potential for helping us to perceive different relationships, to make different connections, and to contemplate different ways of constructing reality. We can, of course, learn from these languages only if they survive, and if they survive without being too heavily semantically influenced by European languages.

A probably less controversial argument that will be more familiar to anthropologists is that the preservation of languages is important for the preservation of cultures. It is not inevitably the case that when a language is lost, a culture is lost with it: nor is it always the case that the survival of a language will inevitably ensure the survival of a culture; but there is a close connection, and language loss does make for greater vulnerability of cultures and will very probably lead towards increasing cultural uniformity. (The reverse case can also be argued, of course: cultural homogenisation can lead to language loss.)

Cultural uniformity would be highly undesirable for a number of reasons. Indeed, it is possible to conceive of it as having rather sinister possibilities. Crocombe (1983) writes, for example:

> Nothing would more quickly stultify human creativity or impoverish the richness of cultural diversity than a single world culture. Cultural uniformity is not likely to bring peace: it is much more likely to bring totalitarianism. A unitary system is easier for a privileged few to dominate. Cultural diversity is one of the world's potential sources of both sanity and fulfilment.

Linguistic and cultural homogenisation would, among other things, make it much easier for alien politicians and advertisers to penetrate other societies. As Mühlhäusler (1989) has also pointed out, language death can also make life easier for advertisers. He cites the example of the Aiwo language of the Santa Cruz Islands, Solomon Islands, which has a complex, semantically based noun-classification system. In the speech of younger speakers, this system is breaking down as a result of language shift, language death, and consequently imperfect learning (see Trudgill 1983). Among the semantic categories that are being lost is the noun class for useless or noxious entities. This loss has the consequence that younger people no longer have to commit themselves grammatically, as it were, to their perception of the usefulness of an entity they happen to be talking about – 'no doubt,' as Mühlhäusler says, 'a great relief to those wanting to advertise their goods in the Aiwo language'.

Finally, I believe that it is important for linguists to argue rather strongly for the thesis that barriers to communication are a Good Thing. I have suggested previously (Trudgill 1975) that such barriers, although penetrable – it is perfectly possible to learn languages other than your native language – help to ensure the survival of different language communities. Thus

> the separation of the world's population into different groups speaking different languages helps the growth of cultural diversity, which in turn can lead to opportunities for the development of alternative modes of exploring possibilities for social, political and technological progress.

That is, a world where everyone spoke the same language would not only be a very boring place; there is a very good chance that it would also be a very stagnant place. If the entire population of the world consisted of native speakers of English, it is probable that we would not only all be watching American soap-operas on TV and drinking Coca Cola, we would also all tend to have the same values, the same ideas, and the same world-view. If it is the case that diversity leads to progress, this is a frightening scenario indeed. (Similar views are expressed in Labov 1972 and in Mühlhäusler 1987).

If we now ask what we can do, as individual human beings, about this catastrophic loss of languages from the world, it is apparent that we need political action to stop language murder. One obvious course of action is to support organisations that fight for the rights of minorities and tribal peoples in different parts of the world, such as Survival International, Die Gesellschaft für gedrohte Völker, Cultural Survival and l'Association Internationale pour la Défence des Langues et Cultures Menacées.

As far as trying to retard language shift is concerned, it is clear that linguists have a rather more special role to play. We can work for the preservation of traditional modes of language transmission from generation to generation. We can argue that it is desirable to maintain viable linguistic communities of children, and we can suggest that societies preserve incentives for young people actually to use the language in question. Perhaps more importantly, however, linguists are in an especially powerful position when it comes to engendering positive ideas about languages and dialects in their speakers. People typically acquire a majority metropolitan, national, or world language for perfectly sound and understandable instrumental reasons, and no linguist would want to discourage them from doing so. Very often, however, speakers cease to be bilingual and fail to retain their original community language for attitudinal reasons: they are ashamed of their tribal, marginal, minority, or unofficial language. Linguists should therefore proclaim as loudly and as frequently as possible not only that bilingualism (for instance in a speaker's vernacular and a language of wider communication) is extremely common and entirely normal and desirable; we should also argue especially strongly that all language varieties are valuable and worthy of preservation if at all possible. We should make it better known that no dialects are linguistically inferior, that no language as such is 'old-fashioned', 'backward', 'primitive', or 'unsophisticated'. Wherever we encounter missionaries, politicians, journalists, business people, or educationists who devalue (deliberately or not) indigenous languages and dialects, we have a duty to oppose their ignorance and their prejudice.

V. ENGLISHES

INTRODUCTION: ENGLISHES

The expansion of English as a native language has been remarkable. As we noted in Section I, 400 years ago it was spoken in a very small area of the globe indeed. Now it has spread to a remarkable extent. This expansion has caused, among other things, a certain amount of angst. In recent years, anyone following discussions in the British press and broadcasting media about the English language will have noticed that among the vast majority of the British intelligentsia who know nothing at all about language – except how to use it – there are a number who are very concerned about its future. There is nothing new about this, of course. As admirably chronicled by Milroy and Milroy (1998), this 'complaint tradition' pattern of concern that younger people are not using the language so well as older people appears to be repeated in every generation. The present worries, however, as expressed by non-expert journalists and writers of letters to the national press, are currently taking a particularly interesting and rather unusual form: they appear to be predicting two very different linguistic catastrophes which, if we are not all very careful, will befall the English language. The interesting thing is that these two catastrophes are so very different from one another as to be exact opposites.

The first of these two conflicting worries we can label the *Americanisation catastrophe*. Those who fear this catastrophe foresee in the English-speaking world a process of cultural and linguistic homogenisation, brought about mainly by the influence of the electronic media, whereby before very long we will not only all be eating Macdonald's hamburgers and wearing our baseball caps backwards but also all speaking a single (and of course, the implication is, undesirable) form of United States English. This does not on the face of it seem a totally unreasonable point of view. After all, increasing communications and travel possibilities are a prominent feature of late twentieth-century life. And it is certainly the case that a number of words and other features which used to be confined to American – or American and Canadian – English are now to be found in British Isles and Australasian English also.

The second scenario we can label the *disintegration catastrophe*. According to this view, the great fear is that English is now used so widely around the world, and is in particular used by so many non-native speakers, that if we are not careful, and very vigilant, the language will quite rapidly break up into a series of increasingly mutually unintelligible dialects, and eventually into different languages. This too seems to be a perfectly sensible point of view. After all, it is true that English is one of the few languages in the world that has more non-native than native speakers. And we know from historical linguistics that languages do over time break up into dialects and then into languages: 2000 years ago English, German and Norwegian were all one language, for example.

Obviously, both these scenarios may be wrong. But, even more obviously, they cannot both be right. English cannot be homogenising and disintegrating at the same time.

In fact, at the lexical level, there does indeed seem to be some truth in the assertion that Americanisation of the English language – homogenisation in the direction of North American usage – is taking place. The first set of worriers, that is, do seem to have some justification, even if we do not have to share their actual worry that this is necessarily in every respect an undesirable development. This trend is not difficult to explain. We learn new words readily and constantly, and it is a simple matter to pick up new items from what one reads and from what one hears on radio, on television, and at the cinema. There is no doubting the American domination of English-language television and cinema around the world, and there can therefore be no surprise that American words are spreading.

At the grammatical level, on the other hand, the picture is not nearly so clear. Grammatical change is much slower than lexical change, and the overall impression much more difficult to determine. There is also the very considerable problem that we cannot be at all sure that just because a grammatical change in American English, say, precedes by some decades an identical change in British English, the change has been introduced into the latter from the former. This is the well-known historical and anthropological problem of diffusion versus independent development, and can be illustrated by the case of *hopefully*. Until the 1970s, this word was in British English simply a manner adverbial, while in American English it had for a number of decades combined this function with that of a sentence adverbial. Rather suddenly, in about 1974, people in Britain started using *hopefully* in the American fashion: *Hopefully it won't rain tomorrow*. At first this attracted quite a lot of negative attention from the usual quarters, but by about 1978 most people had forgotten that it was an innovation, and now nearly everybody in the country uses it. The interesting question is: did this innovation represent a borrowing from American English, or was it an independent development – or both?

The picture in the case of phonology is much clearer. Consider sound changes that are currently taking place in varieties of English around the world. Generally, the trend points to divergence. This is particularly evident in the case of the short vowel system. Perhaps the most dramatic change affecting this subsystem in American English is the Northern Cities Chain Shift. This circular movement of vowels in phonological space, which is associated most closely with Minneapolis, Chicago, Detroit, Cleveland, Buffalo, Rochester, Boston, New York and Philadelphia, involves the fronting of the LOT vowel to a position approaching, at its most extreme, [æ]; the raising and diphthongisation of the TRAP-vowel, at its most advanced to [ɪə]; centralisation of the DRESS-vowel; and the backing of the STRUT-vowel. Notice that not only are these changes not taking place anywhere else in the English-speaking world but that, in many cases, the changes which are taking place elsewhere are in completely the opposite direction. In New Zealand, for instance, the DRESS-vowel is raising to a position closer than [e], giving a contrast between the two varieties of the order of *let* [lɪt] vs. [lʌt]. And in the south of England the STRUT-vowel is fronting, giving a contrast between certain forms of English and American English of *sun* [sæn] versus [sɔn].

So, in the case of phonology, it is the second group of worriers who appear to be correct, although it is among native English speakers that the phonological systems of English show signs of diverging from one another. Again, this is relatively easy to explain. What we are witnessing here is the normal pattern of linguistic change, while the pattern we saw in the case of vocabulary is unusual and recent. The electronic media, contrary to widespread popular belief, do not play a very big role in the diffusion of linguistic innovations. Speakers can, and do, learn new words and phrases from the TV, but sound changes require face-to-face contact for diffusion (through accommodation) to take place. Speakers need to interact with one another for changes in the central phonological and grammatical systems of language to be transmitted – and there is no spoken interaction with the television set.

The conclusion thus has to be a mixed one. English looks set to become increasingly homogenised at the level of lexis, although there is still a long way to go, but at the level of phonology, the dominant national native-speaker varieties of the language are slowly diverging from one another. Since there is still relatively little face-to-face contact, for the vast majority of people, between speakers of American English and Australian English, or between New Zealand English and Irish English, we must expect that this trend will continue for the foreseeable future.

In the chapters that follow in this section, we look at ongoing developments affecting English, both linguistic changes and sociolinguistic changes. We begin with a world-wide perspective, and then narrow the focus down to a more specifically British point of view.

14

ENGLISH AS
AN ENDANGERED LANGUAGE

As we saw in Chapter 13, language death is a serious problem. English, however, is obviously not one of the languages threatened by death. There are, it is true, some people in the USA who, noting an increasing role for Spanish in some aspects of American life, have misguidedly started an organisation called 'English Only' which is designed to defend American English. Of course, if ever a language did not need defending, it is American English. Nothing could be more absurd, unless perhaps it is simliar efforts by certain members of the French establishment to defend French. These are both languages which actually need defending against. French and English are not in danger, they are the danger: they are killer languages (see Chapter 13). There is a danger of French killing off Breton, Flemish, Basque, Alsatian German, Occitan and Catalan in France, and Franco-Provençal has almost disappeared in Switzerland. Many languages are killer languages on a much wider scale: Spanish and Portuguese in the Americas; Russian in Central Asia; Swahili in East Africa; Arabic in North Africa and the Middle East; Indonesian in Indonesia; Chinese in China. And English is the biggest of them all, especially in Australasia and North America.

I therefore need to explain why I have referred, in the title of this chapter, to English as an endangered language. There are some people who see a danger to English in its very success. There are many languages which have played important roles as institutionalised lingua francas: Latin was the lingua franca of the Roman Empire, and continued to play a significant role in European learning until quite recently. But the extent to which English is employed like this is without parallel. Never before has a language been used as a lingua franca by so many people in so many parts of the world. English is also remarkable in having more non-native than native speakers: perhaps 400 million to 300 million. There are, as just mentioned, anglophone people who regard this expansion of English as a danger to the language. One reason is an irrational fear that one just cannot trust foreigners with one's language: who knows what they will get up to with it if native speakers are not at all times totally vigilant? After all, some foreigners seem to think that English is their language: some French and German speakers have invented English words which do not exist in English, such *lifting*, or *wellness*, or *handy*, or *pullunder*. This, however, is not a danger to English. It is on the contrary quite interesting and amusing, and does not make any difference to anything important. It is a even a kind of compliment, perhaps. The true repository of the English language is its native speakers, and there are so many of them that they can afford to let non-natives do what they like with it so long as what they do is confined to a few words here and there. In other words, this is not an area where English is an endangered language, although it is true that it will be interesting to see whether English as a European lingua franca is acquiring any linguistic characteristics of its own, and the extent to which widespread international non-native usage may influence native usage.

There is also a worry that some people have, mentioned already in the introduction to this section, which concerns endonormative varieties. In discussions of varieties of English it is usual to distinguish between countries where English is a *native* language, a *foreign* language, and a *second* language. English-as-a-Foreign-Language nations are countries like Germany, Uruguay or China where English has no official status, and where it is not widely used within the country. In countries where English is a second language, most people do not have it as their mother tongue, but it does play an important role, particularly amongst educated élites, within the country itself, in politics, education, law, the media and business. It may well also have some official status. If such a country is multilingual, like India, English often plays an important role as an internal lingua franca. This means that many educated élite speakers, though they do not have English as their *first* language, may have it as their *primary* language – the one they use most. In this situation, there is a likelihood that English will acquire a set of local norms which are widely adhered to even if they are not officially recognised. This is where some anglophones see a danger. In India, Nigeria, Singapore, Ghana, Kenya and other places in the world where English English was originally used as a model, a series of well-established, focused, national internal forms of English have now developed (see Trudgill and Hannah 1994) which can now be used as local norms. In my view these endonormative varieties are precisely the ones which should be taught and used in the countries concerned: Indian English should be the norm in India, just as Australian English should be the norm in Australia, and Irish English in Ireland. Standard Indian English is not just the variety of English used by educated Indians; it is also more suitable for use in India than English English because speakers of the model variety are close at hand, its phonology is closer to Indian languages, and its vocabulary is adapted to Indian society and culture.

The fear is that if these endonormative varieties take on more and more local characteristics they will become mutually incomprehensible, and the language will disintegrate. It is already true, I accept, that certain forms of Indian English are difficult for British people to understand, but I do not regard this problem as serious. Most anglophones who have been to India will agree that a week in the country is enough to ease comprehension problems. Familiarity is all that is needed: when cinema films first acquired soundtracks in the 1930s, British people complained that they could not understand them, as they had never heard American English before.

In any case, there is much more likelihood of English at the native-speaker level being subject to disintegration. All languages change, and they change because native speakers change them, even though they are not aware of it. And at least at the level of accents it is clear that New Zealand and American and Irish and English English are currently becoming more unlike one another, as discussed in the introduction to this section. It is not impossible that native anglophones in the future will be able to communicate with one another in writing but not in speech, as is already the case with Chinese.

However, there is another side to this 'success' story of English. It is not actually the case that everywhere in the world where English is spoken natively it is on the offensive. The fact is that there are many communities in the world where the reverse is true, and where language shift *from* English is taking place, or likely to take place in the near future. Surprising as it may seem, very few people, incuding academic linguists, know or care about the many parts of the world where English, as a native language, is actually in danger. Obviously, if English does die out in these places, this will not represent the loss of a language as such. But it will represent the loss – and the loss for ever – of distinctive varieties of the languge. These varieties of English constitute fascinating and important forms of the language for many different types of linguistic research, as well as being the repositories of the cultures and histories of the people who speak them. Preserving these varieties of English may not be as important as preserving the 900 languages of Papua New Guinea, but it is important. I argue that we should attempt to preserve linguistic diversity, of all types, wherever we can, and suggest, in the spirit of encouraging diversity, that we should try to preserve not just languages as such, but also as many varieties and dialects of languages as possible.

We will examine first three areas where English may well be in danger because it is spoken by very small and isolated populations. Almost certainly the least-known anglophone community in the world are the Bonin Islands (see also the introduction to Section I). These islands are Japanese-owned and are in the central Pacific Ocean, about 800 km south-east of Japan proper: the population is about 2000. The islands were discovered by the Spanish in 1543, claimed by the US in 1823 and by Britain in 1825, but were formally annexed by Japan in 1876. After the Second World War they were placed under US military control, and were returned to Japan in 1968. The originally uninhabited islands were first settled in 1830 by five seamen: two Americans, one Englishmen, one Dane, and one Italian, together with ten Hawaiians, five men and five women. This founding population was later joined by whalers, shipwrecked sailors, and drifters of many different origins. The English they speak is mainly American in origin and has many similarities with New England varieties. It also resembles a number of other island Englishes around the world in ways which are not very easy to explain, and which are the subject of ongoing historical sociolinguistic research (see Trudgill *et al.* forthcoming).

Recent waves of immigration from Japan are now being followed by a language shift to Japanese. If the Japanese-based American linguist Danny Long (1998, 2000a, b) had not alerted us to this community, only quite recently, it is quite possible that this form of English would have died out without anybody knowing that it even existed, let alone what it was like. In any case, researchers will have to hurry before it is too late.

Second, Tristan da Cunha, a South Atlantic British dependent territory, is about halfway between southern Africa and South America. It is said to be the most remote permanently inhabited settlement in the world, the nearest habitation being St Helena, which is about 2000 km distant. The islands were discovered in 1506 by a Portuguese sailor, Tristão da Cunha. A British garrison was stationed on Tristan in 1816, as a result of fears that it might be used as a base for the rescue of Napoleon from St Helena. When the garrison left in 1817, three soldiers asked to stay, and during the 1800s they were joined by shipwrecked sailors, a few European settlers, and six women from St Helena. By 1886 the population was ninety-seven; the current population is about 290.

The English spoken there is mainly of English dialect origin but shows some signs of pidginisation, though probably not enough to be considered a creoloid (see Chapter 7); and it has a number of features found nowhere else in the anglophone world. This variety is very important for studies of dialect contact and new-dialect formation (see Schreier forthcoming b). There is no worry about the future of this form of English at present, but the population of Tristan is declining, and it is not absolutely clear what its long-term prospects are.

Third, Pitcairn Island is an isolated British colony 2000 km south-east of Tahiti in the South Pacific. As is well known, the population is descended from the mutineers of the British ship *The Bounty* and their Tahitian companions. After a lengthy stay on Tahiti, the crew, led by the first mate Fletcher Christian, mutinied when their voyage to the West Indies had got only as far as western Polynesia. They set their captain William Bligh and a number of loyal sailors adrift, headed back to Tahiti, where they collected a number of local women and a few men, and, fearing discovery by the Royal Navy, set off again. This group reached Pitcairn in 1790, where, in the interests of secrecy, they burnt their ship. The island was uninhabited at the time, but showed signs of previous Polynesian habitation or at least visitation. The island community survived undiscovered until 1808 when American whalers stumbled upon it.

A range of varieties of English is available to the islanders. The most basilectal of these resembles an English-based creole and has many features of Polynesian origin. There is controversy about its status, but I have suggested that the term 'dual-source creoloid' can be applied to it (see Chapter 7). The population of Pitcairn is currently fifty-two. The number of people on the island is declining as a result of emigration to New Zealand, and it is not clear that the dialect will survive.

THE WESTERN HEMISPHERE

Now we come to a rather different kind of case. There is an important linguistic boundary in the Americas between English, on the one hand, and the Romance languages French, Portuguese and Spanish, on the other. English comes up against French in Canada, on the border between Ontario and Quebec, and again in New Brunswick. It confronts Spanish on the border between the USA and Mexico, in Belize, and on the border between Venezuela and Guyana. And English-based creoles meet a French-based creole on the borders between Surinam and Guyane.

This boundary is not static. In the Caribbean islands, some places such as Guadeloupe and Martinique are French-speaking; the Dominican Republic and Cuba are Spanish-speaking; and Aruba, Bonaire and Curaçao speak a Spanish-based creole. Most other islands are anglophone, but some territories which were formerly francophone have become or are on the way to becoming anglophone: Dominica, St Lucia, Trinidad and Tobago, Grenada and the Grenadines; and Spanish is in competiton with English in Puerto Rico. One fact that is not widely known, however, is that English is not everywhere the language which is expanding along this borderline: in some places it is on the defensive. Let us examine some interesting cases which make this point, travelling north to south.

The frontline begins in Canada. The European population of Quebec is French-speaking. It is less well known that there are anglophone communities in Quebec. The most threatened of these are the English-speaking villages of the Magdalen Islands. These islands – Les Îles de la Madeleine – are in the Gulf of St Lawrence between Prince Edward Island and Newfoundland. There are nine main islands which were 'discovered' by Jacques Cartier in 1534, although Basque and Breton fishermen had known about them long before that. They acquired a settled population in 1755, when many of the Acadian French colonists of Nova Scotia who were expelled by the British escaped there. The islands were ceded to Britain in 1763 and were annexed to Newfoundland, but they were made a part of Quebec in 1774. At the end of the 1700s the population was reinforced by more

Acadians who had earlier taken refuge on the French-owned islands of St Pierre and Miquelon, but who now preferred the British monarchy to the French Republicans. Their population today is about 14,000. About 90 per cent of them, as this history would lead one to suspect, are French-speaking, but there is a longstanding community of about 1500 anglophones who are mainly of Scottish and Irish origin.

Further south, the Dominican Republic is basically monolingual Spanish-speaking, but several regions of the country were settled in the 1820s by 6000 American ex-slaves who immigrated through arrangements between the Haitian rulers of Santo Domingo and American religious and philan-thropic agencies. Typhus soon decimated many of these settlements, but a number still exist including one on the peninsula of Samaná. The anglo-phones refer to themselves as 'Americans' and speak fluent English, some of them even now being monolingual. Nearly all cite Philadelphia, New York or New Jersey as the place of origin of their ancestors. Research has been carried out here which is of considerable historical importance for an understanding of the origins of African American Vernacular English (see Poplack and Tagliamonte 2001). There is naturally considerable pressure on the community to shift to Spanish.

The next examples all come from Central America (see Holm 1983). The central American country of Belize, for example, is one of those that is on the frontline: the population of this Commonwealth country is about 220,000, and English is its official language, but only 61 per cent of the population, mainly of African origin, are English-speaking. The rest are speakers of Spanish, as befits a frontline state, or of the original Amerindian Mayan languages. Neighbouring hispanophone Guatemala has recently abandoned its territorial claims to the country,

To the south of Belize lies Honduras. The Bay Islands are a group of eight small islands belonging to northern Honduras, about 55 km offshore in the Caribbean. The islands were first sighted by Columbus in 1502 and were settled in 1642 by English buccaneers. Between 1650 and 1850 Spain, Honduras, and England disputed ownership. The islands were annexed to Britain in 1852 but were then ceded to Honduras in 1859. English-speaking Protestants formed the majority of the population until about 1900, when hispanic Hondurans from the mainland began settling there, but indigenous anglophones still account for 85 per cent of the current population of about 20,000 black, white and mixed citizens.

English is also spoken in many different locations on the Caribbean coast of mainland Honduras where, however, language shift to Spanish seems to be takng place.

The Miskito coast of Nicaragua is the Caribbean coastal area consisting of a strip of lowland about 70 km wide and 350 km long. Columbus visited it in 1502, but there was not much European presence there until the arrival of buccaneers in the 1650s. England established a protectorate over the local Miskito Indians, who the region is named after, and the area was a British dependency from 1740 to 1786.

The British founded the principal Miskito coast city of Bluefields. Spain, Nicaragua and the United States at different times disputed this dependency. The issue was settled by the occupation of the coast by Spain in 1786, and later by a British-American treaty in 1850. There are about 30,000 native speakers of English in this area who look to Bluefields as their centre. Most of them are of African origin. Several hundred, however, are Rama Indians, and another several hundred are so-called Black Caribs, who were transported from their native island of St Vincent by the British in the late 1700s. Since the Nicaraguan revolution, there has been considerable in-migration of Spanish speakers from the Pacific coast of the country.

Nicaragua's Great and Little Corn Islands lie in the Caribbean about 80 km offshore from Bluefields. The population is about 2500 and they are anglophone. On both the mainland and the islands, English is under pressure from Spanish.

In Costa Rica, the Caribbean lowland province of Limón contains about 7 per cent of Costa Rica's population. The main city, Limón, has 40,000 people and all the black inhabitants are anglophone, many of them descendants of workers brought from Jamaica in the 1870s. Anglophones constitute 2 per cent of the total population of Costa Rica. Younger English speakers are now all bilingual in Spanish and English, and recent reports suggest that English is giving way to Spanish.

Further south, English is spoken natively by the black minority in three different areas of Panama. The first is the islands of the Bocas del Toro, where an anglophone community was founded by people who had left the island of San Andres in 1827. The other areas are the two largest cities: Panama City and Colon, where anglophones of Jamaican origin have been living since 1850. Indigenous anglophones make up about 14 per cent of the total population, but the younger speakers are all bilingual in English and Spanish.

Mainland Colombia has no anglophone communities, but its Caribbean islands have. These are San Andrés and Providencia, with a population of 35,000, lying about 180 km off the coast of Nicaragua and about 700 km north-west of mainland Colombia. Colombia controlled Panama until 1903, which explains this geographical anomaly. The islands were settled in 1629 by English Puritans, and subsequently by Jamaican planters and their black slaves. The islands were officially decreed to be Spanish in 1786, and they became part of Colombia in 1822, after Colombian independence, but they are still English-speaking.

Another fascinating and little-known story involves anglophones in Brazil (see also the introduction to Section I). At the end of the American Civil War in 1865, thousands of Americans from the defeated South left the United States for ever. Some went to Mexico and the West Indies, and some even made it as far as Japan and Egypt, but the largest number went to Brazil, perhaps 40,000, where they founded a number of settlements. The best known of these is called Americana, which is near Santa Barbara, about 150 km north-west of Sao Paulo. The language of the community was for many decades a Southern variety of American English, and there are many hundreds of older people today who still speak a conservative form of English which has its roots in Georgia and Alabama. This English is of considerable interest for reconstructing the history of English in the southern United States and for dating a number of linguistic changes (Montgomery and Melo 1990; 1995). Gradually the community have become bilingual in English and Portuguese, and most younger people may be more comfortable in Portuguese.

Finally, we come to the southern end of the frontline, the Falkland Islands. This British colony in the South Atlantic lies about 500 km east of South America. There are two main islands, East Falkland and West Falkland, with a population of British origin. The islands' first settlement was by the French on East Falkland in 1764, followed by a British settlement a year later on West Falkland. The Spanish bought the French settlement, and the British later withdrew from West Falkland without renouncing their claim to sovereignty. The Spanish settlement was in turn withdrawn in 1811. In 1820 the Argentinian government, which had declared its independence from Spain in 1816, proclaimed its sovereignty over the Falklands, but in 1831 an American warship attacked the Argentinian settlement on East Falkland, and in 1833 a British force expelled the few remaining Argentinian officials. In 1841 a British governor was appointed for the Falklands, and by 1885 a British community of about 1800 people had been established on both islands. The Falklands became a British colony in 1892. According to current research, a new focused dialect of English has developed in the capital and only town, Port Stanley. This must be the newest native-speaker variety of English in the world, and it is very important for us to study this variety to make further progress with our theories of new-dialect formation. In rural West Falkland, on the other hand, each village apparently still shows connections with the particular part of England from which it was settled (Sudbury 2000). This frontline community has a population of only about 2100, and its future, while apparently secure at the moment, can obviously not be guaranteed.

CONCLUSION

English is not in any kind of immediate danger as a result of being used as an international lingua franca, or as a result of having developed endonormative second language varieties. On the other hand, there is cause for concern. As we saw in Section II, it can be argued that dialects are just as intimately linked to cultures as languages are. Some European countries such as Norway and Switzerland have succeeded in defending their dialects, and the majority of their inhabitants remain dialect-speaking. I am keen that the anglophone world should also try to defend its dialects. English as such is not an endangered language – nothing could be further from the truth. Yet many varieties of English *are* endangered; the loss of these varieties would not constitute a tragedy to compare with the loss of thousands of the world's truly endangered languages, but it would be a small and avoidable tragedy. If we are serious about honouring and preserving linguistic diversity, and if we believe in countering cultural homogenisation, and if it is important that all speakers should have and receive respect for their own dialects, then these distinctive varieties of our English language deserve to be honoured and preserved also.

15

STANDARD ENGLISH:
WHAT IT ISN'T

There is a reasonably clear consensus in the sociolinguistics literature about the term *a standardised language*: it is a language one of whose varieties has undergone standardisation. *Standardisation*, too, appears to be a relatively uncontroversial term, although the terminology employed in the discussion of this topic is by no means uniform. I myself have defined standardisation (Trudgill 1992) as consisting of the processes of language determination, codification and stabilisation. Language determination 'refers to decisions which have to be taken concerning the selection of particular languages or varieties of language for particular purposes in the society or nation in question' (p. 71). Codification is the process whereby a language variety 'acquires a publicly recognised and fixed form'. The results of codification 'are usually enshrined in dictionaries and grammar books' (p. 17). Stabilisation is a process whereby a formerly diffuse variety (in the sense of Le Page and Tabouret-Keller 1985) 'undergoes focussing and takes on a more fixed and stable form' (p. 70). wrong page.

It is therefore somewhat surprising that there seems to be considerable confusion in the English-speaking world, even among linguists, about what Standard English is. One would think that it should be reasonably clear which of the varieties of English is the one which has been subject to the process of standardisation, and what its characteristics are. In fact, however, we do not even seem to be able to agree how to spell this term – with an upper case or lower case <s> – a point which I will return to later – and the use of the term by non-linguists appears to be even more haphazard.

In this chapter, I therefore attempt a characterisation of Standard English. It should be noted that this is indeed a characterisation rather than a strict definition – language varieties do not readily lend themselves to definition as such. We can describe what Chinese is, for example, in such a way as to make ourselves very well understood on the issue, but actually to define Chinese would be another matter altogether. The characterisation will also be as much negative as positive – a clearer idea of what Standard English is can be obtained by saying what it is not as well as by saying what it is. My discussion of this topic will be both sociolinguistic and linguistic. But it will be specifically linguistic: the word 'ideology' will not appear again in this chapter. And it will also, I hope, be informed by references from time to time to the nature of standard and nonstandard varieties in language situations beyond the English-speaking world.

STANDARD ENGLISH IS NOT A LANGUAGE

Standard English is often referred to as 'the standard language'. It is clear, however, that Standard English is not a 'language' in any meaningful sense of this term. Standard English, whatever it is, is less than a language, since it is only one variety of English among many. It is also the most important variety of English in all sorts of ways: it is the variety of English normally used in writing, especially printing; it is the variety associated with the education system in all the English-speaking countries of the world, and is therefore the variety spoken by those who are often referred to as 'educated people'; and it is the variety taught to non-native learners. But most native speakers of English in the world are native speakers of some nonstandard variety of the language, and English, like other Ausbau languages (see Chapter 11), can be described (Chambers and Trudgill 1997) as consisting of an autonomous standardised variety together with all the nonstandard varieties which are heteronomous with respect to it. Standard English is thus not *the* English language but simply one variety of it.

STANDARD ENGLISH IS NOT AN ACCENT

There is one thing about Standard English on which most linguists, or at least British linguists, do appear to be agreed, and that is that its characterisation has nothing to do with pronunciation. From a British perspective, we have to acknowledge that there is in Britain a high status and widely described accent known as Received Pronunciation (RP) which is sociolinguistically unusual when seen from a global perspective in that it is not tied to any geographical area, being instead a purely social accent associated with speakers in all parts of the country, or at least in England, from upper-class and upper-middle-class backgrounds (see Chapter 16). It is widely agreed, though, that while all RP speakers also speak Standard English, the reverse is not the case. Perhaps 9–12 per cent of the population of Britain (see Trudgill and Cheshire 1989) speak Standard English with some form of regional accent. It is true that in most cases Standard English speakers do not have 'broad' local accents i.e., with large numbers of regional features which are phonologically and phonetically very distant from RP, but it is clear that in principle we can say that, while RP is in a sense standardised, it is a standardised accent of English and not Standard English itself. This point becomes even clearer from an international perspective. Standard

160

English speakers can be found in all English-speaking countries, and it goes without saying that they speak this variety with different non-RP accents depending on whether they come from Scotland or the USA or New Zealand or wherever.

STANDARD ENGLISH IS NOT A STYLE

There is, however and unfortunately, considerable confusion in the minds of many concerning the relationship between Standard English and the vocabulary associated with formal varieties of the English language. We characterise *styles* (see Trudgill 1992) as varieties of language which can be ranged on a continuum ranging from very formal to very informal. Formal styles are employed in social situations which are formal, and informal styles are employed in social situations which are informal – which is not to say, however, that speakers are 'sociolinguistic automata' (Giles 1973) who respond blindly to the particular degree of formality of a particular social situation. On the contrary, speakers are able to influence and change the degree of formality of a social situation by manipulation of stylistic choice.

All the languages of the world would appear to demonstrate some degree of stylistic differentiation in this sense, reflecting the wide range of social relationships and social situations found, to a greater or lesser extent, in all human societies. I believe, with Labov (1972), that there is no such thing as a single-style speaker, although it is obviously also the case that the repertoire of styles available to individual speakers will be a reflection of their social experiences and, in many cases, also their education. It is of course important here to distinguish between individual speakers of languages and those languages themselves, but it is clear that languages too may differ in the range of styles available to their speakers. In many areas of the world, switching from informal to formal situations also involves switching from one language to another. In such cases, it is probable that neither of the two languages involved will have the full range of styles available to speakers in monolingual situations.

English as it is employed in areas where it is the major native language of the community, such as in the British Isles, North America and Australasia, has the fullest possible range of styles running from the most to the least formal. This obviously does not mean to say, however, that all speakers have equal access to or ability in all styles, and it is generally accepted that one of the objectives of mother-tongue education is to give pupils exposure to styles at the more formal end of the continuum that they might otherwise not gain any ability in using.

Stylistic differences in English are most obvious at the level of lexis. Consider the differences between:

Father was exceedingly fatigued subsequent to his extensive peregrination.

Dad was very tired after his lengthy journey.

The old man was bloody knackered after his long trip.

Although one could argue about some of the details, we can accept that these three sentences have more or less the same referential meaning, and thus differ only in style – and that the stylistic differences are indicated by lexical choice. It is also clear that native speakers are very sensitive to the fact that stylistic variation constitutes a cline: some of the words here, such as *was, his* are stylistically neutral; others range in formality from the ridiculously formal *peregrination* through very formal *fatigued* to intermediate *tired* to informal *trip* to very informal *knackered* and tabooed informal *bloody*. It will be observed that, as is often the case, the most informal or 'slang' words are regionally restricted, being in this case unknown or unusual in North American English. It will also be observed that there are no strict co-occurrence restrictions here as there are in some languages – one can say *long journey* and *lengthy trip* just as well as *lengthy journey* and *long trip*.

Formality in English is, however, by no means confined to lexis. Grammatical constructions vary as between informal and formal English – it is often claimed, for instance, that the passive voice is more frequent in formal than in informal styles – and, as has been shown by many works in the Labovian secular linguistics tradition, starting with Labov (1966), phonology is also highly sensitive to style.

As far as the relationship between style and Standard English is concerned, we can say the following: the phonological sensitivity to stylistic context just referred to obviously has no connection to Standard English since, as we have noted, Standard English has no connection with phonology.

Let us then examine lexis. I would like to assert that our sentence

The old man was bloody knackered after his long trip

is clearly and unambiguously Standard English. To assert otherwise – that swear words like *bloody* and very informal words like *knackered* are not Standard English – would get us into a very difficult situation. Do Standard English speakers suddenly switch out of Standard English as soon as they start swearing? Are Standard English speakers not allowed to use slang without switching into some nonstandard variety? My contention is that Standard English is no different from any other (nonstandard) variety of the language. Its speakers have a full range of styles open to them, just as speakers of other varieties do, and can swear and use slang just like

162

anybody else. (It will be clear that I do not agree with the contention which is sometimes heard that 'nobody speaks Standard English'.) Equally, there is no need for speakers of nonstandard varieties to switch into Standard English in order to employ formal styles. The most logical position we can adopt on this is as follows:

The old man was bloody knackered after his long trip

is a Standard English sentence, couched in a very informal style, while

Father were very tired after his lengthy journey

is a sentence in a nonstandard (north of England, for instance) variety of English, as attested by the nonstandard verb form *were*, couched in a rather formal style. It is true that in most English-speaking societies there is a tendency – a social convention perhaps – for Standard English to dominate in relatively formal social situations, but there is no necessary connection here, and we are therefore justified in asserting the theoretical independence of the parameter standard/nonstandard from the parameter formal/informal. This theoretical independence becomes clearer if we observe sociolinguistic situations outside the English-speaking world. There are many parts of the world where speakers employ the local dialect for nearly all purposes, such as Luxemburg, Limburg in The Netherlands, and much of Norway. In such situations, a visit to the Town Hall to discuss important local political problems with the mayor will not elicit a switch to Standard German or Dutch or Norwegian, but it will produce styles of greater formality than those to be found on Friday night in the local bar among a group of close friends. Stylistic switching occurs *within* dialects and not *between* them.

This theoretical independence of the notion of Standard English from style does not mean that there are not problems in individual cases of distinguishing the two, as Hudson and Holmes (1995) have pointed out. For example, I tend to regard the use of *this* as an indefinite in narratives as in

There was this man, and he'd got this gun . . . etc.

as a feature of colloquial style, but other linguists might regard it as a nonstandard grammatical feature.

STANDARD ENGLISH IS NOT A REGISTER

We use the term register in the sense of a variety of language determined by topic, subject matter or activity, such as the register of mathematics, of medicine, or of pigeon fancying. In English, this is almost exclusively a matter of lexis, although some registers, notably the register of law, are known to have special syntactic characteristics. It is also clear that the education system is widely regarded as having as one of its tasks the transmission of particular registers to pupils – those academic, technical or scientific registers which they are not likely to have had contact with outside the education system – and of course it is a necessary part of the study of, say, physical geography to acquire the register – the technical terms – associated with physical geography.

It is, however, an interesting question as to how far technical registers have a technical function – that of, for example, providing well-defined unambiguous terms for dealing with particular topics – and how far they have the more particularly sociolinguistic function of symbolising a speaker or writer's membership of a particular group, and of, as it were, keeping outsiders out. Linguists will defend the use of 'lexical item' rather than 'word' by saying that the former has a more rigorous definition than the latter, but it is also undoubtedly true that employing the term 'lexical item' does signal one's membership of the group of academic linguists. And it is not entirely clear to me, as a medical outsider, that using 'clavicle' rather than 'collar-bone' has any function at all other than symbolising one's status as a doctor rather than a patient.

Here again we find confusion over the term Standard English. Some British National Curriculum documents for English have talked about 'Standard English vocabulary'. It is not at all clear what this can mean. I have argued above that it cannot mean 'vocabulary associated with formal styles'. Is it perhaps supposed to mean 'vocabulary associated with academic or technical registers'? If so, this would not make sense either, since the question of register and the question of standard versus nonstandard are also in principle entirely separate questions. It is of course true that it is most usual in English-speaking societies to employ Standard English when one is using scientific registers – this is the social convention, we might say. But one can certainly acquire and use technical registers without using Standard English, just as one can employ non-technical registers while speaking or writing Standard English. There is, once again, no necessary connection between the two. Thus

There was two eskers what we saw in them U-shaped valleys

is a nonstandard English sentence couched in the technical register of physical geography.

This type of combination of technical register with a nonstandard variety is much more common in some language communities than others. In German-speaking Switzerland, for example, most speakers use their local nonstandard dialect in nearly all social situations and for nearly all purposes. Thus it is that one may hear, in the corridors of the University of Berne, two philosophy professors discussing the works of Kant using all the appropriate philosophical vocabulary while using the phonology and grammar of their local dialect.

It would of course be possible to argue that their philosophical vocabulary is not an integral part of their native nonstandard Swiss German dialects and that the professors are 'switching' or that these words are being 'borrowed' from Standard German and being subjected, as loan words often are, to phonological integration into the local dialect. This, however, would be very difficult to argue for with any degree of logic. All speakers acquire new vocabulary throughout their lifetimes. There seems no reason to suppose that technical vocabulary is the sole prerogative of standard varieties, or that while, if you are a nonstandard dialect speaker, it is possible to acquire new non-technical words within your own nonstandard dialect, it is sadly by definition impossible to acquire technical words without switching to the standard variety. After all, dialects of English resemble each other at all linguistic levels much more than they differ – otherwise interdialectal communication would be impossible. There is no reason why they should not have most of their vocabulary in common as well as most of their grammar and most of their phonology. If the Swiss example tells us anything, it tells us that there is no necessary connection between standard language and technical registers.

SO WHAT IS IT THEN?

If Standard English is not therefore a language, an accent, a style or a register, then of course we are obliged to say what it actually is. The answer is, as at least most British sociolinguists are agreed, that Standard English is a dialect. As we saw above, Standard English is simply one variety of English among many. Subvarieties of languages are usually referred to as *dialects*, and languages are often described as consisting of dialects. As a named dialect, like Cockney or Scouse or Yorkshire, it is entirely normal that we should spell the name of the Standard English dialect with capital letters.

Standard English is, however, an unusual dialect in a number of ways. It is, for example, by far the most important dialect in the English-speaking world from a social, intellectual and cultural point of view; and it does not have an associated accent. It is also of interest that dialects of English, as of other languages, are generally simultaneously both geographical and social dialects which combine to form both geographical and social dialect continua. How we divide these continua up is also most often linguistically arbitrary, although we do of course find it convenient normally to make such divisions and use names for dialects that we happen to want to talk about for a particular purpose as if they were discrete varieties. It is thus legitimate and usual to talk about Yorkshire dialect, or South Yorkshire dialect, or Sheffield dialect, or middle-class Sheffield dialect, depending on what our particular objectives are. Standard English is unusual, seen against this background, in a number of ways. First, the distinction between Standard English and other dialects is not arbitrary or a matter of slicing up a continuum at some point of our own choice, although as we have seen there are some difficulties. This is inherent in the nature of standardisation itself. There is really no continuum linking Standard English to other dialects because the codification that forms a crucial part of the standardisation process results in a situation where, in most cases, a feature is either standard or it is not.

Second, unlike other dialects, Standard English is a purely social dialect. Because of its unusual history and its extreme sociological importance, it is no longer a geographical dialect, even if we can tell that its origins were originally in the south-east of England. It is true that, in the English-speaking world as a whole, it comes in a number of different forms, so that we can talk, if we wish to for some particular purpose, of Scottish Standard English, or American Standard English, or English Standard English. (Bizarrely, at least one British National Curriculum document suggested that American and Australian English are not Standard English!) And even in England we can note that there is a small amount of geographical variation at least in spoken Standard English, such as the different tendencies in different parts of the country to employ contractions such as *he's not* as opposed to *he hasn't*. But the most salient sociolinguistic characteristic of Standard English is that it is a social dialect.

At least two linguists have professed to find this statement controversial. Stein and Quirk (1995), as mentioned in the General Introduction, argue that Standard English is not a social class dialect because the *Sun*, a British newspaper with a largely working-class readership, is written in Standard English. This argument would appear to be a total *non sequitur*, since all newspapers that are written by middle-class journalists in English are written in Standard English, regardless of their readership. Stein and Quirk also fly in the face of all the sociolinguistic research on English grammar carried out in the last quarter of the twentieth century (see for example Cheshire 1982). Standard English is a dialect which is spoken as their native variety, at least in Britain, by about 12–15 per cent of the population, and this small percentage does not just constitute a random cross-section of the population. They are very much concentrated at the top (or, as some would prefer, 'the top') of the social scale. The further down the social scale one goes, the more nonstandard forms one finds.

Historically, we can say that Standard English was selected (though of course, unlike many other languages, not by any overt or conscious decision) as the variety to become the standard variety precisely because it was associated with the social group with the highest degree of power, wealth and prestige. Subsequent developments have reinforced its social character: the fact that it has been employed as the dialect of an education to which pupils, especially in earlier centuries, have had differential access depending on their social class background.

So far we have not discussed grammar. When, however, it comes to talking about the linguistic differences between Standard English and the nonstandard dialects, it is obvious from our discussion above that they cannot be phonological, and that they do not appear to be lexical either (though see below). It therefore follows that Standard English is a social dialect which is distinguished from other dialects of the language by its *grammatical* forms.

STANDARD ENGLISH IS NOT
A SET OF PRESCRIPTIVE RULES

We have to make it clear, however, that these grammatical forms are not necessarily identical with those which prescriptive grammarians have concerned themselves with over the last few centuries. Standard English, like many other Germanic languages, most certainly tolerates sentence-final prepositions, as in *I've bought a new car which I'm very pleased with*. And Standard English does not exclude constructions such as *It's me* or *He is taller than me*.

GRAMMATICAL IDIOSYNCRASIES
OF STANDARD ENGLISH

Grammatical differences between Standard English and other dialects are in fact rather few in number, although of course they are very significant socially. This means that, as part of our characterisation of what Standard English is, we are actually able to cite quite a high proportion of them.

Standard English of course has most of its grammatical features in common with the other dialects. When compared to the nonstandard dialects, however, it can be seen to have idiosyncrasies which include the following

1. Standard English fails to distinguish between the forms of the auxiliary forms of the verb *do* and its main verb forms. This is true both of the present tense, where many other dialects distinguish between auxiliary *I do, he do* and main verb *I does, he does* or similar, and the past tense, where most other dialects distinguish between auxiliary *did* and main verb *done*, as in *You done it, did you?*
2. Standard English has an unusual and irregular present tense verb morphology in that only the third-person singular receives morphological marking: *he goes* versus *I go*. Many other dialects use either zero for all persons or *-s* for all persons.

3. Standard English lacks multiple negation, so that no choice is available between *I don't want none,* which is not possible, and *I don't want any.* Most nonstandard dialects of English around the world permit multiple negation.

4. Standard English has an irregular formation of reflexive pronouns, with some forms based on the possessive pronouns e.g. *myself,* and others on the objective pronouns e.g. *himself.* Most nonstandard dialects have a regular system employing possessive forms throughout, for example, *hisself, theirselves.*

5. Standard English fails to distinguish between second-person singular and plural pronouns, having *you* in both cases. Many nonstandard dialects maintain the older English distinction between *thou* and *you,* or have developed newer distinctions such as *you* versus *youse.*

6. Standard English has irregular forms of the verb *to be* both in the present tense (*am, is, are*) and in the past (*was, were*). Many nonstandard dialects have the same form for all persons, such as *I be, you be, he be, we be, they be,* and *I were, you were, he were, we were, they were.*

7. In the case of many irregular verbs, Standard English redundantly distinguishes between preterite and perfect verb forms both by the use of the auxiliary *have* and by the use of distinct preterite and past participle forms: *I have seen* versus *I saw.* Many other dialects have *I have seen* versus *I seen.*

8. Standard English has only a two-way contrast in its demonstrative system, with *this* (near to the speaker) opposed to *that* (away from the speaker). Many other dialects have a three-way system involving a further distinction between, for example, *that* (near to the listener) and *yon* (away from both speaker and listener).

LINGUISTIC CHANGE

There is also an interesting problem concerning which grammatical forms are and are not Standard English which has to do with linguistic change, in general, and the fact that, in particular, there is a tendency for forms to spread from nonstandard dialects to the standard. Just as there are some difficulties in practice in distinguishing between features of nonstandard dialect and features of colloquial style, as was discussed above, so there are difficulties associated with standard versus nonstandard status and linguistic change. Given that it is possible for nonstandard features to become standard (and vice versa), it follows that there will be a period of time when a form's status will be uncertain or ambiguous. For example, most Standard English speakers are happy to accept the new status of *than* as a preposition rather than a conjunction in constructions such as

He is bigger than me.

but they are less happy, for the time being, to do so in

He is bigger than what I am.

Similarly, American Standard English currently admits a new verb *to got* in

You haven't got any money, do you?

but not (or not yet) in

You don't got any money, do you?

NONSTANDARD LEXIS

I have argued above that there is no necessary connection between formal vocabulary or technical vocabulary and Standard English; that is, there is no such thing as Standard English vocabulary. There is an interesting sense, however, in which this is not entirely true. We can illustrate this in the following way. It is clear that there is such a thing as *nonstandard* vocabulary. For instance, in the nonstandard dialect of Norwich, England, there is a verb *to blar* which means 'to cry, weep'. Not only is this verb regionally restricted to the dialects of this part of the country, it is also socially restricted – the small proportion of the population of Norwich who are native speakers of Standard English do not normally use this word, although they are perfectly well aware of what it means. This means that there is a sense in which we can say that *to cry* is a Standard English word, whereas *to blar* is not. However, *cry* is by no means only a Standard English word, since there are very many other nonstandard dialects elsewhere in which it is the only word available with this meaning, and even in the working-class nonstandard dialect of Norwich, *to cry* is a perfectly common and frequently used word. Because Standard English is not geographically restricted to any particular region, its vocabulary is available to all. In any case, there are also, of course, many instances in which Standard English speakers in different parts of England employ different but equivalent words, and hundreds of cases in which the vocabulary of English Standard English and American Standard English differ, as is very well known. The usage by some contributors to National Curriculum documents of the term 'Standard English vocabulary' in the sense of 'vocabulary that occurs in the Standard English dialect and no other' thus remains problematical.

CONCLUSION

From an educational point of view, the position of Standard English as the dialect of English used in writing is unassailable. We should perhaps add, however, that it has nothing whatsoever to do with spelling or punctuation!

As far as spoken Standard English is concerned, we could conclude that the teaching of Standard English to speakers of other dialects may be commendable – as most would in theory agree, if for no other reason than the discrimination which is currently exercised against nonstandard dialect speakers in most English-speaking societies – and possible, which I am inclined, for sociolinguistic reasons (see Trudgill 1975), to doubt. Either way, however, there is clearly no necessary connection at all between the teaching of formal styles and technical registers, on the one hand, and the teaching of the standard dialect on the other.

16

THE SOCIOLINGUISTICS
OF MODERN RP

RP AS A MINORITY ACCENT

An often cited statistic has it that in Britain RP speakers constitute only 3 per cent of the population. When this statistic first became commonplace in the sociolinguistics literature, it was not unusual for people to dispute it. Certainly, at least in the 1970s, it seemed as if there were many more RP speakers around than that. However, a little reflection showed that this impression was due to the fact that it was much easier to hear speakers of the RP accent in the media than their proportion in the population would indicate. If people disputed the 3 per cent figure, it was only necessary to ask them how many RP speakers they had had face-to-face contact with recently. Since most readers of sociolinguistic literature were not members of the Royal Family, the point was, in the end, well taken.

Perhaps, therefore, it will be as well to discuss where this statistic came from. The guilty party was myself. I popularised the 3 per cent figure in Trudgill (1974). (Incidentally, I also suggested that only 12 per cent of the population were speakers of Standard English, implying that 9 per cent of the population normally speak Standard English with a regional accent, as mentioned in Chapter 15.) I did not, however, pick this figure out of thin air. It was, on the contrary, rather carefully considered, and was arrived at in the following way. My sociolinguistic urban dialect study of the city of Norwich, some of the findings of which were presented in Trudgill (1974), was based for the most part on interviews with a random sample of fifty people taken from the population of the city. This was a genuine random sample in which the entire voting-age population, at that time people aged twenty-one and over, had an equal chance of selection. As is normal with such samples, a small number of people refused to help, and one person had died. These were replaced in the normal way by others also selected randomly. I also rejected from my sample people who had not been brought up in Norwich and its vicinity – there was no point in investigating the phonology of Norwich English by talking to Lancastrians. The number of people rejected in this way was also very small – it would certainly have been much larger today. Out of this sample of fifty people, only one was an RP speaker. (None of the rejected out-of-towners was an RP-speaker either). In other words, the evidence from my random sample was that the population of Norwich contained only 2 per cent of RP speakers.

In considering to what extent I could generalise from this finding to Britain as a whole, I had to bear in mind a number of factors: sampling error could have meant that the true proportion of RP speakers in Norwich might actually have been as high as, say, 5 per cent; then I had to consider the probability that there were more RP speakers in some places, such as Cheltenham or Bath, say, than there were in Norwich; equally I also had to take into account that there were yet other places, such as Glasgow or Hull, where the proportion might have been lower. In the end, I decided that 3 per cent was approximately correct, but if anybody wishes to say that we should raise the figure to, say, 5 per cent, I would have no objection. The point is that RP speakers have always represented a very small proportion of the population of native speakers of English in Britain.

This raises the interesting question: if RP is so very much a minority accent, why do we spend so much effort teaching it to non-native speakers, especially since, as David Abercrombie (1956: 55) pointed out, it would make much more sense on purely phonetic grounds to teach, for example, Scottish pronunciation? My own response to the question 'why teach RP?' is 'why not?' After all, we have to teach something.

THE SOCIOLINGUISTIC ORIGINS OF RP

It is widely agreed that from a sociolinguistic point of view, this minority accent is rather unusual, and indeed it is perhaps unique. In many languages in the world that have been heavily standardised, the standardisation extends from lexis, orthography and grammar into phonology to a certain extent, and it is not at all unusual to find a particular regional accent that has higher status than others. What is unusual about RP, as discussed in the previous chapter, is that it is the accent of English English with the highest status and that it is totally non-regional. It is a defining characteristic of the RP accent that, while it is clearly a variety that is associated with England, and to a certain extent also with the rest of the United Kingdom, it otherwise contains no regional features whatsoever. Of course, typologically it has its origins in the south-east of England. Unlike accents from the south-west of England, for example, it is a non-rhotic accent. And unlike the accents of the north of England, it has /aː/ rather than /æ/ in the lexical sets of *bath* and *dance*. The point is, however, that it is not possible to ascribe any geographical origins to a genuine native RP speaker other than that they are almost certainly British, and probably English. This peculiar lack of regionality must be due to a peculiar set of sociolinguistic preconditions, and has in fact often been ascribed to its origin in British residential, and therefore also non-regional, schools for the children of the upper classes: the so-called Public Schools.

REGIONAL AND SOCIAL VARIATION

The relationship between social and regional accent variation in Britain has often been modelled as having the form of an equilateral triangle (following Daniel Jones, as reported in Ward (1929) where, however, the diagram takes the form of a cone). The base of the triangle is broad, implying considerable amounts of phonological variation between the different regional accents spoken by the lower social classes. Going upwards from the base, the increasing narrowness of the triangle implies decreasing regional variation between the accents of speakers higher up the social scale. Similarly, the point at the top of the triangle indicates the total lack of regional variation we have already noted as characteristic of the RP accent, spoken as it is by people at the top of the social scale. There is no doubt that this model is an effective one. It is impossible, as we have said, to tell where an RP speaker comes from. It is usually possible to tell which broad region of the country middle-class speakers come from. And working-class speakers can usually be pinpointed even more accurately as to their geographical origins. Thus, an unskilled manual worker might be recognisable by anybody having the appropriate sort of linguistic knowledge as coming from Bristol, a non-manual worker as coming from the West Country, a middle-class professional person as coming from somewhere in the south of England, and an upper-middle class RP speaker as coming simply from England, even if all of them had their origins in Bristol. Equally, a typical middle-class person from Birmingham will obviously have an accent which is phonetically and phonologically different from that of a middle-class person from Bristol, but the differences between the accents of two working-class speakers from the same places will be even greater.

There is a further interesting complication which we can add to the model, which has to do with a number of varieties of English spoken outside Britain, notably in Ireland and in the southern hemisphere – South Africa, New Zealand and Australia. In Australia, it is usual for linguists to claim that Australian English phonology demonstrates no, or very little, regional variation, but some considerable social variation. It has also become usual to refer to Australian accents as falling into one of three social accent types: cultivated, general and broad. These terms are rather unfortunate since they suggest that there are three discrete varieties rather than the continuum of varieties which obviously exists, but the status-ordering is clear from the terminology: cultivated Australian consists of the accents with the highest status, while broad Australian consists of those with the lowest status, and general Australian comes in between.

How does one recognise these accents linguistically? The answer is quite straightforward. Until relatively recently, RP had a role to play in Australian society as the accent with the highest status, and RP speakers were the people who were employed in broadcasting. Now, RP as such has more or less disappeared from Australia. It is associated in the minds of Australians with upper-class Britain, and increasing Australian national self-confidence and cultural independence *vis-a-vis* the 'mother country' has meant that there are now very few, if any, native speakers of RP left in the country. However, the influence of the legacy of RP in Australia is still vitally important: cultivated Australian is precisely the accent type which most closely resembles RP, while broad Australian is the one which resembles it least. We should, that is, make a place in our triangle for regional varieties from beyond Britain as well.

The triangle model is also accurate in that it implies, correctly, that the situation is one which involves continua – both a social accent continuum, from high status to low status accents, and a geographical accent continuum, from one end of the country to another. Accurate, that is, with one exception: like standard dialects, RP is a standard accent which has undergone, albeit implicitly rather than explicitly, codification. The point is that speakers either have an RP accent or they do not. There are many people who have a so-called 'near-RP' accent, but this is by definition not an RP accent. When it comes to employing a codified language variety, a miss is as good as a mile. Just as someone who otherwise uses only grammatical forms associated with Standard English but habitually says *I seen it* cannot be said to be a speaker of Standard English, it takes only one non-RP feature for a speaker not to be a speaker of RP.

INNOVATIONS IN RP

This raises the interesting quasi-philosphical question of what is and is not an RP feature. RP, like all accents and dialects of all languages, is subject to changes, some of which are certainly internally generated. Descriptions of some of these can be found in Gimson (1962) and Wells (1982), and probably include the fronting of the GOAT vowel, and lowering of the TRAP vowel. Other changes, however, clearly make their way into RP over time by diffusion upwards from lower-status accents. Features which used not to be RP and now are RP probably include:

(a) the employment of intrusive /r/;
(b) the replacement of /ɔː/ by /ɒ/ in the lexical set of *lost, cloth, off*;
(c) glottaling of syllable-final /t/ before another consonant;
(d) the merger of /ʊə/, /ɔə/ and /ɔː/;
(e) the fronting of /uː/ from [uː] towards [ʉː].

174

As the discussion above suggested, the criterion for the inclusion of any feature in RP must be that it is not a regional feature. This implies that there will be features that for a period of time, while a change is taking place, may have an indeterminate status. One good example is provided by the case of what Wells (1982) has called HAPPY-tensing. This involves the replacement through time of word-final unstressed /ɪ/ by /iː/, so that /hæpɪ/ becomes /hæpiː/. At the level of regional accents, this innovation appears to be one which is most characteristic of southern accents but which has been spreading northwards for many decades. For example, the *Survey of English Dialects* records show that many counties in the south of England which now have -/iː/ had -/ɪ/ in the speech of rural traditional dialect speakers in the 1950s and 1960s.

RP has always had /ɪ/ in such items. This was the one respect in which it resembled north of England rather than south of England accents. It was also the case that there were many people who had near-RP accents in that they had RP accents except that they had HAPPY-tensing. We could define such people as non-RP speakers because HAPPY-tensing was a regional feature – they were obviously from somewhere in the south of England. However, there is now some evidence that HAPPY-tensing is, or at least is going to be, a feature of RP. The conclusive evidence would be if we could show that younger speakers who otherwise have only RP features and who come from areas of the north of England which do not have HAPPY-tensing nevertheless do have it, unlike their – we could now say – regionally accented colleagues. HAPPY-tensing will now no longer be a regional feature, though absence of HAPPY-tensing will be. Note that this will force us into the position of having to say either that certain people aged, say, fifty who have HAPPY-tensing are not RP speakers, while certain people aged, say, twenty who have HAPPY-tensing are RP speakers; or, perhaps alternatively, that fifty-year-old people who used not to be RP-speakers have now become RP speakers without changing the way they speak at all. I would personally not find either of these solutions ridiculous.

CHANGES IN THE SOCIOLINGUISTIC SITUATION OF RP

Phonetic and phonological changes are not the only changes which have been taking place involving RP. In the last few decades there have also been a number of changes in the sociolinguistic situation of RP, and in its relationship to other accents. Much of this appears to stem from a change in attitudes towards RP and other accents of British English on the part of the British population as a whole. Most of what we know about attitudes to English accents derives from a whole series of research programmes carried out by the social psychologist Howard Giles and his associates, particularly in the 1970s. Giles (see, for example, 1987), very skilfully using a whole range of research techniques, most notably matched-guise experiments, showed that it was a reasonably straightforward matter to gain access to peoples' attitudes to different accents of English without asking them directly – something which would naturally have produced a series of skewed results.

It was apparent from Giles' work that RP was perceived as being an accent associated, in the absence of information to the contrary, with speakers who were competent, reliable, educated and confident. It was also perceived as being the most aesthetically pleasing of all British English accents. On the other hand, RP speakers scored low on traits like friendliness, companionability and sincerity, and messages couched in RP also proved to be less persuasive than the same messages in local accents. (Notice also that there is a long history in American science-fiction and horror films for sinister, menacing characters to be given RP accents.)

As far as changes in the last twenty years are concerned, we lack reliable research on most of these issues, but it is a matter of common – and not necessarily unreliable – observation that the RP accent is no longer the necessary passport to employment of certain sorts that it once was. Non-RP accents are very much more common on the BBC, for example, than they were forty years ago, and telephone sales companies, as I know from frequent requests from such companies for advice, now think about which regional accents will be most effective rather than automatically employing non-regional RP.

Discrimination on the grounds of accent still, unfortunately, occurs in British society. But this discrimination is no longer against all regional accents but only against those from, as it were, lower down the triangle. And it is also no longer permitted in British society to be seen to discriminate against someone on the basis of their accent – it has to masquerade as something else. This hypocrisy is a sign of progress, of an increase in democratic and egalitarian ideals. This has also, probably, though again we lack the research, had the consequence that an RP accent can be even more of a disadvantage in certain social situations than was formerly the case. In many sections of British society, some of the strongest sanctions are exercised against people who are perceived as being 'posh' and 'snobbish'. These factors also mean that many fewer people than before are now speakers of what Wells (1982: 283–5) has called *adoptive RP*: that is, many fewer people than before who are not native speakers of RP attempt, as adolescents or adults, to acquire and use this accent. Even Conservative Party politicians no longer have to strive for RP accents, as a recent Conservative Prime Minister once did.

THE DEATH OF RP?

In spite of these observations, it is necessary to be sceptical about reports of two different types that appear to be rather common anecdotally, especially on the part of journalists in need of something to write about. The first is that RP is disappearing; the second is that RP is being replaced by a new, potentially non-regional accent. I will now discuss these two scenarios, which are largely myths, in turn.

There seem to be a number of reasons for the erroneous but under-standable misperception that RP is disappearing. First, non-RP accents are now found, as we have already noted, in situations from which they would have been excluded only a few decades ago. It is therefore easy to gain an impression that there are fewer RP speakers than formerly. Second, the kind of people who in earlier generations would have been speakers of adoptive RP no longer are, as we have already observed. So there actually are fewer RP speakers, though not necessarily fewer native speakers. Third, RP itself, again as we have already seen, has changed. It has acquired – as it always has over the generations – forms that before were part of local, notably south-east of England accents. This is what leads journalists to report that Public School pupils now 'speak Cockney'. It is true that RP now admits certain types of /t/-glottaling which were formerly associated with local accents only – but that most certainly does not mean that it is Cockney. This perception resembles the belief now current in my own home city, Norwich, where older people frequently complain that the youngsters 'talk like Londoners'. When asked why they say this, they invariably reply: 'Young people say *fing* instead of *thing*'. This is quite true (see Chapter 6) but otherwise they still sound as Norwich people have sounded for decades. One salient phonological feature can lead to utterly inaccurate stereotypical reports.

As far as RP is concerned, the ongoing work of Fabricius (2000) shows that the younger generations of those sections of the community one would expect to be RP speakers still are RP speakers. Pupils at Eton, and under-graduates at Cambridge University who are former pupils at the major Public Schools, are still for the most part RP speakers. Their RP has some new features, but these features are all, including /t/-glottaling, non-regional features and therefore must still be considered as being RP. (Non-region-ality is a necessary but not sufficient condition for a feature to be considered RP. For instance, if all regions of England were to acquire /h/-dropping, something which will actually happen if, as seems possible, this phenom-enon eventually reaches the north-east of England, that would not make it an RP feature!)

A COMPETITOR FOR RP?

As far as the second myth is concerned, this has to do with the development of so-called 'Estuary English'. This is an inaccurate term which, has however, become widely accepted. It is inaccurate because it suggests that we are talking about a new variety, which we are not; and because it suggests that it is a variety of English confined to the banks of the Thames Estuary, which it is not. The label actually refers to the lower middle-class accents of the Home Counties which surround London: Essex and Kent, which do border on the Thames Estuary, but also parts or all of Surrey, Berkshire, Buckinghamshire and Hertfordshire, which do not. Early 'descriptions' using this label were by non-linguists. However, as described by John Wells, and by Altendorf (1999), Estuary English has obvious southeast of England features such as diphthong-shift, /l/-vocalisation and merger of vowels before /l/, but it does not have features typical of working-class accents only, such as th-fronting.

It is easy to obtain an impression from reading some of the commentators that 'Estuary English' is advancing on all fronts. I would like to dispute this, in some measure. There are a number of explanatory factors for this perception. First, as we have already seen, many people who in earlier generations would have become speakers of adoptive RP no longer become so. People who are upwardly socially mobile or who come into the public eye may still in fact reduce the number of regional features in their accents – they will move themselves up the triangle, as it were – but they will no longer remove all such features. It is therefore undoubtedly true that many more people than was formerly the case can be heard in public situations, especially in the media, speaking with lower middle-class regional accents. And of course the most prominent of these are from the south-east of England (a) because this is the largest region of England in terms of population, and (b) because there is a considerable metropolitan bias in the media, with most nationally available media being broadcast from or published in London. Secondly there has been a certain amount of upward social mobility in the last twenty years which has found people from lower middle-class backgrounds in socially prominent positions in which it would have been unusual to find them previously. Thirdly, at least some of the phonological features associated with 'Estuary English' are currently spreading, as London-based features have done for centuries, outwards into surrounding areas. In East Anglia, for example, /l/-vocalisation has not yet reached Norwich, but, as discussed (with maps) in Trudgill (1986), it reached Cambridge and Colchester some decades ago and is beginning to affect Ipswich. It is therefore undoubtedly the case that lower middle-class south-eastern accents cover a wider geographical area than was formerly the case, and will probably continue to spread for some time to come.

What I would strenuously dispute, however, is that this means that 'Estuary English' is going to be the 'new RP'. It is unlikely that it will ever become anything more than a regional accent, albeit the accent of a rather large region covering, together with its lower-class counterparts, the Home Counties plus, probably, Sussex, Hampshire, Bedfordshire, Cambridgeshire, Suffolk and parts of Northamptonshire. The sociolinguistic conditions are not such that it could turn into the new RP. There is no parallel here to the nationwide network of residential Public Schools which gave rise to RP. What we know about the geographical diffusion of linguistic innovations, moreover, indicates that there is no way in which the influence of London is going to be able to counteract the influence of large centres such as Liverpool and Newcastle which are at some distance from London. And we also know that linguistic innovations are not spread by radio and television (see Trudgill 1986).

Reports that a few individual features such as th-fronting are spreading across Britain northwards and westwards from London, though undoubtedly true, do not invalidate this point. This spreading of individual features is something which has always happened, and in any case th-fronting is not to be considered an 'Estuary English' feature. The fact that young people in Cardiff are now using /t/-glottaling does not mean that they are speaking London English, or RP. And the fact that young people in Sheffield are now using th-fronting does not mean that they are speaking Cockney. As anyone who has been to Sheffield recently can attest, people there do not sound remotely like Cockneys – or even like 'Estuary English' speakers.

This leads me again to raise the topic of which model to employ for teaching so-called 'British English', in reality English English, to non-native learners. It has been suggested that it would now make more sense to teach learners 'Estuary English' rather than RP. Of course, it must be true that there are more speakers of 'Estuary English' in England than there are of RP. And of course it is a good idea if twenty-four-year-old Poles, say, sound as much as possible like twenty-four-year-old, rather than ninety-four-year-old, English people. I would therefore advocate rather strongly teaching intrusive /r/ and some forms of /t/-glottaling at least to advanced students. But I would not advocate the teaching of 'Estuary English' or of features associated solely with it, such as diphthong-shifted vowels or /l/-vocalisation, since these are specifically regional features.

NEW DIALECT AND ACCENT REGIONS

The geographical spread of 'Estuary English' is part of a much bigger trend. What is happening in Britain, and probably not only there, as far as regional linguistic variation is concerned, is rather complicated. On the one hand, much regional variation is being lost as the large number of traditional dialects covering small geographical areas gradually disappear from most, though by no means all, parts of the country. These, however, are being replaced by a much smaller number of new modern dialect areas covering much larger areas. The dialects and accents associated with these areas are much less different from one another, and much less different from RP and Standard English, than the traditional dialects were. However, and this is crucial, in terms of phonology they are for the most part currently diverging, not converging. The work of the European Science Foundation

Network on Dialect Divergence and Convergence paints a very similar picture Europe-wide. Work in large urban centres such as Liverpool, Newcastle and Cardiff shows that, although these places are adopting some nationwide features such as labio-dental /r/, /t/-glottaling and th-fronting, they also demonstrate independent divergent developments, such as voiceless-stop affrication in Liverpool and, from my own work in Norwich, the fronting of the GOAT-vowel from [uː] to [ʉː], the widespread smoothing of triphthongs as in *doing* /dɜːn/, *knowing* /nɒːn/, and the merger of the vowels of NEAR and SQUARE (see Trudgill 1999). This is probably part of a much larger scale world-wide pattern where varieties of English around the world, while they may demonstrate lexical convergence, are diverging phonologically: accents of English from New Zealand to the United States are getting less like one another, not more (see the introduction to this section).

Parallel to the development of a large dialect region centred on London, whose lower middle-class accents have been referred to as 'Estuary English', we are seeing the development of similar areas elsewhere, as yet not much studied by linguists, focusing on centres such as Belfast, Dublin, Cardiff, Glasgow, Newcastle, Nottingham, Leeds, Liverpool, Manchester, Birmingham and Bristol. Mats Thelander (1979) reported similar developments twenty years ago from northern Sweden.

London-based journalists have not noticed this kind of development, but this is no reason for linguists to ignore it. To focus pedagogically on one of the newer, larger regional accents of British English to the detriment of all the others, just because it happens to be spoken in London, would be the worst kind of metropolitan bias, of which there is far too much in Britain already.

CONCLUSION

I am a non-RP speaker, but I believe that it is convenient that students learning English English still have a non-regional model available to them. The fact is that in spite of the developments just outlined, the triangle model remains an accurate one for a description of social and regional patterns of accent variation in Britain. The development of a network of regional varieties in Britain is taking place, as it were, underneath a non-regional, nationwide layer provided by RP. This layer is thinner than it was – the minority is probably even smaller than it was – but it is likely to remain intact until British society undergoes even more radical changes in its social structure than it has already undergone in the last twenty years.

REFERENCES

Abercrombie, David (1956) *Problems and Principles in Language Study*. London: Longman.

Abercrombie, David, D. Fry, P. MacCarthy, N. Scott and J. Trim (eds) (1964) *In Honour of Daniel Jones*. London: Longman.

Aikhenvald, Alexandra (1998) Physical properties in a gender system: a study of Manambu. *Language and Linguistics in Melanesia* 27 (1996).

Aitchison, Jean (1981) *Language Change: Progress or Decay?* London: Fontana.

Altendorf, Ulrike (1999) Approaching the notion of Estuary English: /t/-glottalling and /l/-vocalisation by the Thames Estuary. In: Carita Paradis (ed.) *Recent trends in the pronunciation of English: social regional and attitudinal aspects*. Stockholm: Almqvist & Wiksell, pp. 15–31.

Andriotis, N. (1966) *The Federative Republic of Skopje and its Language*. Athens.

Angelopoulos, A. (1979) Population distribution of Greece today according to language, national consciousness and religion. *Balkan Studies* 20; 123–32.

Avis, W. S. (1961) The 'New England short o': a recessive phoneme. *Language* 37; 544–58.

Bailey, Beryl (1965) Toward a new perspective in Negro English dialectology. *American Speech* 40; 171–7.

Bailey, Guy, Natalie Maynor and Patricia Cukor-Avila (1989) Variation in subject-verb concord in Early Modern English. *Language variation and change* 1; 285–300.

Bakker, Peter (1996) Language contact and pidginisation in Davis Strait, Hudson Strait, and the Gulf of Saint Lawrence (northeast Canada). In: Jahr and Broch (eds) 261–310.

Baugh, Albert C. and Thomas Cable (1993) *A History of the English Language*. London: Routledge.

Benham, Charles (1960) *Essex Ballads*. Colchester: Benham Newspapers.

Bloomfield, Leonard (1933) *Language*. New York: Henry Holt.

Breatnach, D. (ed.) (1991) *Contact Bulletin 8*. Dublin: European Bureau for Lesser Used Languages.

Bright, William (ed.) (1992) *International Encyclopedia of Linguistics*. Oxford: Oxford University Press.

Britain, David (1991) *Dialect and Space: a Geolinguistic Study of Speech Variables in the Fens*. Unpublished PhD thesis, University of Essex.

Broch, Ingvild and Ernst Håkon Jahr (1984) *Russenorsk: et pidginspråk i Norge*. 2nd edn. Oslo: Novus.

Brook, G. L. (1958) *A History of the English Language*. London: Deutsch.

Browning, R. (1969) *Mediaeval and Modern Greek*. London: Hutchinson.

Burling, Robbins (1973) *English in Black and White*. New York: Holt, Rinehart & Winston.

Bybee, Joan (1985) *Morphology: A Study of the Relation between Meaning and Form*. Amsterdam: Benjamins.

Cedergren, Henrietta (1990) Linguistic change in Panama. In: Ash, S. (ed.) *Papers from NWAVE-14*. Philadelphia: University of Pennsylvania.

Chambers, J. K. (1991) Canada. In: Cheshire (ed.)

Chambers, J. K. and Peter Trudgill (1997) *Dialectology*. 2nd edn. London: Cambridge University Press.

Cheshire, Jenny (1982) *Variation in an English Dialect*. Cambridge: Cambridge University Press.

Cheshire, Jenny (ed.) (1991) *English Around the World: Sociolinguistic Perspectives*. Cambridge: Cambridge University Press.

Clarke, Sandra (1991) Phonological variation and recent language change in St John's English. In: Cheshire (ed.)

Clarke, Sandra (1997) The role of Irish English in the formation of New World Englishes: the case of Newfoundland. In: Kallen (ed.)

Clogg, Richard (1979) *A Short History of Modern Greece*. Cambridge: Cambridge University Press.

Comrie, Bernard (1988) Coreference and conjunction reduction in grammar and discourse. In: Hawkins (ed.) 186–210.

Comrie, Bernard and Greville Corbett (eds) (1993) *The Slavonic Languages*. London: Routledge.

Corbett, Greville (1991) *Gender*. Cambridge: Cambridge University Press.

Crocombe, R. (1983) *The South Pacific*. Suva: University of the South Pacific.

Croft, William (1990) *Typology and universals*. Cambridge: Cambridge University Press.

Croft, William (1994) Semantic universals in classifier systems. *Word* 45; 145–71.

Crystal, David (1971) Prosodic and paralinguistic correlates of social categories. In: E. Ardener (ed.) *Social Anthropology and Language*. London: Tavistock, pp. 185–208.

Cuthbertson, B. (1998) The peoples of Nova Scotia. In: S. Poole and A. Kingsbury (eds) *Nova Scotia*. Halifax: Formac.

Dawkins, R. (1916) *Modern Greek in Asia Minor*. Cambridge: Cambridge University Press.

Deme, László (1998) Bomlott gondolkodású nyelvészek!? Magyar nyelvmü-velés = terápia nélküli diagnózis?! [Half-witted linguists!? Hungarian language cultivation = diagnosis without therapy?!] In: Kontra, Miklós and Noémi Saly (eds) *Nyelvmentés vagy nyelvárulás? [Saving the Language or Language Treason?]* Budapest: Osiris.

Derbyshire, D. (1977) Word order universals and the existence of OVS languages. *Linguistic Inquiry* 8; 590–99.

Dillard, J. L. (1970) Principles in the history of American English: paradox, virginity and cafeteria. *Florida FL Reporter* 8.

Dillard, J. L. (1972) *Black English*. New York: Random House.

Dixon, R. M. W. (1980) *The Languages of Australia*. Cambridge: Cambridge University Press.

Dorian, N. (ed.) (1989) *Investigating Obsolescence*. Cambridge: Cambridge University Press.

Dressler, Wolfgang U., Katarzyna Dziubalska-Kolaczyk and Malgorzata Fabiszak (1998) Polish inflectional classes within natural morphology. *Bulletin de la Société Polonaise de Linguistique* 53; 95–119.

Edwards, V. K. (1979) *The West Indian Language Issue in British Schools*. London: Routledge.

Ellis, A. J. (1874) *Early English Pronunciation*. London.

Emeneau, Murray (1935) The dialect of Lunenburg, Nova Scotia. *Language* 11; 140–7.

Exarchos, G. (1992) Afti ine i Vlachi: 5. *Eleftherotypia* 29 August 1992.

Fabricius, Anne H. (2000) *T-glottaling between Stigma and Prestige: a Sociolinguistic Study of Modern RP*. Unpublished PhD thesis, Copenhagen Business School.

Fasold, Ralph (1972) *Tense Marking in Black English*. Arlington: Center for Applied Linguistics.

Fisiak, Jacek (1968) *A Short Grammar of Middle English*. Warsaw: Panstwowe Wydawnictwo Naukowe.

Fisiak, Jacek (1975) Some remarks concerning the noun gender assignment of loanwords. *Bulletin de la Societé Polonaise de Linguistique* 33; 59–63.

Fisiak, Jacek (1990) Domesday book and late Old English dialects. In: H. Andersen and K. Koerner (eds) *Historical Linguistics 1987*. Amsterdam: Benjamins, pp. 107–28.

Fodor, István (1959) The origins of grammatical gender. *Lingua* 8; 1–41; 186–214.

Foldvik, Arne Kjell (1979) Endring av uttale og spredning av ny uttale: generasjonsskilnader i Brunlanes, Vestfold. In: J. Kleiven (ed.) *Språk og Samfunn*. Oslo: Pax.

Foley, William A. (1997) *Anthropological Linguistics: An Introduction*. Oxford: Blackwell.

Foley, William A. and Robert Van Valin (1984) *Functional Syntax and Universal Grammar*. Cambridge: Cambridge University Press.

Forby, Robert (1830) *The Vocabulary of East Anglia*. London: Nichols.

Giles, Howard (1973) Accent mobility: a model and some data. *Anthropological Linguistics* 15; 87–105.

Giles, Howard (1987) Our reactions to accent. In: B. Mayor and A. Pugh (eds) *Language, Communication and Education*. London: Croom Helm, pp. 64–72.

Gimson, A. C. (1962) *An Introduction to the Pronunciation of English*. London: Edward Arnold.

Givón, Talmy (1979) *On Understanding Grammar*. New York: Academic Press.

Givón, Talmy (1984) *Syntax: a Functional Typological Introduction*. Amsterdam: Benjamins.

Golovko, Evgenij (1996) A case of nongenetic development in the Arctic area: the contribution of Aleut and Russian to the formation of Copper Island Aleut. In: Jahr and Broch (eds) 63–78.

Golovko, Eugeni and Nikolai Vakhtin (1990) Aleut in contact: the CIA enigma. *Acta Linguistica Hafniensia* 22; 97–125.

Gordon, Elizabeth, and Peter Trudgill (1999) Shades of things to come: embryonic variants in New Zealand English sound changes. *English World-Wide* 20; 1.

Grace, George (1990) The 'aberrant' (vs. 'exemplary') Melanesian languages. In: P. Baldi (ed.) *Linguistic change and reconstruction methodology*. Berlin: Mouton de Gruyter, pp. 155–173.

Green, Barbara and Rachel Young (1964) *Norwich: The Growth of a City*. Norwich: Museums Committee.

Greenberg, Joseph (1966) Some universals of grammar with particular reference to the order of meaningful elements. In: J. Greenberg (ed.) *Universals of Language*. 2nd edn. Cambridge, MA: MIT Press, pp. 73–113.

Grosjean, Francois, Jean-Yves Dommergues, Etienne Cornu, Delphine Guillelmon and Carole Besson (1994) The gender-marking effect in spoken word recognition. *Perception and Psychophysics* 56; 590–98.

Haas, Mary R. (1944) Men's and women's speech in Koasati. *Language* 20; 142–9.

Hancock, Ian (1986) The domestic hypothesis, diffusion and componentiality; an account of Atlantic creole origins. In: Pieter Muysken and Norval Smith (eds) *Substrata vs universals in creole genesis*. Amsterdam: Benjamins, pp. 71–102.

Hancock, Ian (1988) Componentiality and the origins of Gullah. In: J. Peacock and J. Sabella (eds) *Sea and Land: Cultural and Biological Adaptation in the Southern Coastal Plain*. Athens: University of Georgia Press.

Hancock, Ian (1996) The special case of Arctic pidgins. In: Jahr and Broch (eds) 15–32.

Harris, Alice and Lyle Campbell (1995) *Historical Syntax in a Cross-Linguistic Perspective*. Cambridge: Cambridge University Press.

Hasluck, M. and G. Morant (1929) Measurements of Macedonian men. *Biometrika* 21; 322–6.

Hawkins, John (ed.) (1988) *Explaining Language Universals*. Oxford: Blackwell.

Heath, Jeffrey (1975) Some functional relationships in grammar. *Language* 51; 89–104.

Hecht, S. and A. Cockburn (1989) *The Fate of the Forest*. London: Verso.

Herbert, R.K. and B. Nykiel-Herbert (1986) Explorations in linguistic sexism: a contrastive sketch. *Papers and Studies in Contrastive Linguistics* 21.

Hickey, Raymond (forthcoming) The phonology of gender in Modern German.

Hill, P. (1992) Language standardisation in the South Slavonic area. *Sociolinguistica* 6; 108–50.

Hogg, Richard (1993) *A Grammar of Old English I: Phonology*. Oxford: Blackwell.

Holm, John (ed.) (1983) *Central American English*. Amsterdam: Benjamins.

Holm, John (1997) Passive-like constructions in English-based and other creoles. In: Edgar Schneider (ed.) *Englishes around the World* vol.1; pp. 71–86. Amsterdam: Benjamins.

Holmqvist, Erik (1922) *On the History of English Present Inflections*. Heidelberg: Winter.

Hudson, Richard and J. Holmes (1995) *Children's Use of Spoken Standard English*. London: School Curriculum and Assessment Authority.

Hughes, Arthur and Peter Trudgill (1995) *English Accents and Dialects*. 3rd edn. London: Edward Arnold.

Hughey, Ruth (ed.) (1941) *The correspondence of Lady Katherine Paston 1603–1627*. Norwich: Norfolk Record Society.

Ihalainen, Ossi (1987) Towards a grammar of the Somerset dialect. *Neuphilologische Fennica* 15; 71–86.

Jahr, Ernst Haakon and Ingvild Broch (eds) (1996) *Language Contact in the Arctic: Northern Pidgins and Contact Languages*. Berlin: Mouton.

Jahr, Ernst Haakon and Peter Trudgill (1993) Parallels and differences in the linguistic development of modern Greece and modern Norway. In: E. H. Jahr (ed.) *Language Conflict and Language Planning*. Berlin: Mouton de Gruyter, pp. 83–98.

Jaworski, Adam (1986) *A Linguistic Picture of Women's Position in Society: a Polish-English Contrastive Study*. Frankfurt: Peter Lang.

Jaworski, Adam (1989) On gender and sex in Polish. *International Journal of the Sociology of Language* 78; 83–92.

Jespersen, Otto (1924)*The Philosophy of Grammar*. New York: Norton.

Jolivet, Rémy (ed.) (1998) *Cahiers de l'Institut de Linguistique et de Sciences du Langage* 11. Festschrift for Morteza Mahmoudian, Lausanne.

Kallen, Jeff (ed.) (1997) *Focus on Ireland*. Amsterdam: Benjamins.

Karakasidou, A. (1993) Politicising culture: negating ethnic identity in Greek Macedonia. *Journal of modern Greek studies* 11; 1–28.

Keller, Rudi (1994) *On Language Change: The Invisible Hand in Language*. London: Routledge.

Kett, John (n.d.) *Tha's a rum'un, bor!* Woodbridge: Baron.

Ketton-Cremer, R. W. (1957) *Norfolk Assembly*. London: Faber.

Kloss, Heinz (1967) Abstand languages and Ausbau languages. *Anthropological Linguistics* 9; 29–41.

Kökeritz, Helge (1932) *The Phonology of the Suffolk Dialect*. Uppsala: Uppsala University Press.

Kondosopoulos, N. (1974) Etude instrumentale de quelques sons du dialecte crétois. *Travaux de l'Institut de Phonétique de Nancy* 1; 171–85.

Kondosopoulos, N. (1988) *Glossikos atlas tis Kritis*. Iraklio: Panepistimiakis Ekdoseis Kritis.

Konstantinov, Y., G. Alhaug and B. Igla (1991) Names of the Bulgarian Pomaks. *Nordlyd* 17; 8–117.

Krapp, George (1924) The English of the Negro. *American Mercury* 2; 190–5.

Kryk-Kastovsky, Barbara (1998) Norm vs. use: on gender in Polish. In: M. Rissanen (ed.) *Gender*. Berlin: Mouton de Gruyter.

Kurath, Hans (1928) The origin of the dialectal differences in spoken American English. *Modern Philology* 25; 385–95. Reprinted in: J. V. Williamson and V. M. Burke (eds.) *A Various Language: Perspectives on American Dialects*. New York: Holt, Rinehart and Winston, 1971, pp. 12–21.

Kurath, Hans (1964) British sources of selected features of American pronunciation: problems and methods. In: D. Abercrombie *et al.* (eds.) 146–55.

Kurath, Hans (1965) Some aspects of Atlantic seaboard English considered in their connection with British English, *Communications et Rapports du Centre International de Dialectologie Générale de l'Université de Louvain* 3; pp. 236–40. Reprinted in: J. V. Williamson and V. M. Burke (eds.) *A Various Language: Perspectives on American dialects*. New York: Holt, Rinehart & Winston, 1971, pp. 101–7.

Kurath, Hans and Raven I. McDavid (1961) *The Pronunciation of English in the Atlantic States*. Ann Arbor: University of Michigan Press.

Kytö, Merja (1993) Third-person singular inflection in early British and American English. *Language Variation and Change* 5; 113–40.

Labov, Wiliam (1966) *The Social Stratification of English in New York City*. Washington, DC: Center for Applied Linguistics.

Labov, William (1972) *Sociolinguistic Patterns*. Philadelphia: University of Pennsylvania Press.

Labov, William (1975) On the use of the present to explain the past. In: L. Heilmann (ed.) *Proceedings of the 11th International Congress of Linguists*. Bologna: Mulino.

Labov, William (1982) Objectivity and commitment in the linguistic sciences: the case of the Black English trial in Ann Arbor. *Language in Society* 11; 165–202.

Langacker, Ronald W. (1987) *Foundations of Cognitive Grammar: Theoretical Prerequisites*. Stanford: Stanford University Press.

Lass, Roger (1990) How to do things with junk: exaptation in linguistic change. *Journal of Linguistics* 26; 79–102.

Lass, Roger (1997) *Historical Linguistics and Language Change.* Cambridge: Cambridge University Press.

Laycock, Donald C. (1965) *The Ndu Language Family.* Canberra: Pacific Linguistics.

Lazarou, A. (1986) *L'aroumain et ses rapports avec le grec.* Thessaloniki: Institute for Balkan Studies.

Le Page, Robert B. and Andrée Tabouret-Keller (1985) *Acts of Identity.* Cambridge: Cambridge University Press.

Lee, Michael (1988) Language, perception and the world. In: Hawkins (ed.) 211–46.

Leigh-Fermor, Patrick (1966) *Roumeli: Travels in Northern Greece.* London: Murray.

Lewandowska-Tomaszczyk, Barbara (1992) Cognitive and interactional conditioning of semantic change. In: G. Kellerman and M. D. Morrissey (eds) *Diachrony Within Synchrony: Language History and Cognition.* Frankfurt: Peter Lang, pp. 229–50.

Long, Daniel (ed.) (1998) *The Linguistic Culture of the Ogasawara Islands.* Japanese Language Centre Research Reports 6. Osaka: Shoin Women's College.

Long, Daniel (2000a) Evidence of an English contact language in 19th century Bonin Islands. *English World-Wide* 20; 251–86.

Long, Daniel (2000b) Examining the Bonin (Ogasawara) Islands within the Contexts of Pacific Language Contact. In: S. Fischer and W. B. Sperlich (eds) *Leo Pasifika: Proceedings of the Fourth International Conference on Oceanic Linguistics,* pp. 200–17.

Lunden, T. (1993) *Språkens landskap i Europa.* Lund: Studentlitteratur.

Lyons, John (1977) *Semantics.* Cambridge: Cambridge University Press.

McElhinny, Bonnie (1993) Copula and auxiliary contraction in the speech of White Americans. *American Speech* 68; 371–99.

Mackridge, Peter (1985) *The Modern Greek Language.* Oxford: Oxford University Press.

Makri-Tsilipakou, M. (ed.) (1992) *Proceedings of the sixth International Symposium on the Description and/or Comparison of English and Greek.* Thessaloniki: Aristotle University.

Mallinson, Graham (1988) Rumanian. In: M. Harris and N. Vincent (eds) *The Romance Languages.* London: Routledge.

Mansfield, Peter F. (1964, revised 1992) *The Dialect of Sfakia.* Unpublished ms.

Mansfield, Peter and Peter Trudgill (1994) A sex-specific linguistic feature in a European dialect. *Multilingua* 13; 4: 181–6.

Miller, D. Gary (1977) Tripartization, sexism, and the rise of the feminine gender in Indo-European. *The Florida Journal of Anthropology* 2; 3–16.

Milroy, James and Lesley Milroy (1998) *Authority in Language.* London: Routledge.

Mirambel, A. (1965) Remarques sur les systèmes vocaliques des dialectes néo-grecs d'Asie Mineure. *Bulletin de la société linguistique de Paris* 51; pp. 18–45.

Moens, William (1888) *The Walloons and their Church at Norwich 1565–1832*. London: Huguenot Society.

Montgomery, Michael, Janet Fuller and Sharon DeMarse (1993) 'The black men has wives and Sweet harts [and third-person plural -*s*] Jest like the white men': evidence for verbal -*s* from written documents on 19th-century African American speech. *Language Variation and Change* 5; 335–57.

Montgomery, Michael and C. A. Melo (1990) The Phonology of the Lost Cause. *English World-Wide* 10; 195–216.

Montgomery, Michael and C. A. Melo (1995) The language: the preservation of southern speech among the colonists. In: C. B. Dawsey and J. M. Dawsey (eds) *The Confederados: Old South Immigrants in Brazil*. Tuscaloosa: University of Alabama Press, pp. 176–90.

Mufwene, Salikoko, John Rickford, Guy Bailey and John Baugh (1998) *African-American English: Structure, History and Use*. London: Routledge.

Mühlhäusler, Peter (1977) *Pidginisation and Simplification of Language*. Canberra: Pacific Linguistics.

Mühlhäusler, Peter (1987) The politics of small languages in Australia and the Pacific. *Language and Communication* 7; 1–24.

Mühlhäusler, Peter (1989) On the causes of accelerated linguistic change in the Pacific area. In: L. E. Breivik and E. H. Jahr (eds) *Language Change: Contributions to the Study of its Causes*. Berlin: Mouton de Gruyter.

Nandris, J. (1987) The Aromani: approaches to the evidence. In: R. Ruhr (ed.) *Die Aromunen: Sprache, Geschichte, Geographie*. Hamburg: Buske.

Newmeyer, Frederick (1986) *The Politics of Linguistics*. Chicago: University of Chicago Press.

Newton, Brian (1972) *The Generative Interpretation of Dialect*. Cambridge: Cambridge University Press.

Nichols, Joanna (1992) *Linguistic Diversity in Space and Time*. Chicago: Chicago University Press.

O Baoill, D. (1997) The emerging phonological substratum in Irish English. In: J. Kallen (ed.)

Paddock, Harold (1981) *A Dialect Survey of Carbonair, Newfoundland*. Tuscaloosa: University of Alabama Press.

Platt, John and Heidi Weber (1980) *English in Singapore and Malaysia*. Oxford: Oxford University Press.

Poplack, Shana (ed.) (1999) *The English History of African American English*. Oxford: Blackwell.

Poplack, Shana and Sali Tagliamonte (1989) There's no tense like the present: verbal -*s* inflection in early Black English. *Language Variation and Change* 1; 47–84.

Poplack, Shana and Sali Tagliamonte (1993) African American English in the diaspora: evidence from old-line Nova Scotians. In: S. Clarke (ed.) *Focus on Canada*. Amsterdam: Benjamins.

Poplack, Shana and Sali Tagliamonte (2001) *African American English in the Diaspora*. Oxford: Blackwell.

Rickford, John (1999) *African American Vernacular English*. Oxford: Blackwell.

Rickwood, Douglas (1984) The Norwich Strangers, 1565–1643: a problem of control. *Proceedings of the Huguenot Society* 24; 119–28.

Ross, A. S. C. and A. W. Moverley (1964) *The Pitcairnese Language*. London: Deutsch.

Rothstein, Robert (1993) Polish. In: Comrie and Corbett (eds) 686–758.

Ruhlen, M. (1987) *A Guide to the World's Languages*. Stanford: Stanford University Press.

Scarlatiou, E. (1992) Les parlers des minorités roumanophones du nord de la Grèce et leurs rapports avec le grec. *Plurilinguismes* 4; 192–202.

Schneider, Edgar (1983) The origin of verbal -*s* in Black English. *American Speech* 58; 99–113.

Schreier, Daniel (forthcoming a) Third-person singular zero in Tristan da Cunha English.

Schreier, Daniel (forthcoming b) *The English of Tristan da Cunha*. PhD thesis, Fribourg University.

Selinker, Larry (1972) Interlanguage. *IRAL* 10; 209–231.

Sella-Mazi, E. (1992) La minorité turcophone musulmane du nord-est de la Grèce et les dernières évolutions politiques dans les Balkans. *Plurilinguismes* 4; 203–31.

Shilling, Alison (1982) Bahamian English – a non-continuum? In: R. Day (ed.) *Issues in English Creoles*. Heidelberg: Julius Groos, pp. 133–46.

Sikkenga, Elizabeth (1992) Structural influence of Turkish on Asia Minor Greek. Paper presented at NWAVE 21 Conference, University of Michigan, Ann Arbor.

Singler, John (1997) The configuration of Liberia's Englishes. *World Englishes* 16; 205–31.

Stein, Gabrielle and Randolph Quirk (1995). Standard English. *European English Messenger* 4; 2.

Stone, Gerald (1993) Cassubian. In: Comrie and Corbett (eds) 759–94.

Story, G., William Kirwin and John Widdowson (1982) *Dictionary of Newfoundland English*. Toronto: University of Toronto Press.

Stucky, Susan U. (1978) How a noun class system can be lost: evidence from Kituba lingua franca Kikongo. *Studies in the Linguistic Sciences* 8; 217–33.

Sudbury, Andrea (2000) *Dialect contact and koineisation in the Falkland Islands: the development of a southern hemisphere English?* PhD thesis, University of Essex.

Sullivan, William J. (1981) English as a (non-)sexist language. In: James E. Copeland and Philip W. Davis (eds) *The Seventh Lacus Forum 1980*. Columbia: Hornbeam, pp. 444–56.

Thelander, Mats (1979) *Språkliga variations modeller tillämpade på nutida Burträsktal.* Stockholm: Almqvist & Wiksell.

Thomason, Sarah and Terence Kaufman (1988) *Language Contact, Creolisation and Genetic Linguistics.* Berkeley: University of California Press.

Tressou-Milona, E. (1992) I didaskalía tis ellinikís glóssas se pedhiá Rom. In: M. Makri-Tsilipakou (ed.)

Trudgill, Peter (1972) Sex, covert prestige and linguistic change in the urban British English of Norwich. *Language in Society* 1; 179–95.

Trudgill, Peter (1973) Linguistic change and diffusion: description and explanation in sociolinguistic dialect geography. *Language in Society* 3; 215–46.

Trudgill, Peter (1974) *The Social Differentiation of English in Norwich.* Cambridge: Cambridge University Press.

Trudgill, Peter (1975) *Accent, Dialect and the School.* London: Arnold.

Trudgill, Peter (1977) Creolisation in reverse: reduction and simplification in the Albanian dialects of Greece. *Transactions of the Philological Society 1976–7.* Reprinted as 'Language contact in Greece' in P.Trudgill *On dialect: Social and Geographical Perspectives.* Oxford: Blackwell, pp. 108–26.

Trudgill, Peter (ed.) (1977) *Applied Sociolinguistics.* London: Academic Press.

Trudgill, Peter (1978) Sociolinguistics and sociolinguistics. In: P. Trudgill (ed.) *Sociolinguistic Patterns in British English.* London: Arnold.

Trudgill, Peter (1983) *On Dialect: Social and Geographical Perspectives.* Oxford: Blackwell.

Trudgill, Peter (1986) *Dialects in Contact.* Oxford: Blackwell.

Trudgill, Peter (1989) Contact and isolation in linguistic change. In: L. Breivik and E. H. Jahr (eds) *Language Change: Contributions to the Study of its Causes.* Berlin: Mouton de Gruyter.

Trudgill, Peter (1992) *Introducing Language and Society.* London: Penguin.

Trudgill, Peter (1995) Grammaticalisation and social structure: nonstandard conjunction formation in East Anglian English. In: F. R. Palmer (ed.) *Grammar and Semantics.* Cambridge: Cambridge University Press.

Trudgill, Peter (1996) Dialect typology: isolation, social network and phonological structure. In: G. Guy *et al.* (eds) *Towards a social science of language: Papers in honour of William Labov.* Vol. 1: Variation and change in language and society. Amsterdam: Benjamins, pp. 3–22.

Trudgill, Peter (1998) The great East Anglian merger mystery. In: Rémy Jolivet (ed.) 1–10.

Trudgill, Peter (1999a) Norwich: endogenous and exogenous linguistic change. In: P. Foulkes and G. Docherty *Urban voices: Accent Studies in the British Isles.* London: Edward Arnold.

Trudgill, Peter (1999b) *The Dialects of England.* 2nd edn. Oxford: Blackwell.

Trudgill, Peter (1999c) A southern hemisphere East Anglian: New Zealand English as a resource for the study of 19th century British English. In: U. Carls and P. Lucko (eds) *Form, Function and Variation in English: Studies in Honour of Klaus Hansen.* Berlin: Peter Lang, pp. 169–74.

Trudgill, Peter (2000) *Sociolinguistics: An Introduction to Language and Society*. 4th edn. London: Penguin.

Trudgill, Peter (2001) Lesser-known Englishes. In: P. Trudgill and R.Watts (eds) *Alternative Histories of English*. London: Routledge.

Trudgill, Peter and Jenny Cheshire (1989) Dialect and education in the United Kingdom. In: J. Cheshire, V. Edwards, H. Münstermann and B. Weltens (eds) *Dialect and Education: Some European Perspectives*. Clevedon: Multilingual Matter, pp. 94–109.

Trudgill, Peter and Tina Foxcroft (1978) On the sociolinguistics of vocalic mergers: transfer and approximation in East Anglia. In: P. Trudgill (ed.) *Sociolinguistic patterns in British English*. London: Edward Arnold, pp. 69–79.

Trudgill, Peter and Jean Hannah (1994) *International English: A Guide to Varieties of Standard English*. 3rd edn. London: Edward Arnold.

Trudgill, Peter, Elizabeth Gordon and Gillian Lewis (1998) New-dialect formation and Southern Hemisphere English: the New Zealand short front vowels. *Journal of Sociolinguistics* 2; 1: 35–51.

Trudgill, Peter, Elizabeth Gordon, Gillian Lewis and Margaret Maclagan (2000a) Determinism in new-dialect formation and the genesis of New Zealand English. *Journal of Linguistics* 36; 299–318.

Trudgill, Peter, Elizabeth Gordon, Gillian Lewis and Margaret Maclagan (2000b) The role of drift in the formation of Southern Hemisphere Englishes: some New Zealand evidence. *Diachronica* 17; 1: 111–38.

Trudgill, Peter and George Tzavaras (1975) *A Sociolinguistic Study of Albanian Dialects Spoken in the Attica and Biotia areas of Greece*. London: Social Science Research Council.

Trudgill, Peter and George Tzavaras (1977) Why Albanian-Greeks are not Albanians. In: H. Giles (ed.) *Language, Ethnicity and Intergroup Relations*. London: Academic Press. Reprinted as 'Language contact, language shift and identity: why Arvanites are not Albanians' in P. Trudgill *On Dialect: Social and Geographical Perspectives*. Oxford: Blackwell, pp. 127–40.

Trudgill, Peter, Daniel Schreier, Danny Long and Jeffrey P. Williams (forthcoming) On the reversibility of mergers: /v/, /w/, and evidence from lesser-known Englishes.

Tsiouris, E. (1989) *Modern Greek: A Study of Diglossia*. PhD thesis, University of Exeter.

Tsitsipis, L. (1983) Language shift among the Albanian speakers of Greece. *Anthropological Linguistics* 25; 288–308.

Tynch, Milton (1994) Analysis of the verb system of the AAVE of Edenton, North Carolina. Unpublished paper, English Department, North Carolina State University.

Vane, Christine (1984) The Walloon community in Norwich; the first hundred years. *Proceedings of the Huguenot Society* 24; 129–40.

Videnov, Michail (1999) The present-day Bulgarian language situation: trends and prospects. *International Journal of the Sociology of Language* 135; 11–37.

Wakelin, Martyn (1972) *English Dialects: an Introduction*. London: Athlone.

Ward, Ida (1929) *The Phonetics of English*. Cambridge: Heffer.

Weist, Richard, Hanna Wysocka and Paula Lyytinen (1991) A cross-linguistic perspective on the development of temporal systems. *Journal of Child Language* 18; 67–92.

Wells, J. C. (1982) *Accents of English*. Cambridge: Cambridge University Press.

Whinnom, Keith (1971) Linguistic hybridisation and the 'special' case of pidgins and creoles. In: Dell Hymes (ed.) *Pidginisation and Creolisation of Languages*. Cambridge: Cambridge University Press.

Wierzbicka, Anna (1992) *Semantics, Culture and Cognition: Universal Human Concepts in Culture-Specific Configurations*. Oxford: Oxford University Press.

Williams, Colin (1992) On the recognition of minorities in contemporary Greece. *Planet* 94; 82–90.

Williamson, Juanita V. and V. M. Burke (1971) *A Various Language: Perspectives on American Dialects*. New York: Holt, Rinehart & Winston.

Winford, Donald (1992) Back to the past: the BEV/creole connection revisited. *Language, Variation and Change* 4; 311–58.

Winnifrith, T. (1987) *The Vlachs: The History of a Balkan People*. London: Duckworth.

Winnifrith, T. (1993) The Vlachs of the Balkans: a rural minority which never achieved ethnic identity. In: D. Howell (ed.) *Roots of Rural Ethnic Mobilisation*. Dartmouth: New York University Press.

Wolfram, Walt and Donna Christian (1976) *Appalachian Speech*. Arlington: Center for Applied Linguistics.

Woodhouse, C. (1984) *The Story of Modern Greece*. 3rd edn. London: Faber.

Wright, Joseph (1905) *The English Dialect Grammar*. Oxford.

Wyld, H. C. (1936) *A History of Modern Colloquial English*. London.

Zubin, D. A. and K. M. Köpcke (1981) Gender: a less than arbitrary grammatical category. In: R. A. Hendrick, C. A. Masek and M. F. Miller (eds), *Papers from the Seventeenth Regional Meeting, Chicago Linguistic Society*. Chicago Linguistic Society, pp. 439–49.

INDEX

Abstand languages, 112, 114–15, 116, 121–4
accents, 152, 160–1, 171–2, 179–80
admixture, 66, 67, 68, 69
African American Vernacular English (AAVE), 9
  Black Florida English, 13
  hypercorrection, 102
  origins, 9, 21–5, 155
  third-person singular -s/zero, 93–4
Afrikaans, 67, 71, 74, 116
Aikhenvald, 82
Aiwo, 143
Albanian, 77, 122, 123–4, 136, 139
Aleutian, 73–4, 139
Alvanika, 123
Amazonia, 142
Americanisation, 147–9
anglophones, 150, 151, 152–7
Angloromani, 75
Arabic, 150
Arumanian, 123, 133, 135; *see also* Vlachika
Arvanitika, 77, 78, 123, 136
attitudinal factors, 30, 53, 82, 175–6
Ausbau languages, 111, 114–16, 117–21
Australia, 34, 35, 139–40, 173–4
autonomy, 116–17

Basque, 112, 115, 139
Bay Islands, 155
be, 42
Belize, 155
Belorussian, 79, 119
bilingualism, 138, 144
Bislama, 95
Black Florida dialect, 13
Bluefields, 156

Bokmal, 79
Bonin Islands, 152
borrowing, 66, 100, 165
Bosnian, 112, 120
Brazil, 156–7
Breton, 122, 139
British English model, 179
British Isles dialects, 9, 94, 104
Bulgarian, 119, 120, 132, 133, 139

Canadian English, 23, 25, 154
Caribbean English creoles, 78, 95, 102, 104
Cassubian (Kashubian), 79, 119, 139
Catalan, 112, 116, 118, 139
Central America, 155
centralisation, 59, 60
checked vowels, 34, 38
Chinakuan, 139
Chinese, 91, 141, 150
Chora Sfakion, 44
Cockney, 45, 57
codification, 159, 174
complexification, 70
Corsican, 118
Costa Rica, 156
creoles, 45, 70, 77–9, 84, 95
creolisation, 67, 69, 70, 78
creoloids, 71, 74–5, 79, 107, 154
Crete, 44–5
Croatian, 112, 119, 120
culture, 142–3
Czech, 119

Danish, 90, 92, 112, 122
decreolisation, 70
dedialectalisation, 19, 20, 32, 33–9, 41–7

Dhimotiki, 127, 128, 131
dialect change, 29–32
dialect continua, 115, 118–21
dialect death, 29, 30, 32, 33–9, 41
dialect formation, 40–1, 179–80
dialect literature, 37, 38, 45, 95–6,
    101
dialect survival, 21–5
Dialectologists, 93, 94
dialects, 114, 163
*Dictionary of American Regional
    English* (DARE), 13
disambiguation, 83, 85
disintegration, 148, 152
do/don't, 10–14
Dominican Republic, 22, 155
Dutch, 30, 97, 122, 139

East Anglia
    dialects, 94
    do, 10–13
    short vowel system 33–9; *o*, 16–20
    third-person -s/zero, 94, 100–2, 107
    verb forms, 100–2
    vestigial variants, 41–3
    see also Norwich
Easter Island, 140
El Salvador, 138
Ellinika, 125–9
embryonic variants, 40–1
endonormative varieties, 151
English
    -as-a-Foreign-Language, 151
    -as-a-Second-Language, 151
    and gender, 80, 83, 86
    native speakers, 141, 147, 151
    present-tense verb systems, 94–5
English Dialect Dictionary, The, 10
Englishes, 147–58
entrenchment, 92
Eskimo, 139
Essex dialect, 42, 94, 100
Estuary English, 177–9
ethnolects, 75
European Science Foundation
    Network, 179–80
exclaves, 21–5
expansion, 67, 69, 78

Falkland Islands, 157
Fiji, 140
Finnish, 72, 79, 80, 81, 122
Flemish, 118
focusing, 66, 68, 69
Fodor, 82, 83

FOOT vowel, 17, 19, 20
French, 97, 139, 150
    gender, 84, 86, 87, 88, 90
Frisian, 118, 139
Friulian, 118

Gaelic, 122, 138, 139
Galician, 118
gender, 76–92
gender-marking systems, 79–80, 84, 86
German
    and Dutch, 30
    in France, 122, 139
    gender, 80, 83, 84
    Low German (Plattdeutsch), 112,
        116, 118
    and Lunenbourg dialect, 23, 24
    self-reference, 86
    Swiss German, 119, 164
Ghana, 151
glottal stop, 58, 59
GOAT vowel, 17, 19, 20
GOOSE vowel, 18, 19
grammatical categories, 76–9
grammatical change, 148
grammatical constructions, 162–3,
    167–8
grammatical gender, 82–4, 86, 87
Great Yarmouth, 94, 101
Greece, 77, 120, 123, 125–36
Greek, 44–5, 81, 122, 139

Haida, 139
HAPPY-tensing, 175
Hawaiian, 140
heteronomy, 116–17
Hindi, 141
Hixkaryana, 142
Home Counties, 33, 53, 178
homogenisation, 32, 147, 148
Honduras, 155
Hungarian, 79, 81, 84, 86, 122
hyperadaptation, 100
hypercorrection, 100, 102
hyperdialectism, 35, 100

imperfect learning, 66, 68, 69, 71
impoverishment, 66, 68
Indian languages, 88, 138, 151
Indonesian, 150
interdental fricatives, 57
interference, 66, 68, 100
interlanguage, 100, 106
International Helsinki Federation for
    Human Rights, 130

Inuit, 139
Ipswich, 94, 101
Irian Jaya, 140
Irish, 74, 122, 138
Italian, 89, 118

Jamaican Creole, 70, 78
Japanese, 153
jargon, 72, 73

Kashubian (Cassubian), 79, 119, 139
Katharevousa, 127, 128, 131
Kenya, 151
kinship terms, 86
Kituba (Kikongo), 78
Koasati, 88
koinés, 92
Kutenai, 139

Ladin, 118, 139
Ladino, 74, 121, 139
language, 114, 160
language contact, 65–7, 95, 97–9,
    104–7
language creation, 111–13
language death, 111–13, 137–41,
    176–7
language murder, 138, 140, 150
language shift, 74, 138, 140, 149, 152
language status, 112, 114–24
Lemko, 119
lexis, 53, 161–2, 164, 169
Limburg, 163
lingua francas, 69, 71, 97, 150, 151
linguistic change, 168–9
linguistic diversity, 29, 31, 141, 152,
    158
linguistic innovations, 174–5, 179
linguistic minorities, 111, 114, 144
London, 57, 103
Low Countries, 96–7
Low German (Plattdeutsch), 112, 116,
    118
Lunenburg, 22–5
Lusatian (Sorbian), 121, 122, 139
Luxemburgish (Letzeburgisch), 31,
    112, 118, 163

Macedonia, 130, 131, 133, 135
Macedonian, 112, 116, 119, 120, 132
Magdalen Islands, 154
Malaya, 95
Manambu, 82
Maori, 140
Megleno-Rumanian, 133, 135

merging, 54, 55, 57, 60
methodology, 48, 51, 54, 57, 60, 61
Metsif, 74
Micronesian languages, 140
Middle English vowels, 17, 37, 38
minorities *see* linguistic minorities
minority languages, 116, 117–24,
    129–30
Moldavian, 123
morphology, 77
multilingualism, 105, 129
Muslims, 126, 130, 132

National Curriculum, 164
nationalism, 128, 129, 135
natural gender, 80–2, 85
Navaho, 139
NEAR vowel, 41
Netherlands, 30, 163
New Caledonia, 140
New England, 16–20, 24
New Guinea, 83, 87
New Zealand, 40, 41
Newfoundland, 25
Ngala, 87, 88, 89
Nicaragua, 155–6
Nigeria, 151
Norfolk, 33, 43, 94, 100
Norfolk Island, 95
North Slavic continuum, 119
Northern Cities Chain Shift, 149
Norwegian, 31, 46, 72, 79, 87, 163
Norwich
    1968 Study, 38–9, 40, 48–61
    1974 Study, 102, 171
    1983 Study, 48–61
    dialect, 18, 35, 169
    third person -s/zero, 94, 101, 107,
        108
Nova Scotia, 21–5
NURSE vowel, 41, 47
Nynorsk, 79

object-initial languages, 142

Pacific, 139, 152
Panama, 156
Papua New Guinea, 82, 140
phonetic drift, 60
phonological divergence, 148–9
pidginisation, 66, 68–9, 99, 153
pidgins, 66–7, 69, 71–3, 77–9, 84
Pitcairnese, 73, 95, 104, 153
Plattdeutsch (Low German), 112, 116,
    118

polarity, 12, 13
Polish
  gender-marking systems, 79, 80
  grammatical gender, 83, 88, 89, 91
  as minority language, 121
  natural gender, 81
  self-reference, 87
Polynesian languages, 140
Pontic, 126
Port Stanley, 157
Portuguese, 86, 150
post-creoles, 70
pre-pidgins, 69
pronouns, 42–3, 79
Provençal, 112, 116, 118
Providencia, 156
public schools, 173, 177, 179
purification, 70

Quebec, 154

reallocation, 108
Received Pronunciation (RP), 37, 160, 171–80
reduction, 10, 13, 66, 67, 68, 69
redundancy, 66, 69, 90
reference-tracking function, 81, 83, 85
register, 163–5
regularisation, 66, 69
rhoticity/non-rhoticity, 22, 47
Ritwan, 139
Romance languages, 86, 154
Romansch, 118, 139
Romany, 122, 139
RP (Received Pronunciation), 37, 160, 171–80
Rumanian, 122, 123, 135
rural dialect, 53, 108
Russenorsk, 72, 73
Russian, 72, 74, 79, 88, 91, 141
Rusyn, 119
Ruthenian, 119

St. Helena, 95
Samaná, 155
Sami, 72, 122, 139
San Andrés, 156
Santa Cruz Islands, 143
Sapir-Whorf hypothesis, 142
Sardinian, 118
Scandoromani, 75
Scania, 112
Scots, 74, 112, 116
second-language acquisition, 68

self-reference, 86
Serbian, 112, 119, 120
Serbo-Croat, 119, 120
short vowels, 16–20, 33–9, 149
simplification, 66, 67, 69
Singaporean English, 71, 95, 151
slave communities, 67
Slavic, 79, 86, 91, 130–3
Slavika, 130–3
Slavomacedonian, 112, 133
Slovak, 119
Slovene, 119, 122
social class, 102, 108, 178
sociolinguistics, 1–3
Solomon Islands, 95, 140, 143
Sorbian (Lusatian), 121, 122, 139
South Atlantic States, 13–14
South Pacific, 95
South Slavic continuum, 119–21
Spanish, 79, 91, 141, 150, 155
Spanish persecution, 96–7
SQUARE vowel, 41
Sranan, 70, 72, 78
stabilisation, 159
stability, 69, 71, 72
Stammbaum theory, 138
Standard English, 95, 96, 102, 159–70
standardisation, 30, 139, 159
status *see* language status
stereotypes, 44, 45, 46
Strangers, 106, 107
styles, 58, 59, 101, 108, 161–3
Suffolk, 94, 100
Survey of English Dialects (SED), 17, 32, 45, 47, 100, 175
Swahili, 150
Swedish, 90, 92, 112, 122
Swiss German, 119, 164

Tahitian, 140
Tasmania, 138
tense-marking, 12, 13
third-person -s/zero
  African American Vernacular English (AAVE), 93–4
  East Anglia, 94, 100–2, 107, 108
  history in English, 102–4, 107
Tlingit, 139
Tok Pisin, 72, 95
transfer, 36, 100
transparency, 66, 69
triangle model, 174, 180
Tristan da Cunha, 153
Tsakonian, 126

Tuamotuan, 140
Turkish, 81, 122, 126, 139
typology, 65, 104

Ukrainian, 79, 119
United States, 139
urban dialect, 48–61, 108
urbanisation, 139

Valencian, 118
Vanuatu, 140
variability, 107–8
variables, 49, 50, 59, 61
variation, 50, 173–4
varieties, 113, 163

verb forms, 100–2
vestigial variants, 41–7, 54
Vlachika, 123, 133–5; *see also*
     Arumanian
Vojvodina, 119
vowel systems, 33–9, 149

Welsh, 122, 139
West German dialect continuum, 115,
     118–19
West Romance continuum, 118

Yiddish, 74, 121, 139
Yimas, 83, 84
Yugoslavia, 119, 120